ZONE PLAY

A TECHNICAL AND TACTICAL HANDBOOK

Library of Congress Cataloging - in - Publication Data

Di Cesare, Michele and Pereni, Angelo
 ZONE PLAY -A Technical and Tactical Handbook
  Original Title "Calico: Il manuale tecnico e tattico dell'allentore"

ISBN No. 1-890946-18-4
Library of Congress Catalog card Number 98-067117
Copyright © September 1998

First published 1997 by Editoriale Sport Italia Milan

Reedswain Books are available at special discounts for bulk purchase. For details, contact Reedswain at 1-800-331-5191.

Editorial coordination
Marco Marchei

Art Direction, Design and Layout
Kimberly N. Bender

Translated from Italian by
Maura Modanesi

Editing and Proofing
Bryan R. Beaver

Technical coordination
Ferretto Ferretti

Printed by
DATA REPRODUCTIONS
Auburn Hills, Michigan

Photography (cover)
EMPICS

Graphic artist
Roberto Santandrea

REEDSWAIN BOOKS and VIDEOS
612 Pughtown Road
Spring City, Pennsylvania 19475 USA
1-800-331-5191 • www.reedswain.com

A story is the shortest distance
between a human being and the truth.
This book is dedicated to two young players
I have met during my soccer adventures.
I do hope I have been able to show them the right way
- I don't mind how short it is, since even the longest
journey always begins with a simple step.
Unfortunately, life does not always allow us
to cover the same distance.
The death of one of them has left a void in our hearts.
Goodbye Federico and good luck Domenico.

Angelo Pereni

Our heartfelt thanks
to Danila Tarsetti Bonisolo
for she patiently read our work.

ZONE PLAY

A TECHNICAL AND TACTICAL HANDBOOK

by
Angelo Pereni • Michele Di Cesare

Published by
REEDSWAIN INC

ZONE PLAY

Table of Contents

ZONE PLAY

FOREWORD

The book you are about to read is the result of a singular combination of a journalist's knowledge and all the experiences a coach has gradually acquired during his long soccer career. For a long time we had been thinking of writing this work, but for many different reasons we had always been forced to put it off.

Many of you would undoubtedly wonder how a coach and a journalist can cooperate to draw up a technical handbook. In reality, Angelo Pereni and I have been working together for many years and have published many articles in the soccer magazine "Il Nuovo Calcio", always trying to combine our complementary skills and experiences to offer the readers simple texts, easy to understand and particularly close to modern soccer reality.

In this work, we have tried to provide the readers with the main concepts to help them create their own ideas on the technical and tactical organization of a soccer team. Please note that these are simply suggestions. We are reluctant to accept that a coach takes an article or a book as absolute gospel or, still worse, as the perfect solution to all his problems, thus reading it with a very dogmatic approach. We do hope we can offer you a practical tool to reflect upon, since what is truly useful is not what is written in the book, but what you can get from it and adapt to your own experiences and ideas.

A work is valuable only if it leads the reader to think, debate, put himself under discussion or even question the authors. This is the reason why I hope this book can be fully appreciated or maybe have its detractors; anyway, I hope it does not pass unnoticed or is not approached in a very superficial manner, only used to copy one particular training program or a few specific exercises. I believe this would be the worst way for you to wrong us.

There is one last thing I would like to specify: this book does not include any chapter specifically dedicated to goalkeepers. As a matter of fact, after thinking it over, we have come to the conclusion we do not have the suitable specific knowledge to offer you particularly innovative suggestions on the subject; for this reason, we have thought it better to refer the reader to other works by much more competent authors.. However, almost all the exercises suggested in this text also include the goalkeeper, so that he can practice all the technical and tactical skills he requires in modern soccer, where he often becomes a type of sweeper.

Michele Di Cesare

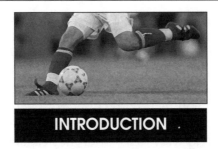

INTRODUCTION

Some of us are awakened by the harsh reality of facts only when they knock against our being. We keep on moving in a state of general stupor and we do not realize that there could be another way for us to act, coach and educate.

Nevertheless, there is a possible way to get out of this stupor and wake up: reading and listening. It is not important whether you agree or not with what you are going to read, because agreeing and disagreeing have nothing to do with the substance everyone has inside himself. The real behavior does not result from simple words; it appears suddenly and gradually grows into a certain kind of attitude. Once again, you can contest what we are going to explain and, nevertheless, still recognize a new path which will allow you to work out your own nature and knowledge. For this to be possible, you need to have a receptive and open-minded attitude and, above all, the strong will to discover something new. This is the only important thing.

What you are going to read in this book is nothing but pure theory and, therefore, it does not represent the practical absolute truth. I cannot tell you about "the truth" - which is inevitably different for every one of you - but I can speak of the obstacles on the path to reaching it.

Are you reading something which supports your ideas, or something new?

In this sense, your personal approach is of critical importance. Remember that we all unconsciously deny anything new. Change, at the beginning, is always opposed, questioned and then, probably, worked out and finally accepted.

Approaching newness usually means approaching doubt and mystery, since nobody knows where it can lead. If we are ready to follow it, that is if we are open-minded, which means neither being ingenuous nor passively accepting everything we are suggesting, and, in particular, if we are willing to put everything we are told into discussion - starting from an attitude of total receptiveness to the reading - only then can we really believe we have embarked on the right path.

You may not accept my theories out of respect, but hopefully you will analyze them deeply and meticulously, cutting out, polishing, refining and merging with them until they become your own convictions. Only then can you suggest these theories to your players.

Only in this way will this book be useful and your proposal certainly positive.

Angelo Pereni

(Inspired by "Messaggio per un'aquila che si crede un pollo" by A. De Mello)

Legend for field diagrams

○	player
A B C	players
A1 B1 C1	players points of arrival
P	goalkeepers
⊛ ●	the ball
⌄⌐⌐→	dribble
⟶	path of the ball
⌒⟶	path of the ball in air
------▶	path of the player without the ball
⌒⌐	final position of the player
●	focal areas where the ball should be played
◉	player standing in the ideal position in the focal area

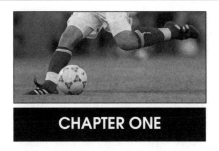

CHAPTER ONE

THE EVOLUTION OF SYSTEMS OF PLAY

Soccer play was born at the dawn of all civilizations in very distant days, but the most reliable and enlightening evidence comes from the Chinese civilization. The most ancient document dates back to 1697 BC, when the Chinese emperor Huang-Ti invented the so-called Tsu-Chu, which literally means "leather ball moved with one's foot".

In reality, soccer as it is seen and played today was born in London in **1863**, when the representatives of eleven English Clubs met to found the Football Association of England and came to a revolutionary decision: players were definitively forbidden to use their hands. The first teams usually fielded nine attackers and one single defender - or *goal cover*. This 1-9 system (see **diagram 1**) involved total offside (the players standing in front of the ball) and no collective play at all. Moreover, a series of precise and strict laws were established to punish rough and unfair play which characterized soccer at that time. Other clubs, which were in favor of the violent nature of medieval competitions (always within a certain range, however), founded the Rugby Football Union, thus partly maintaining roughness, body contact and allowing the use of hands.

At that time, the teams played a very primitive style, characterized by embryonic rules and defined as *kick and yusc* - in other words: "kick and run" - where all the players run to win the ball, thus creating chaotic crowds on the field. This kind of play immediately became very popular, among young students in particular, who favored fair play during the competitions, even without a real judge (the referee). As a matter of fact, in that period the presence of a

2

judge to oversee the play was thought to hurt the honorableness of the contestants. Any sports competition was inspired by such feelings as fairness and sincerity and, therefore, it was up to the captains to take decisions.

The need for a match judge was particularly felt when the rules of the game increased in number, thus becoming too complex to be directly interpreted by players on the field. For this reason, two referees and a judge were introduced at first (each referee controlled one half of the field, while the judge solved controversial situations). Only later, starting from **1890** on, was the modern distribution of specific tasks introduced, thus involving the presence of one single referee and two linesmen.

As tactics began to evolve, another player was moved into the covering area, thus resulting in the 1-1-8 system (see **diagram 2**). In **1870**, the Scottish removed two players from the offensive line to play them in a withdrawn position, thus creating the 1-2-7 formation (see **diagram 3**). For the first time, the two midfielders were responsible for covering and acting as links between the defenders (the goalkeeper and a wing back) and the seven attacking players. By choosing this team organization, the Scottish were the first to understand the importance of team play and passing; in this way, there was a situation - though rather approximate - of relative balance between defense and attack.

The match between England and Scotland, played at Kensington Oval in London in **1873**, was a sign of the evolution soccer was gradually undergoing at that time: most teams were no longer satisfied with playing instinctively with long passes and chaotic runs. Moreover, the corner kick law was introduced on that occasion; England played that match with a 2-1-7 formation, while the Scottish withdrew another player from their offensive line, so that they entered the playing field with a goalkeeper, two wing backs, two central midfielders (balance players) and six attacking players (that is a 2-2-6 system as you can see in **diagram 4**). In this way, the Scottish highlighted the importance of passing and their strategy immediately appeared to be successful.

Technique, which was extremely rudimentary at the beginning, was gradually becoming increasingly refined, and soon reached good levels; moreover, teams slowly began to focus their attention on team organization, so that every player was progressively assigned specific tasks. Passing, dribbling and shooting skills rapidly improved. Nevertheless, play was still mostly based on individual initiatives rather than on real team strategies; every player performed - and often overused - dribbling, ball possession and personal action to try to shoot at goal. In that period, therefore, "individualists" usually prevailed to the detriment of collective team play. The pleasure of individual play excited the creativeness of the individual players, thus preventing the action from developing in a much wider, more rational and effective way.

Defenders gradually began to nullify the attackers' dribbles by means of more and more resolute challenges and tackles and, consequently, dribbling skills - which had often been of crucial importance until then - inevitably appeared less and less efficient. Moreover, increasingly higher attention was focused on the final score in tournaments and championships. Although the concept of team play became more and more successful and was at the base of the incredible evolution and success of soccer all over the world - "individualists" have always played a critical role in this discipline and we hope they always will.

Soccer constantly underwent transformations and, in **1880**, many teams began to play the so-called "pyramidal method" or "system" with a 2-3-5 formation: the goalkeeper, two central defenders, two wide half backs, one central half back and five attackers (see **diagram 5**). The central half back, the playmaker, played a very important role in the team, since he had to cover the defense and prepare the actions for the offensive line; in this way, he slowly became the real hinge of the whole play. That was the first real team play performance. This playing method was also regulated by the offside rule: the attacking player could not move without the ball into the space between the two backs (three-player offside). This rule was skillfully exploited by the defenders who usually positioned vertically - one standing in a withdrawn position and the other as close to the midfielders as possible - so as to keep the opposing attackers away from their goal.

For many years most teams played this pyramidal system, which soon resulted in two different styles of play:
• **the Scottish play** - where technique and individual play prevailed; it was based on short, ground passing tactics, combined with speed in eluding the opponent's marking (this

system was adopted by Austria, Danubian European clubs and in part by Germany),

- **the English play** - based on air and long passing technique; it was a clearly athletic and dynamic play system (this method was mainly adopted by Denmark, Scandinavian countries and partly by Germany).

THE ORIGINS OF SOCCER IN ITALY

Soccer was introduced in Italy by the major gymnastics clubs at the end of the 19th century. In September **1896**, Udinese Fencing and Gymnastics Club won the first national soccer tournament taking place in Treviso (Veneto) – with Ferrara Gymnastics Club runner up. Genoa won the first Italian soccer championship in 1898.

In the beginning, Italian soccer was inspired by the English school, but the Danubian method got the upper hand starting from **1920**. However, at the beginning of the century soccer play was already undergoing radical changes, which gradually led to the combination of individual skills in a sort of primitive collective play.

In **1907** the International Committee slightly modified the offside law: it could be applied only in the opposing half of the field. This innovation caused most teams to change their formations on the playing field: the concave arc arrangement was gradually preferred to the linear formation, so that two attacking players were withdrawn in a back position. That was the origin of the 2-3-2-3 system (see **diagram 6**), which slowly became the classical method of most teams in Danubian Europe.

Since defenders' tactical intelligence was constantly improving, in **1925** the International Committee further modified the offside rule (two players) and, consequently, play systems were immediately revolutionized.

When the two-player offside rule was introduced, the tactical side of soccer really began to evolve. Defensive lines became increasingly large (the backs learned to exploit their territorial advantage) and this fact inevitably influenced offensive play, too. As a matter of fact, the changes in the offside rule brought about incredibly high scores which definitely favored spectacular play and performances. Offensive play increased in speed and mostly developed in depth. Rapid play therefore prevailed over continuous dribbles and over slow and involved play. The 1-3-1-2-3 formation (see

Diagram 1 • 1863

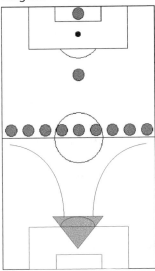

1-1-9 formation
One defender (or goal-cover) in front of the goal-keeper. Total offside (those who are standing in front of the ball).

Diagram 2

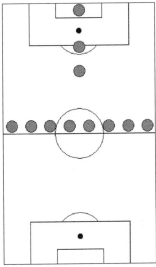

1863 . . .
1-1-1-8 formation

Diagram 3 • 1870

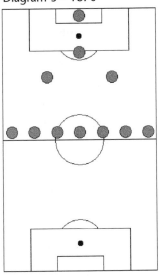

1-1-2-7 formation
Scotland: Two midfielders covering and acting as links between the defensive line (goalkeeper and central back) and the seven attacking players

Diagram 4 • 1873

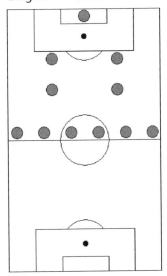

1-2-2-6 formation
Scotland's system of play in the match Scotland vs England played at Kensington Oval in London.

diagram **7**) - also known as "practical method" with three midfield-ers forming a triangle - soon became the most popular.

Instead of marking vertically, defenders began to position hori-zontally, so that man-to-man marking gradually prevailed over a zonal system.

In **1930**, once again the English were the first to perform a new system of play (see **diagram 8**) involving close marking on defense (two marking backs on the opposing wingers and the half back on the opposing central attacker) and the diagonal play (see **diagram 9**). In addition, in this arrangement the famous "quadrilateral" - two wing half backs and two inside forwards, who had to move in a very homogeneous and compact manner - acted as a support for the defensive line and built up the offensive action at the same time.

This system, based on a 3-2-2-3 formation, was conceived by *Herbert Chapman* and was first performed by Arsenal. The London team's play was carried out all over the field and this method inevitably required excellent physical skills, exceptional resistance to prolonged effort and marked offensive vocation. The attacking line was made up of seven players (the three forwards and the two mid-field pairs). Their system was particularly elegant, but it sometimes left the rear guard uncovered, even though **Chapman** - thanks to his players' training - theoretically thought that he could also defend with the four midfielders, who needed to withdraw at the right moment.

All the European clubs soon imitated that system of play, better known as the "WM" formation because of the players' arrangement on the field, defenders forming a W and attackers forming an M (see **diagram 9**). The first Italian team to play with that formation was Genoa, coached by the English coach *Garbutt*.

Soccer began to develop vertically and different variations of the pure "WM" system were almost immediately implemented. In **1932**, most teams shifted to the so-called Riegel method by modifying the defensive disposition and by assigning one player the task of cover-ing and supporting the defenders in difficulty during the match. This play system - which had Swiss origins - introduced a new figure - the sweeper - behind the defenders (one central and one wing back); it resulted in a 1-3-1-2-3 formation where the quadrilateral was broken up and only the M disposition of the offensive line remained (see **diagram 10**). In Italy, the WM method was then

Diagram 5 • **1880**

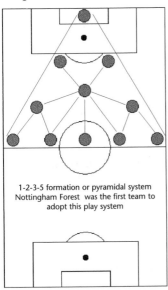

1-2-3-5 formation or pyramidal system
Nottingham Forest was the first team to
adopt this play system

Three-player offside - The player who has
three other players standing in front of him
in any part of the field is not offside.

Diagram 6

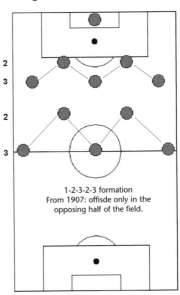

1-2-3-2-3 formation
From 1907: offisde only in the
opposing half of the field.

Diagram 7 • **1925**

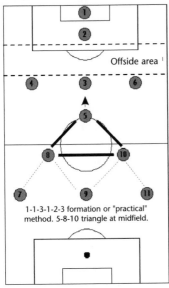

Offside area

1-1-3-1-2-3 formation or "practical"
method. 5-8-10 triangle at midfield.

Two-player offside - Two players
(instead of three) are now sufficient for
applying the offside rule.

Diagram 8 • **1930**   WM

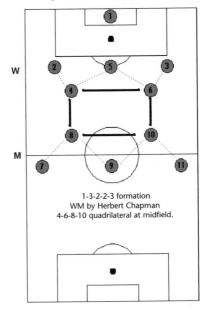

W

M

1-3-2-2-3 formation
WM by Herbert Chapman
4-6-8-10 quadrilateral at midfield.

replaced by the System introduced by *Aitken* and finally gained full popularity in the '40s thanks to Torino soccer club. As a matter of fact, they performed the System in an absolutely exemplary manner, thus making very successful scores, also thanks to the players' technical skills. The quadrilateral at midfield is the fundamental geometric figure in the System.

In **1948**, *Rappan* further refined this arrangement and created the *Verrou*, based on a 2-3-2-3 formation (see **diagram 11**), with two sweepers standing at the back of the defenders (very compact defense system).

The tactics of play implemented by the coach of the Swiss national team corresponded to a definitely defensive soccer philosophy; in practice, he played two sweepers behind the defenders, the right winger in a withdrawn covering position and only two forwards who usually moved a lot to avoid giving specific references to the opposing marking backs. This arrangement, which immediately became very popular after the famous 1-0 win of the Swiss national team over the English masters in Zurich, consisted of large numbers in defense with counterattack its fundamental and successful weapon.

Tactics were then breaking out everywhere in soccer and each country gradually worked out new systems of play which immediately turned into important soccer philosophies. Technical and tactical play solutions developed in different ways in various countries, in relation to the particular physical features, the temperament and the social and cultural background of each people. In that period, most clubs in Northern Europe mainly relied on athletic skills, methodical interpretation of the performance and on tactical discipline often characterized by exemplary self-control in order to achieve success.

Other peoples - generally less endowed from the physical point of view - looked for different solutions, by utilizing their dribbling abilities and creativeness; as a matter of fact, their play mainly resulted from their imagination and improvisation (always characterized by a certain tactical accuracy) rather than from the strict performance of set schemes. This solution was mostly chosen by those countries, particularly South American, where:

- soccer is the expression and the translation of a particular cultural spirit;

Diagram 9 • **1830** • diagonal WM

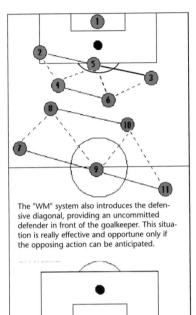

The "WM" system also introduces the defensive diagonal, providing an uncommitted defender in front of the goalkeeper. This situation is really effective and opportune only if the opposing action can be anticipated.

Diagram 10 • **1932**

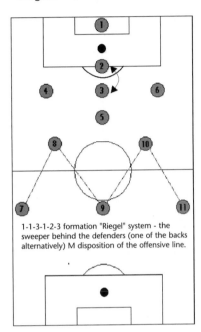

1-1-3-1-2-3 formation "Riegel" system - the sweeper behind the defenders (one of the backs alternatively) M disposition of the offensive line.

Diagram 11 • **1932**

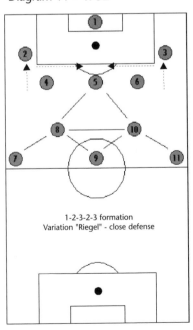

1-2-3-2-3 formation
Variation "Riegel" - close defense

Diagram 12 • **1948**

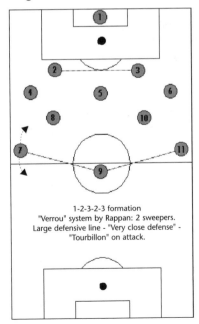

1-2-3-2-3 formation
"Verrou" system by Rappan: 2 sweepers.
Large defensive line - "Very close defense" -
"Tourbillon" on attack.

- culture cannot ignore the figure of the soccer hero with whom supporters inevitably identify themselves;
- soccer is mainly intended for highly spectacular purposes;
- individuality is still a form of social achievement;
- natural skills make up for the lack of a real soccer philosophy.

THE DANUBIAN SCHOOL

There is a third way - the Danubian School - which combines part of the North European technical and tactical conception and part of the South American soccer lesson; the Danubian School was particularly successful in the years immediately after the First World War.

It can also be defined as "Euro-Latin school", since it developed in the countries of Central and Southern Europe. Although it cannot be compared to South American soccer philosophy, it is definitely more refined than that of Northern Europe in terms of play planning and performance, and it is also supported by a considerable dose of creativeness. On the contrary, as far as rhythm (athletic abilities) and tactical discipline are concerned, the improvisation and dribbling skills are much more similar to the North European school than to the South American philosophy.

1950: in response to the success of the 3-2-3-2 formation (see **diagram 12**), or "M" system involving the arrangement of a pentagon at midfield and the implementation of the offside trap, Hungary introduced a variation (see **diagram 13**) by playing with three defenders, two midfielders covering the defense, two advanced midfielders and a withdrawn striker (the famous Hidegkuti), acting as a link between the two forwards.

1952: in Italy, FC Internazionale revolutionized everything by shifting player number 7 to a covering position on the right flank (and therefore acting as a wing back) and player number 2 to the position of the sweeper (see **diagram 14**).

1958: in the World Cup Champion Brazil team, the diagonal disappeared and a new system of play - the 4-2-4 formation - was introduced, which turned into 4-3-3 in the defensive phase. No player was forced to mark his own opponent, but simply controlled the area he was previously assigned.

This method obviously included covering mechanisms and mutual supporting strategies. When a player moved forward, one of his

Diagram 13 • **1950**

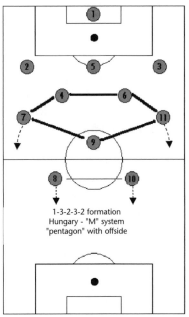

1-3-2-3-2 formation
Hungary - "M" system
"pentagon" with offside

Diagram 14 • **1952**

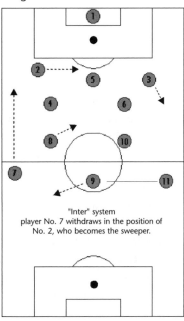

"Inter" system
player No. 7 withdraws in the position of
No. 2, who becomes the sweeper.

Diagram 15 • **1958**

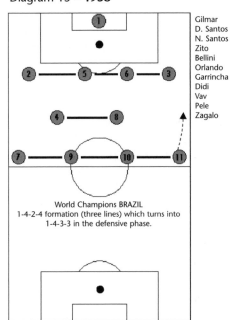

Gilmar
D. Santos
N. Santos
Zito
Bellini
Orlando
Garrincha
Didi
Vav
Pele
Zagalo

World Champions BRAZIL
1-4-2-4 formation (three lines) which turns into
1-4-3-3 in the defensive phase.

Diagram 16 • **1962**

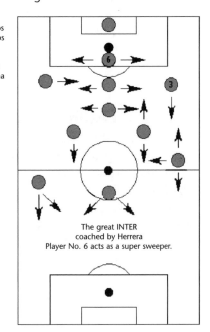

The great INTER
coached by Herrera
Player No. 6 acts as a super sweeper.

teammates immediately positioned so as to cover that unguarded area. Some teams also began to perform a sort of double teaming mechanism, although they appeared to be mostly dictated by pure instinct.

1962: FC Internazionale coached by *Helenio Herrera* (whose saying "Taca la bala" - attack the ball - made him very popular), played number 6, Picchi, as a super sweeper, by performing very close man-to man marking on the forwards and on the withdrawn strikers. Moreover, player number 3, *Giacinto Facchetti*, was allowed to attack on the left flank of the field (see **diagram 16**).

1966: The World Cup Champions England adopted a 4-1-3-2 system with *Stiles* playing in front of the defensive line - (see **diagram 17**), which was nothing but a modified version of Brazil's 4-3-3 formation, with the center of gravity slightly brought forward towards the attacking line (see **diagram 18**).

1969: many Italian clubs began to field the offensive sweeper (see **diagram 19**) who both shielded the defense and actively took part in the organization of offensive action (*Cera*, in Cagliari coached by **Scopigno** and in the National team).

1970: Brazil, the World Cup Champions, changed its 4-3-3- system into a 4-4-2 formation (see **diagram 20**), involving zone marking and more double teaming actions.

Italy, the runner up, also played the 4-4-2 system (see **diagram 21**), but, unlike Brazil, their play was based on man-to-man marking.

EUROPE'S LEADING ROLE IN SOCCER

Starting from the final match between England and Germany in **1966**, Europe gradually acquired a leading role in the evolution of the tactical organization of play compared to South American soccer, despite Brazil's win over Italy (characterized by the famous turnover between *Mazzola* and *Rivera*) at the **1970** World Cup in Mexico City. The European system of play, characterized by quick offensive actions, tactical movements without the ball, rapid play rhythm and combining long and short passes, was destined to gain more and more success.

European soccer reached its peak during the **1974** World Cup, when the Netherlands (see **diagram 22**) succeeded in combining

Diagram 17 • **1966**

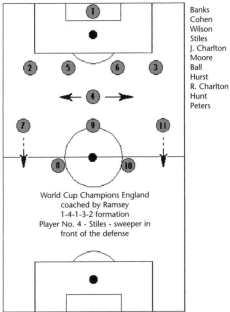

Banks
Cohen
Wilson
Stiles
J. Charlton
Moore
Ball
Hurst
R. Charlton
Hunt
Peters

World Cup Champions England
coached by Ramsey
1-4-1-3-2 formation
Player No. 4 - Stiles - sweeper in
front of the defense

Diagram 18 • **1966**

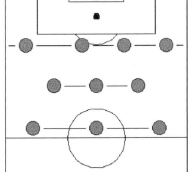

BRAZIL
1-4-3-3 arrangement
(three lines)

Diagram 19 • **1969**

"OFFENSIVE SWEEPER"

Diagram 20 • **1970**

Felix
Carlos
Alberto
Everaldo
Brito
Piazza
Clodoaldo
Jairzinho
Gerson
Tastao
Pelé
Rivelino

World Cup Champions BRAZIL

1-4-4-2 formation
Zone marking

14

creative organization with tactical play mechanisms, individual maturity with team strategies (double teaming, supports...), considerable changes of pace with ball possession, the balance between the defensive and the offensive lines (always with a typically offensive play philosophy) and a perfect fusion of individual skills and collective play solutions.

The most surprising aspect of that great team was not their system of play, that is the arrangement of players on the field (which was nevertheless extremely important), but their team play combined with individual performances in the critical phases of the match. Dutch play was, and still is, characterized by an evident offensive disposition, by accurate and skilled passes, by continuous changes of positions and by constant pressure on the opponent in his half of the field (offensive pressure).

The Dutch constantly performed play combinations based on the incessant movements of all the players both along the width and the depth of the field and on the defenders' frequent penetration on attack. In the defensive phase, as soon as the opposition achieved possession (won the ball, bad pass, tackle, shot...), the Dutch could immediately and nearly always exploit the advantages offered by their own play philosophy. This was possible because the players were all ready to prepare and to get into the offensive action in a very dynamic way (shifting or transition from defense to attack was instant). That system involved the active movement and participation not only of the players who successfully interrupted the opposition's attack, but of all the team members as a whole.

That dynamic approach created a wide range of possible solutions in the development of offensive tactics. In addition, in most cases the team could exploit the important numerical advantage in the central area of the pitch. Outnumbering the opposition in midfield allowed them to practice increasingly sudden and original offensive solutions, while also exalting their creativeness as well as passing skills and variety. In **1978**, the Netherlands slightly modified their tactical formation on the field (see **diagrams 22b and 22c**), while always maintaining their tactical organization.

In the **80s**, soccer players having generally improved their individual technical skills, play actions and combinations considerably increased in speed (in increasingly restricted spaces) since most teams played very aggressive zone systems and applied pressing

Diagram 21 • **1970**

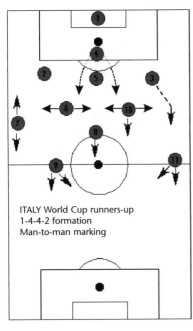

Albertosi
Burgnich
Facchetti
cera
Rosato
Bertini
Domenghini
Mazzola
Boninsegna
De Sisti
Riva

ITALY World Cup runners-up
1-4-4-2 formation
Man-to-man marking

Diagram 22 • **1970**

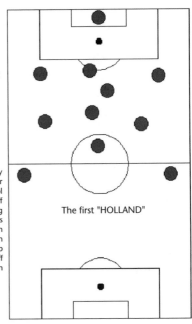

Stuy
Suurbier
Krol
Hulschoff
Brankerburg
Neeskens
Haan
Muhren
Rep
Cruyff
Keizen

The first "HOLLAND"

Diagram 22b • **1974**

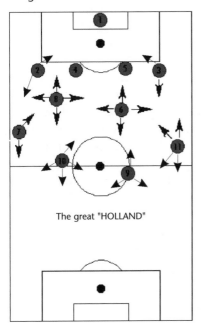

The great "HOLLAND"

Diagram 22c • **1978**

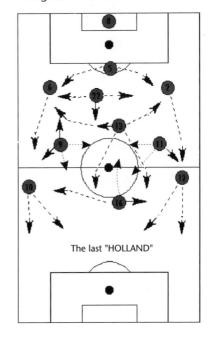

The last "HOLLAND"

strategies more and more frequently. Furthermore, the average level of individual technique was definitely higher and increasingly high attention began to be focused on fitness training.

In the course of the European Championship - held in Italy in 1980 - West Germany, the winners, practiced high-pressure soccer all over the field, but without systematically resorting to pressing and offside strategies.

That team, fielding such great players as *Stielike, Rummenigge, Schuster* and *Müller*, could easily shift from player-to-player defense (always and only on the central opposing forwards) to zone marking, by covering the wings with Kaltz and Briegel. That European Championship clearly highlighted (in a much more evident way than in The Argentina World Cup) the tendency to drop back into one's own half once the offensive play had been made, so as to create space, prepare for the counterattack and prevent the opposition from counterattacking. Therefore, twenty players were rapidly moving from one half of the field to the other, which resulted in a more and more popular compact disposition.

In that period, Belgium was the country that most performed offside tactics, both at club levels (Bruges and Anderlecht) and in the National team, applying this strategy even more than Holland. Thanks to constant offside tactics Belgium reached the European final in 1980 where they were defeated 2-1 by Germany.

The French school was another important parenthesis in the history of soccer, especially thanks to the "champagne" play performed by the team coached by Hidalgo and led by Michel Platini directly on the field. That group included such important top-class players as *Giresse, Tigana, Fernandez...* (see **diagram 24**) and won the European Championship in 1984, playing a midfield quadrilateral which was reminiscent of Chapman's WM formation, although it was based on different tactical principles. That tactical strategy was greatly supported by the undeniable skills and technical-tactical features of Hidalgo's players.

At the **1990** World Cup Championship, the teams playing a mixed-zone system usually fielded larger defensive lines, so that the number of defenders increased from four to five (see **diagram 25**); while those teams playing zone marking generally modified the formation at midfield or on attack if necessary (4-4-2 or 4-3-3 or 4-5-1). In practice, the 5-3-2 or 5-4-1 system (overturned pyramidal sys-

Diagram 23 • **1980**

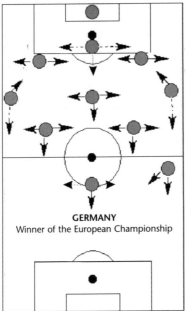

Shumacher
Kaltz
Dietz
Briegel
Forster K.
Stielike
Rummenigge
Schuster
Hrubesch
Muller
Allofs

GERMANY
Winner of the European Championship

Diagram 24

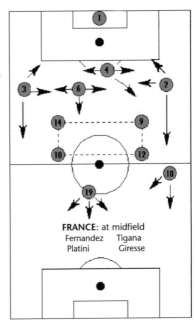

FRANCE: at midfield
Fernandez   Tigana
Platini   Giresse

Diagram 25

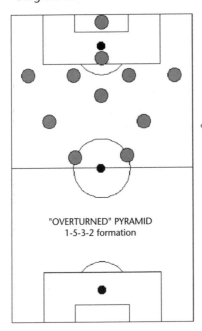

"OVERTURNED" PYRAMID
1-5-3-2 formation

Diagram 26

Galli G.
Tassotti
Maldini
Galli F.
Baresi
Colombo
Donadoni
Ancellotti
Van Basten
Gullit
Virdis

on the bench:
Evani
Massaro
Bortolazzi
Mussi
Costacurta
Bianchi

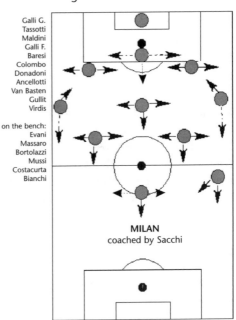

MILAN
coached by Sacchi

18

tem) was gradually becoming the most successful. It included a sweeper, two central marking backs (man-to-man or zone marking), and two zone offensive wingers. Moreover, the figure of the linkman almost completely disappeared, while the wide back and the offensive half back progressively became more and more important.

The **1987/88** soccer season opened the so-called "*Sacchi* era": his Milan won the Italian championship, which was mainly characterized by their incredibly catching Maradona's Napoli (the defending champions). In that season, "Dutch" Milan (see **diagram 26**) mostly trusted to *Ruud Gullit*, because of the serious injury affecting *Marco Van Basten*.

That formation represented a much more advanced and refined expression of the system performed by the Netherlands a few years before. In practice, *Sacchi* succeeded in creating a still more compact team, by focusing increasingly high attention on the team as a whole and on collective play. He mainly insisted on offside mechanisms, ultra-offensive pressing strategies (compared to Holland's slightly empirical offensive pressure), double teaming, supporting play... This tactical attitude allowed AC Milan to press the opponents in their own half of the field, while imposing their own pace and rhythm to regain possession of the ball immediately, by means of an extraordinary filter at midfield and the participation of the whole team in pressing actions.

The team usually imposed their play, forcing the opposition to apply constant adjustments which inevitably neutralized their tactical game plan. They generally managed to get the better of their opponents also from the physical point of view, by dictating rhythm and pace of the match. Sacchi's teams also highlighted the critical importance of the fitness coach in soccer and a strong relationship developed between *Arrigo Sacchi* and *Vincenzo Pincolini*, the fitness coach. In addition, Sacchi's Milan club achieved great success also because of their general organization and management, in which a top-level coaching staff, managers and medical team all played a crucial role.

However, it is curious and interesting to observe that their successful cycle definitely corresponded to the choice of foreign players, all of Dutch nationality.

The arrival of *Marcello Lippi* at FC Juventus opened a new cycle in soccer whose main feature was the combination of collective play organization and personal initiative and flair.

Personal creativeness became a critical support to tactical schemes in the offensive phase. Juventus has embraced the principle that those who have the best players from the technical and mental point of view generally win in modern soccer. Nevertheless, everything must be combined with and supported by perfect general organization both at the coaching personnel and club staff levels.

It is evident that play organization is still undergoing constant changes and will undoubtedly continue its metamorphosis in the future. Each country has always proposed and advocated its school of thought and each coach his own ideas; all this has gradually led to modern total soccer, regardless of the single system of play, zone playing strategies or not.

Championships, Tournaments, Cup and World Cup contests have always been won by teams performing different play methods - zone play, mixed-zone system or man-to-man marking - different soccer philosophies and different cultures. What is really important is:

- to develop skillful players and, above all, maturity in their play;
- to have an open mind, that is to be willing to consider new experiences and ideas;
- to be ready to consider innovations and changes;
- to exalt creativeness
- to play a role in the development of sport disciplines as cultural events;
- to love and enjoy one's job.

It is important to include a new reality in the world of modern soccer: the African continent, which is gradually acquiring an increasingly important position worldwide and whose achievement has culminated with Nigeria winning the 1996 Olympic games. There are several reasons for their escalation, but the social and cultural development of the African continent is undoubtedly playing a crucial role.

The United States are the sole reality where soccer is still experiencing its embryonic phase and can hardly take off, even though its success at the youth and college levels and the positive response of the public to the new professional league generally give people hope for the future.

AN INEXORABLE SUCCESS

There are many different reasons for the success of the soccer phenomenon: this sport discipline can be practiced at any latitude, its success is neither connected to particular physical or temperamental features, nor to specific social and cultural characteristics. Moreover, it is fundamental that each people interpret soccer according to the average athletic, psychological and cultural values of its own youths.

The history of soccer clearly shows us that bad imitations have always disappointed and failed; those who follow their own nature, those who adjust their play to specific goals and use common sense, can always hope of finally achieving success.

Theories and tactical strategies tend to channel soccer into fixed schemes, to bind it to long studied formulae and to reduce the role of hazard on the final scores, but its charm always lies in its unpredictable and irrational nature which constantly rebels against the bonds some would like to impose to this game. These conditions and qualities inevitably make soccer increasingly charming.

CHAPTER TWO

PLAY ORGANIZATION

THE MAIN CHANGES IN SOCCER

The first important changes in the play organization mainly resulted from the changes in the offside rules. The pioneers in the field of soccer soon understood that play should concentrate and develop near the player in possession of the ball and that it was necessary to prevent the anarchy deriving from players positioning in any area of the field, regardless of the position of the ball. This is the reason why the International Committee immediately passed the first **total off-side** law: "Those who stand before the line of the ball in any area of the playing field are in an offside position".

However, that rule was soon modified so as to prevent play from resulting in chaotic bunches of players, where nothing but dribbling skills were exalted. The new law stated that: "Those who have three other players standing before them in any part of the field, are not in offside positions". For this reason, most teams were obliged to rethink their formation on the field, mainly in the vertical sense, and to focus the attention on a sort of play organization.

Nevertheless, the first crucial tactical advance resulted from the evolution of the pass, which consequently brought about substantial changes in the positioning of players on the pitch. These "tactical" modifications were not always positive in terms of play quality and, furthermore, wide defenders playing in a more advanced position, this inevitably appeared as an obstruction to the offensive action. Since the situation was gradually becoming more and more exasperating, the International Board resolved to modify the offside law once again, in order to try to encourage offensive play.

According to this new rule, offside was applied only in the opposing half of the field; this involved much more dynamism in most teams' play and, in particular, the creation of:

- "through passing" tactics, that is the pass towards the teammate who is running forward, and movement without the ball gradually became fundamental in soccer;
- "wall passing" tactics, supported by another teammate for the return pass.

Two important innovations, the **pass** and the **triangle**, considerably affected the way most teams played soccer and inevitably forced players to greatly improve their basic technical skills.

The offside law underwent further changes from that moment on: in particular, the number of players necessary to apply the offside rule dropped from three to two.

NOT ONLY OFFSIDE

Until that moment, the main changes in soccer all, or nearly all, resulted from the evolution of the offside law. But starting from that moment on, crucial transformations were gradually inspired by the importance of the final score, especially in leagues and tournaments, by the various defensive formations (man-to-man or zone marking) and by each particular play philosophy (long passes and predominance of the athletic aspect or short passes and exaltation of technical skills). Therefore, play organization underwent modifications which increasingly privileged the defensive phase. The number of players on defense slowly increased, while their offensive mentality and inclination gradually grew weaker.

These rules and tactical attitudes have characterized soccer for nearly forty years. Apart from the system of play (player-to-player or zone marking - long or short passes - tactical formation) the **Netherlands** substantially modified the arrangement of the team on the playing field, both in width and in depth, as well as the players' mentality. This wave of innovations also enriched soccer jargon with new terms: pressure, mentality, double teaming, regaining possession of the ball, collective and team play, vertical, compact team, physical condition, mind and action speed, tactical mobility, universality of positions, eclecticism, total player... With the help of mass-media, these terms gradually became an integral part of soccer vocabulary, although the choice of man-to-man or zone marking always remained an open question. Because of their nature, these two tactical solutions also influenced the way coaches coached soccer.

Zone tactics: the teams performing these tactics are strictly influenced by their own coaches' ideas and practice in order to improve their play system and refine it, regardless of the features of the opposing teams they are going to play.

Man-to-man tactics: the teams choosing this defensive formation practice so as to refine their system of play and eventually make suitable changes in both players and tactics according to the teams they are going to play in the coming matches, especially in case of teams performing zone tactics.

Each country and each soccer philosophy constantly tries to sublimate these tactical concepts according to their own mentality and culture and choose discipline, hard work and team moral strength as their basic principles. Their main goal is to coach and perform positive, creative and spectacular soccer, combining technical skills with perfect physical and athletic conditioning.

In the last few years, soccer has been undergoing considerable changes; this is partly due to the fact that this sport, which is by far one of the richest, has been provided with incredible means, although its enormous resources are not always conveyed in the right direction.

How many clubs have suitably equipped training facilities which effectively meet their real needs, especially for youth soccer?

How many clubs can provide their coaches with a suitable library of coaching books, videos and computer software?

How many clubs help their coaches to travel abroad in order to study and investigate the organization of the most important foreign clubs and their youth teams?

The strong will of most coaches combined with the possibility of travelling to visit professional clubs' training facilities and investigate their training methods and improve their knowledge supported by computer, specific books, videotapes, cable and satellite TV programs is now beginning to bear fruit.

Soccer players should also be involved in this important growth, since they often - or nearly always - play their role passively and do not behave as great athletes who live their sports lives in an active manner, always bringing themselves up to date, studying, being active protagonists of the training session and so forth.

All these elements have brought about an important evolution in soccer:

from the physical point of view, especially as a consequence of introducing the fitness coach who - despite the numerous difficulties he always has to cope with – has helped to make considerable improvements in the traditional training methods. Although there are still serious difficulties, this evolution in planning fitness training is starting to bear fruit at all levels of the game;

at technical and tactical levels: with play becoming increasingly fast paced, this causes coaches to rethink systems of play and tactics and players to refine their technical skills since the speed of each skill has increased considerably.

This aspect is of critical importance, because if a coach aims at improving the tactical skills of his team as a whole, he cannot neglect the technical facet; in particular, he needs to concentrate on how his players practice each exercise, that is:

*   with the greatest intensity
*   with maximum attention, concentration and diligence
*   in a way that players are forced to perform all the various technical skills (stop, control, pass...) at the same or higher speed than they are asked during official games.

Let's go back to the '70s and '80s - when soccer pressure (both on and off the field) was not so high, when spaces on the field were definitely wider (longer teams) and when players could still look for and perform aesthetic technical skills - the sequence of the receiver of the ball developed as follows:

Technical Skills (Action)	**Choosing** (Thought)	**Performing** (Action)
⇩	⇩	⇩
Basic technical skill (Space and time support)	**Tactical solution** (Understand, Choose, Assess)	**Applied technique**

In practice, there were two technical "moments" (actions): the first one was basic technique (stop, ball control...) and the second was applied technique (pass, dribbling the ball, beating an opponent...); these two moments were separated by the **tactical solution** (thought), whose length was directly influenced by the opposition's pressure (space and time). In this space and time the player had to **understand - assess- choose** all the various possibilities of play (unmarked teammates, their movements, the best solutions and so forth), and then play the ball or, in the worst (or the best) case (that is no solution at all), start an individual action (by dribbling the ball or taking on a 1 versus 1 situation).

The first technical skill was usually performed (in midfield in particular) in a non-pressure or semi-calm situation; this is the reason why players sometimes chose the aesthetic skill (like an instep stop and so on).

As years went by, and nowadays in particular, new tactical situations and the considerable improvement in training methods from the physical point of view have gradually imposed a different sequence, so that the order technical skill-choosing-performing was replaced by:

Choosing	**Technical skill**	**Performing**
(Thought)	(Action)	(Action)
⇩	⇩	⇩
Tactical solution	**Basic technical skill**	**Applied technique**
(Understand and assess)	(Space and time)	

This is due to the strong pressure which is carried out by the opposition in the area where the ball is, to the increasingly small spaces which do not allow players to move freely and, consequently, to the increasingly short time players have to properly perform the three different sequences. For this reason, **choosing** (thought, tactical solution) becomes much more complex and articulate. The **technical skills** and **the performance**, which were previously almost

always separated by the **choice** and were therefore two distinct moments, are now extremely close together. In practice, basic technical skill and applied technique combine in one single skill. This is the reason why, today more than ever, technique needs to be trained in a much more specific and refined manner.

Pressure areas: in the '70s and '80s soccer play was characterized by a sort of "static pressure". Most teams performed pressing strategies, but mainly in the two defensive areas and almost exclusively individually, as a consequence of players' disposition on the field (only the sweeper could double team). Therefore,

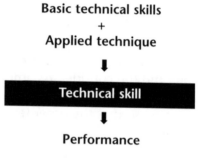

the two pressure areas were well-defined and never shifted into other parts of the playing field, regardless of the position of the ball.

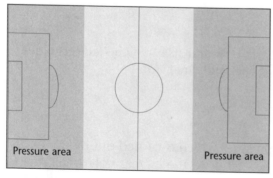

Pressure groups: today, new tactical situations and different psycho-physical conditions have gradually helped the development of pressing or "dynamic pressure", involving the whole team to move continuously. Each single unit acts as a whole; the team is gathered in about 40 yards and - unless the coach makes particular tactical choices - players are asked to perform continuous pressure.

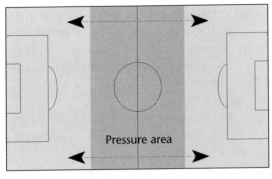

Pressure area

For a team to be really successful and definitely stand out, they need to have:
• skillful players both at the technical and tactical level who are able to "read" the game;
• psychological and physical balance (one component cannot prevail over the other);
• strong motivations, which really are of critical importance.

In-line player: FIFA has once again re-thought the offside rule according to the position of the ball. It has been decided that when the attacking player is standing in line with the defender, he cannot be considered offside. This change is aimed at favoring offensive play and partly undoes the systematic use of the offside tactics, which has become particularly risky not only in consequence of the new rule, but also because of the ability of most teams to adopt increasingly effective countermeasures.

Back pass to the goalkeeper: television requires fewer "off" periods in the performance and, if possible, a larger number of goals. Therefore, FIFA has thought of preventing any waste of real play time - which usually resulted from continuous passes to the goal-keeper - by introducing a new law, which completely changes the role of the goalkeeper and, consequently, the behavior of the players on the field. This has inevitably caused coaches to make tactical adjustments. Each time a player voluntarily plays the ball towards his goalkeeper, the goalie cannot touch the ball with his hands, otherwise he is penalized with an indirect free kick against. This is the first time FIFA has structurally worked on the figure of the goalkeeper, since this role has always been affected only marginally by important changes. This means that he is constantly involved in the play action but only with his feet.

Expulsion: in the last few years, the increasingly strong desire for more excitement and spectacular play has influenced most of the decisions made by FIFA and has finally led the official committee to punish by an immediate expulsion the foul committed on a player running towards the opposing goal with a clear possibility of scoring, when the player committing the foul is the last one before the goalkeeper. Expulsion is the punishment inflicted also to those players charging their opponent from behind; this disciplinary measure has been taken to prevent these kinds of fouls, which have unfortunately become too frequent and dangerous.

It is also important to remember that the player intentionally handling and the goalkeeper touching the ball with his hands outside the penalty area are also punished by immediate expulsion.

These disciplinary modifications have gradually forced coaches to also teach their teams how to play with a numerical disadvantage, by assessing the most suitable adjustments according to their system of play and to the opponents' tactics.

ZONE PLAY

The player is the protagonist of the various soccer situations, especially when he is expected to solve technical and tactical problems at any time during the competition. The coach is responsible for organizing his players' tactics on the playing field - by following effective systems which can be easily understood by everybody - optimizing the potential of every single player and using coaching methods aimed at stimulating a winning mentality both in each player and in the group as a whole. The coaching and teaching systems used in modern soccer are based on theoretical premises which can be brought together as follows:

a) players position on the playing field according to the position of the ball and of their own goal;

b) each player is assigned one particular opponent to mark or a specific area to control: in this area he is supposed to mark any opponent and win any ball arriving there;

c) the players in the team all take part in both the defensive and offensive play;

d) players are mentally and physically trained for the transition, that is the immediate shifting from the defensive to the offensive game and vice versa;

e) the player works for the whole team and the whole team works for every single player.

There are three main principles on which zone play in soccer is based:

- the concept of marking tactics and, consequently, the way to defend
- pressing, which means cutting off the opponents' playing spaces (both vertically and horizontally)
- offside, which means preventing the opposition from playing in depth

Implementing these principles directly on the field consequently results in an increasingly high speed of play both vertically (when it is possible) and horizontally - involving very quick changes of direction - and winning of the ball more quickly so that the defensive action immediately turns into an offensive maneuver. This ultimately results in a much more spectacular and exciting game.

For a coach to get the best out of this system of play, he needs to have players who are cooperative (they should be ready to cooperate in this kind of game which causes players to spend a great deal of energy), clever (which means they must be able to rapidly adapt to all the different tactical situations, after properly assessing the development of the physical action) and able to read the match they are playing.

Therefore, it is very important to have:

- fast defenders able to play both long and short balls
- tactically skilled midfield players
- cooperative spirit and strong will to learn
- marked team spirit

ZONE MARKING

Unlike the man-to-man defensive system, in the zone defense each player is responsible for challenging any opponent entering the area he is assigned. Since there are no specific reference points on which the general defensive strength can be conveyed (and the word defense refers to the active participation of all the players in the non-possession phase), the tactical arrangement of the team - if they are not in possession of the ball - will inevitably tend to cut off the spaces or the passing lanes, both vertically and horizontally, in order to better control the opposition, and to immediately win the ball so as to quickly shift from defensive to offensive play (the quicker the transition, the greater its effectiveness).

The team should be as short as possible (thirty or forty yards of the playing field) playing four defenders in line (but not excessively, especially the two central backs who will play in a withdrawn position compared to the outside backs), three or four midfielders who, one at a time, will position in the central area by moving horizontally and two or three attacking players forming the offensive line. When I speak of three attacking players I do not necessarily refer to three forwards, because team play is offensively effective and successful when the whole group has a "winning" mentality and an "offensive" will and not just because the coach fields three or four attackers.

Real Madrid, winner of 1985/86 UEFA Cup, used to play three forwards: Sanchez, Valdano and Butragueno who, one at a time, withdrew so as to support the midfield and the defense.

In the 1984/85 European Champions final match, Liverpool played with two forwards - Dalglish and Rush - one of whom was always more retracted than the other.

In the 1986/87 European Cup-Winner's Cup final, Ajax practically played one single forward on attack - Van Basten - always supported by the midfielders and especially by the most advanced one, that is Bosman. Moreover, do not forget the early A.C. Milan coached by Arrigo Sacchi; they played two forwards but were the best expression of team offensive play, along with the Ajax of Van Gaal, fielding one single striker as offensive reference.

Therefore, there are numerous tactical formations (see **diagrams 1 - 2 - 3 - 4**) each one translating both the fashion and the mentality of the country as well as the tactical philosophy of the coach, while always respecting the basic principles characterizing zone play. It is possible to play one, two or three forwards, but what is really and always fundamental is the organization of the midfield and the defensive line in particular (which can be more or less aggressive according to the mentality of the coach and consist of three, four or five players).

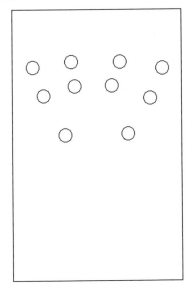

Diagram 1

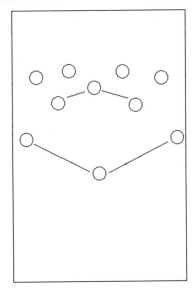

Diagram 2

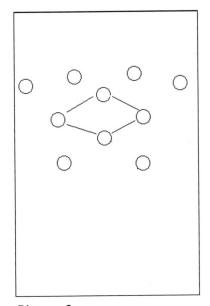

Diagram 3

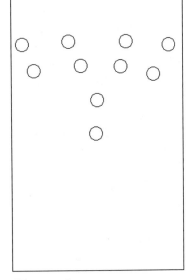

Diagram 4

Four-player zone defense: the defenders position in line, but not excessively. What is really fundamental is the position of the two central backs who stand slightly behind the two outside backs (semi-circle-like position - see **diagram 5**), ready (during the offensive phase) to support their teammate pressed by his opponent, so as to give him the possibility to play the ball (see **diagram 6**). Furthermore, the defenders should be ready (in the defensive phase) to double team the opposition on the flanks, by using the defensive diagonal (see **diagram 7**).

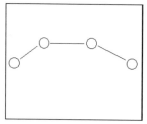 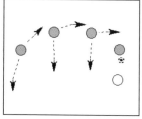 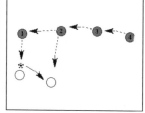

Diagram 5   Diagram 6   Diagram 7

The defensive diagonal can be performed in three different ways, as you can see in the **diagrams 8 a-b-c:**

- **four-line defense** - the outside defender presses the area of the ball, while the other members of the defensive unit position in different lines to cover their teammate, by mutually supporting each other; this arrangement is not particularly helpful when the players need to implement the offside trap;
- **three-line "Eagle" defense** - three players acting on their strong side position diagonally: one of them presses the opponent, while the others stand and act as supporting players. Their teammate placed on his weak side positions along the second defensive line and should take care not to be found uncovered behind his back;
- **two-line defense** - the outside back presses the area of the ball, while the other members of the defensive unit position along one single line; the goalkeeper is asked to be much more attentive since he can sometimes be asked to act as a sweeper.

The position of the goalkeeper - who also plays a crucial role in these defensive arrangements - can never be neglected during the teaching stage and the training sessions.

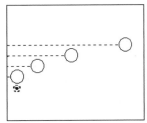
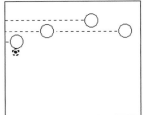
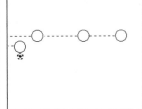

Diagram 8a   Diagram 8b   Diagram 8c

In order to check the central attack by the opposition, the defensive line should form a triangle, where the central back presses the area of the ball, while the others stand along one single line in a covering position (see **diagram 9**). The teammate standing on the weak side moves towards the center so as to increase the compactness of the defensive wall.

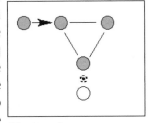

Diagram 9

In addition, the two central backs must be ready:

- to recover on through passes;
- to accurately and quickly play the ball to the mid-fielders and, if it is possible (and if they are able to do so), to the forwards;
- to penetrate centrally any time there is an opening in the mid-field of the opposition;
- to call the offside trap (by means of a gesture or the voice) since they are the last line of defense, but only when it is necessary.

Not only is it important to pay attention to all these movements, but the central backs also need to keep the greatest concentration in case they are forced to defend in the last twenty yards, because in this area of the field the defense shifts from zone marking to man-to-man marking on the last opponent entering the area which the defender was previously assigned to. As a matter of fact, we all know that it can be very dangerous to leave room (even a few inches) to an attacking player in the penalty area; this is the reason why the defenders can never be doubtful about who is going to challenge the opponent when he has the possibility to receive the ball and shoot at goal.

Five-player zone defense: exactly like in the four-player defensive arrangement, the defenders move according to the position of the ball (goal side of the playing field) by making diagonal, in line and triangular tactical movements (like in the four-player defense). This defensive system can combine the principles of zone marking and those of player-to-player marking. One of the central backs can act as a sweeper or as a supporting player for his teammates, in relation to the development of the action and of the opponents' movements or apart from them. The behavior of the outside backs strictly respects the principles of zone play.

The five-player system allows the defensive line to cover better, both outside and in the central position, and increases the possibility of supporting play. The area each player has to cover is much smaller than in the four-player defense (see **diagrams 10 a-b-c-d**).

Three-player zone defense: the concepts of diagonal, lines and triangle are always the same; the space each player has to cover is much larger and this causes the defenders to be more attentive. The defenders' movement emphasizes the system of the four-player zone defense, but, at the same time, it is very important that in this tactical context the three backs are able to positively face one versus one situations, as in man-to-man marking.

The midfield players: they act as filters in front of the defense, as motors of the whole team and are usually technically skillful, so that they support their teammates and help them to play in depth and are always ready to give the last pass.

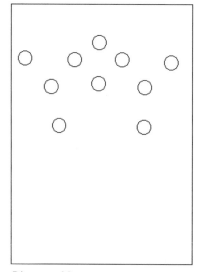

Diagram 10a

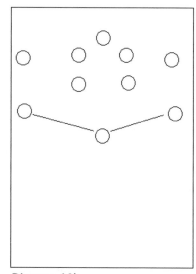

Diagram 10b

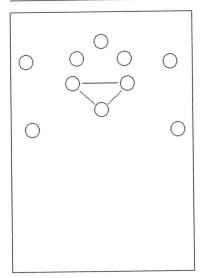

Diagram 10c

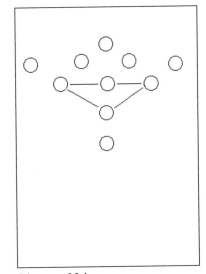

Diagram 10d

Moreover, they should:

- maintain the distances from one unit to the other (see **diagram 11**);
- move and act so as to always maintain the team shape (short - close – compact);
- act as covering players for their teammates who move forward to support the offensive maneuver (see **diagram 12**);
- help the defensive line to get free from the opposition's pressing: the central midfielder moves between the two central backs, trying to help one of them to elude the opponent and sprint forward (see **diagram 13**), or covers one of the two outside backs who has moved forward on the flanks (see **diagram 14**).

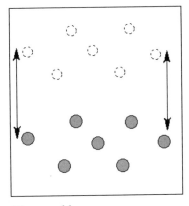

Diagram 11

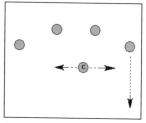
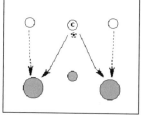
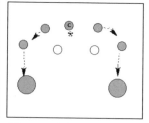

Diagram 12   Diagram 13   Diagram 14

If the four defenders are particularly skillful at dribbling the ball, they should exploit the available spaces in the best possible way, so that one of them can penetrate forward to set up a new offensive action, and create a numerical advantage for his team. It is necessary to remember that, like the defenders, the midfield players should also press and therefore double team the opponent in possession of the ball (see **diagram 15 and 16**), when the whole team has found the right tactical formation.

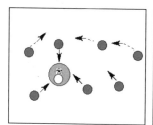
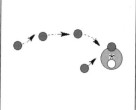

Diagram 15   Diagram 16

The forwards: they are responsible for finishing the play, but they are also the first to defend and press when the team has to regain possession of the ball, the first to slow down the opposition's play, and they should always be ready to push up the team, thus making it much more compact in the defensive phase. Apart from their dribbling skills, the attacking players should also be particularly skillful in:

- maintaining possession of the ball to help the whole team get out of the defensive line and set up the attack;
- the "wall pass", so as to support the sudden penetrating movement of one of their teammates;
- creating room for the various penetrating runs without the ball and playing the ball backward so as to immediately re-create an

offensive situation and shoot at goal after two or more passes.

PRESSING

This English word is used in soccer to refer to a specific tactical attitude which lies in pressing, attacking and forcing the opponent either to win the ball (so as to immediately shift from the defensive action to the offensive one) or not to allow the player in possession time to freely assess the situation. In this way, the opponent is constantly kept under pressure and forced to think and act very quickly. Finally, pressing also means committing a foul so as to interrupt the opposition's offensive maneuver when it is becoming dangerous (a tactical foul).

The advantages of pressing:

- While it is difficult for ten players (considering the width of the field) to cover the whole playing field, pressing allows them to mark one particular area or one side of the field (the one we are most interested in) and therefore reduce the size of the playing area;
- controlling the ball with one's feet in close quarters does not help players to comfortably master the ball (and consequently a smaller field, with more opponents very close around, causes much more difficulty);
- it prevents the players starting the offensive action from freely doing whatever they want (they are forced to act under pressure and with a certain uneasiness);
- it causes the opponent to make more mistakes (wrong passes, forced shots, it creates general nervousness...);
- it forces the opponents to be much more active and to play at a different pace from which they are accustomed;
- it causes serious problems to those teams who do not have skilled passers, dribblers and players able to control and time their runs;
- it is difficult to get accustomed to playing teams using this tactical strategy and it can therefore disturb one's play;
- it forces the opposition to re-organize and adapt their own tactical strategies and, consequently, their psychological attitude cannot be at its best;
- by using zone-pressure there are more favorable possibilities of

double teaming (different players stand ready in the various areas of the playing field);
- it favors a better system to cover the whole field and, therefore, a larger number of safe reference points;
- it causes the opponents to play in unusual positions which they are not accustomed to.

The most important thing to remember when using zone-pressure is to set specific rules which should be applied automatically during the match thanks to the special work carried out in the course of the training sessions. This does not mean that the player cannot think by himself. As a matter of fact:
- the defenders can never exceed their possibilities (double teaming, intercepting, marking);
- the best organization is of critical importance, it is necessary to talk from behind (goalkeeper - sweeper - central midfielder), with respect and take one's responsibilities;
- the coach should help the player become familiar with the movements he is asked to make;
- it is important to set symmetrical responsibilities for each player, so that nobody can try to excuse oneself when making a mistake (everybody will know who is responsible for that mistake);
- in the starting position the players must all see the ball (remember that, because of the offside rule, no attacking player can stand behind the last defender).

Here are the reference points every player should have:
- the ball (the area where it is);
- the opponent (whoever he is);
- the goal to defend;
- forcing the opponent with the ball (pressure on the player in possession) or the ball (pressure on the area of the ball) in some specific areas of the playing field (especially where players are in position to double team);
- stopping the opposing play as far as possible from one's goal or at least slowing it down so as to allow the team to get into a better position to defend;
- never allowing the opponents to attack centrally (this is by far the most dangerous position); there will always be one strong side (the side the ball is on) and one weak side of the field;
- standing in front of the attackers cutting either towards the ball

or the goal, preventing them from eluding the marking (beating the opponent with positioning);

- the penalty area is a fortress;
- when the ball is moving the players should all move simultaneously and as quickly as possible;
- forcing the opponents, but especially the attacker or player in possession, to play in a 1 versus 10 situation.

Pressing zones: in order to better simplify the question, imagine drawing two horizontal lines dividing the playing field into three different sectors (see **diagram 17**) and one vertical line splitting it in two symmetrical sides (the strong side and the weak side - see **diagram 18**).

The ability of our team (and of the defense) to carry out pressing strategies lies in pressing the opposition in two fixed areas of the field (when our team is compact, short and with the right distances between the different units) and on the flanks of the pitch as soon as the ball is played (see **diagram 19**).

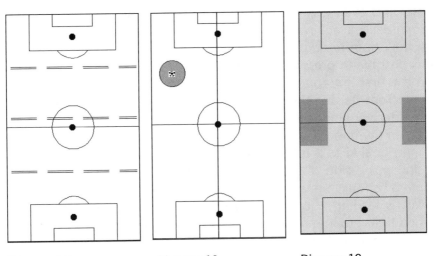

Diagram 17   Diagram 18   Diagram 19

If the ball is played by two central backs who are particularly skillful at playing and dribbling the ball, it is very difficult for us to press in a really effective manner unless we form 'covering pressing' - that is one player on the opponent in possession and his covering teammate standing in a slightly diagonal position to him.

This tactic can be dangerous as it involves the risk of leaving the outside back free or creating a void in the middle of the field. Therefore, it is up to the central forward - moving as a pendulum between the two central defenders, to try to force the least technically skillful back to play the ball and to decide the right moment to start pressing the opponent by forcing him to play the ball sideways towards one outside back or one of the midfielders (see **diagram 20**).

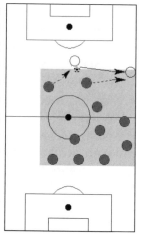

Diagram 20

This is the moment when it can be easier and more profitable to disturb the opposition, because generally they will all sprint along the diagonal by leaving the opponent farthest from the ball in the horizontal direction unguarded while also double teaming the player in possession. There are very few players able to switch the point of attack with a fifty or sixty yard accurate pass, and even if this happens, the players have enough time to organize their defensive action by moving diagonally and covering on the opposite side.

It is possible to press the opponents:

on the first line (offensive or high pressing) - it prevents the opponents from starting the play and is particularly dangerous and effective after winning the ball. It is fundamental to push up the whole team in the opposing half of the field to force the goalkeeper to take a long goal kick. It is important to be particularly aggressive when losing possession of the ball as well as at throw-ins. This pressing strategy should be used when playing weak teams and when the team is leading - it is extremely risky, but sometimes necessary, when trying to immediately gain possession of the ball;

on the second line (midfield or middle pressing) - in the opposing half of the field, because the play of the team is aimed at playing the ball forward to the penalty box, players must be:

- skillful at heading the ball;
- clever when anticipating the defenders;
- opportunistic but not excessively quick to counterattack in very wide spaces.

We will push up our opponents nearly as far as their half of the field and we will try to force them to make long passes, trusting the ability of our defenders and midfielders to immediately win the ball and set up the offensive maneuver. Our tactical strategy should be based on:

- ball possession
- movements on the flanks to dribble the ball as far as the goal line and then cross or center the ball;
- technical skills and creativeness of our players.

On the other hand, when the opponents try to leave their half of the field and set up the attack by maintaining possession of the ball and imposing their play, our players no longer stand close to the opponent but are supposed to immediately press, double team and use the tactical foul and the offside trap, when they are necessary, but without overusing them;

on the third line (defensive or low pressing) - we can use it if the features of our forwards are completely different from those described in the first example, which means that the attackers prefer to move in large spaces because of their excellent speed and good shooting ability from outside the penalty area, while they are not particularly skillful at heading the ball. Moreover, we can also choose this strategy when we are ahead and the match either allows us to change our tactical system or suggests us to be more cautious because the opposition are very strong or there are some problems or because some players are not in perfect condition.

Pressing in our half of the field favors a better cover for our defensive line and is a more cautious tactical behavior, which is much more difficult to break through but is as effective if it is based on an excellent counterattack made by players with particular features fitting this system of play.

In short, the choice of the pressing zone is strictly influenced by:

- the specific features of our forwards;
- the strengths of the opposition
- any particular situation occurring during the match.

As explained above, in order to plan pressing tactics it is necessary to divide the playing field into "two vertical areas" which help us to identify the strong side (where the player in possession of the ball is standing) and the weak side. What are players supposed to do on the two vertical flanks?

On the strong side:
- it is important to put the greatest pressure on the ball;
- constantly press the player in possession of the ball;
- it is fundamental to influence and force the opponents' play so as to press in the favorite position (pressing on request);
- the defenders should all withdraw and be ready to double team;
- while double teaming, the defenders should always anticipate the opponents running towards the ball, or those closest to them;
- make horizontal movements.

On the weak side:
- it is helpful to support the teammates in an open triangle;
- be ready either to support the teammates or to intercept the opponents' passes;
- it is important to anticipate the opponents moving towards the ball;
- move diagonally (in relation to the position of the ball).

Double teaming: it is obvious that pressing is much more effective when supported by suitable double teaming. Double teaming is aimed at:
- causing the opposition to make passing mistakes;
- forcing the opponents to pass backwards (which means losing forward space);
- forcing the opponents to make shooting mistakes (because they act with a certain precipitation);
- favoring interception (2 versus 1 situation);
- keeping the ball and the opponents off the danger areas.

For players to properly double team, they should observe some special rules:
- drive the opponent towards the side lines, by closing the movement angle;
- cover the largest space possible;
- avoid committing a foul if possible (especially if we are not beaten, otherwise the positive situation immediately turns into an adverse one), make faking movements and feints, delay if our teammates are not properly positioned and keep the opponent under constant pressure;
- mark the pass (prevent the most dangerous pass from being made);

- put the greatest pressure on the ball while the covering team-mate is arriving to support the double team.

For supporting play to be really successful it is always necessary:
- to see the position of the ball;
- to move away (the defender) if our opponent is far from the ball;
- to move to the ball so as to prevent the opposition from easily playing the ball and shooting or giving decisive passes;
- to help a teammate who has been beaten;
- to immediately stop the ball, cover the largest space as possible and rapidly take the starting position.

As far as positioning is concerned, it is also fundamental to remember that recovery movements are of critical importance. They should be made at full speed and players should always know how to recover once they have been beaten, which means they have to sprint behind the line of the ball - so that the ball is in front of them and start to build the action again from this position. The sequence of the recovery movement involves: covering the goal area - the ball - the critical area - controlling the weak side.

The recovery movement is always based on a rotation which involves:
- never leaving the goal (and, consequently, the goalkeeper) unguarded;
- performing a complete (low) rotation in a clockwise direction (see **diagram 21**);
- performing this movement simultaneously in the shortest possible time;
- pressing the ball while making the rotation.

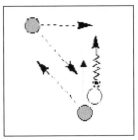

Diagram 21

THE OFFSIDE TRAP

Theoretical plans cannot always be perfectly translated into practice, because players are likely to make frequent mistakes. While pressing and double teaming the opponents, players are sometimes beaten by a more skilled opponent, who may be in better condition or simply luckier on that occasion. Consequently, the whole team is in a dangerous situation and outnumbered by the opposition (or are in a situation of numerical equality at best). Our players mostly resort to tactical fouls, especially in the central lane of the field and far from our own goal.

This tactical attitude is becoming less and less frequent today, since referees often punish it with cards which can have a negative effect both on the course of the match and on the following competitions.

This fact, which is now very common in modern soccer, has gradually stimulated all the teams to train and specialize in set play situations, so that an increasingly high percentage of the goals scored today result from free kicks and corner kicks. Moreover, players sometimes fail to stop the opponent by means of a tactical foul and must therefore be ready to apply the offside trap.

The defensive third of one's team is the best area for the offside strategy to be applied. The defenders withdraw by moving centrally (see **diagram 22**) while one of the midfield players endeavors to disturb and stop the opponent in possession of the ball. However, the midfielder must take care not to be beaten on his turn - either by a wall pass or 1 on 1 - while the last defender gives the starting signal for the offside trap (with his voice or a gesture).

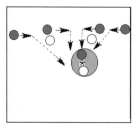
Diagram 22

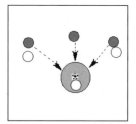
Diagram 23

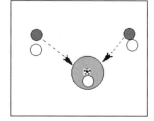
Diagram 24

The defenders all sprint upward and the midfield players (or one midfielder) run to press the opponent in possession of the ball. The other midfielders and the forwards recover on their opponents and the goalkeeper must be ready to act as a sweeper in case the opponent in possession manages to break through the defensive line or to help one of his teammates to arrive in front of the goal. The offside trap is particularly helpful when the defenders are in numerical equality (that is in a 1 v 1 situation when they need to recover from the unfavorable situation - see **diagram 23**) and it is absolutely necessary when outnumbered by the opposition (see **diagram 24**). Offside is a tactical strategy which should be used moderately and carefully, and it should always be something unexpected. Otherwise, the countermeasures of our opponents, and therefore their possibilities to shoot at goal, increase considerably.

HOW TO DISTURB ZONE PLAY

It is possible to create serious difficulties to zone play by exploiting any human mistake but also in the following ways:

- by playing very close and suddenly sprint to counterattack any time there is the possibility to do that;
- by leaving one of the teammates uncommitted behind the central midfielder: if he is particularly skillful from the technical point of view, he can offer his team various solutions;
- by exploiting the whole width of the attacking line: it is fundamental to have attacking outside midfield players (one at least) who often succeed in getting to the goal line and crossing the ball;
- with the goalkeeper taking long and well directed goal kicks.

How to attack zone play: as suggested above, there are several play situations which can seriously disturb the zone system more than others and counterattack is undoubtedly the first which we have previously referred to. It is difficult to set up the offensive play against the opposing squad gathered very close in their half of the field. It is much easier to spot an uncommitted forward when the opposition is playing zone defense rather than when he is marked very closely by one opponent.

When speaking of the defenders' tasks, we should remember that one of the two central backs should always press the most advanced forward behind the central midfield player, both when the opposition is under our pressure and when we experience their pressing (in a different play phase).

This attacking player must be particularly skillful at playing the ball in a neutral area, behind the central midfielder and in front of both the stopper and the sweeper (see **diagram 25**), while also trying to maintain possession of the ball and defend it so as to help his team counterattack very quickly. When the team is forced to set up a "slow" offensive maneuver, the attacking player is supposed to move as a "pendulum" between the two central defenders. This movement is important in order to try to upset their in-line position;

46

the forward will run to receive the ball in this zone, he will then play it towards his midfield teammate at the right moment and will finally sprint forward to receive it again (if it is possible) in the free space resulting from his "rotation" movement (see **diagram 26**).

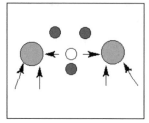
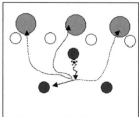

Diagram 25   Diagram 26

In this tactical situation, the team playing zonally will immediately take suitable countermeasures by pressing the opposing forward very closely (man-to-man marking), thus changing part of their defensive arrangement. For this reason, when a coach chooses the zone system he obviously needs players who are able:
- to read the game;
- to adapt to sudden tactical changes;
- to sacrifice themselves, by modifying their play in favor of a common goal.

Moreover, the zone system can also be attacked by playing two forwards. The two attacking players will stand very close to the two opposing central backs so as to prevent them from supporting on the flanks and covering in the central position (the sweeper in the previous case). Therefore, a certain feeling of insecurity will undoubtedly arise in the opposing defense who will be forced to open the offensive scheme by playing the ball to the outside backs: this will inevitably offer us more opportunities to press in the favorite position (pressing on request).

In this case, our goalkeeper can become the first assist-man, because by kicking the ball in the central area of the field, he can create a 2 v 2 situation which is particular risky for the opposition (see **diagram 27**). The movement of the two forwards while counterattacking is aimed at eluding the opponents' marking in the "neutral" zone behind the outside defenders (as soon as one of them has moved from his position either to start the play or to support it - see

diagram 28) when their team gains possession of the ball, so as to drive one of the central backs to move wide open on the flank to mark, thus creating free space.

On the other hand, if the team is setting up the play quite "slowly", the two forwards are supposed to get free from the marking of the two central backs by moving directly towards the ball (eluding the marking in a slightly side position - see **diagram 29**).

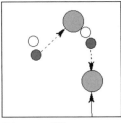 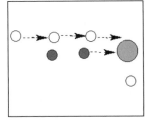 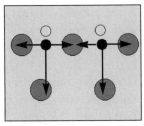

Diagram 27   Diagram 28   Diagram 29

As one of the two forwards wins possession of the ball, they will both try to create a 2 v 2 situation (one player in possession and the other without the ball) and to exploit it by forming a triangle or wall pass (see **diagram 30**).

The team adopting the zone system immediately needs to take specific countermeasures; in particular they should:

- use the offside trap increasingly often, in order to force the two forwards to withdraw, thus making their movement more difficult;
- work to keep one of the two outside backs in a covering position or even drive him near one of the two attackers, so that one central defender becomes the "sweeper" (see **diagram 31**);
- move the central midfield player (playmaker) between the two forwards to mark one of them, while the corresponding central defender provides the necessary cover to his teammate (see **diagram 32**).

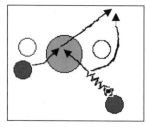

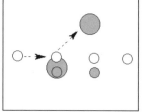

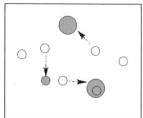

Diagram 30   Diagram 31   Diagram 32

If we have two fast attacking players, very quick to counterattack and particularly skillful at dribbling, we could decide to play them on the two outside backs (outside defenders) rather than on the two central backs. However, remember that if we choose this solution, we also need an advanced midfield player able to play the ball to them (see **diagram 33**) - so as to get the best out of their possibilities and best exploit their skills - and midfielders skillful at making penetrating movements.

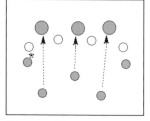

Diagram 33

If the team plays wide open by exploiting the flanks, the width of the attacking line is obviously larger and it is more difficult for the opposition playing zonally to apply the offside trap.

Moreover, by exploiting the speed of the two wingers we will try to dribble to the goal line to cross the ball - especially if one of the two forwards or one midfield player is particularly skillful at heading the ball - or to play excellent balls to our midfield players, who will quickly penetrate in the central area and shoot at goal.

It is also possible to play three forwards to upset the opposition's zone tactics. The three attacking players must however be ready to: sacrifice themselves to follow their respective opponents, press the defenders during the defensive phase or while winning the ball, create space for the penetrating runs of their midfield and back teammates, suitably cover and support them and make all the movements we have previously explained when referring both to one and two forwards in the various offensive areas.

Going back to the previous example where the zone strategy is upset by two forwards (they can play either both wide open or one on the flank and the other in a central position), the defending squad should take specific countermeasures; in particular they should:

- apply the defensive "diagonal" in the best way possible
- double team on the flanks as much as possible
- cover their central midfield teammate in the area in front of the stopper and the sweeper; this will help the central defenders to communicate a stronger feeling of safety to the outside backs and obstruct the opposing midfield players any time they try to perilously penetrate centrally.

It is obvious that the forwards can attack the opposition's zone tactics by playing at their pace, or still better at a higher rhythm, by pressing and maintaining possession of the ball at the right moment, by adapting suitable tactics to our players and always using "common sense" in each competition.

ZONE PLAY TODAY

Modern soccer is increasingly characterized by formations whose extremely offensive play does not depend on the number of attackers entering the playing field, but directly results from the mental attitude of the players. They practically play a 3-3-3-1 system or a 3-3-1-3 formation (see **diagram 34**), which is nothing but a pyramid similar to that characterizing English play at the end of the 19th century. This is obviously just a geometrical similarity (most teams played a 2-3-5 system at that time) since the roles of the various players on the field are now completely different.

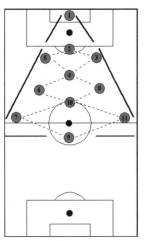

Diagram 34

The defensive line consists of three players particularly skillful both at marking the opponent and mutually covering each other. They are all marking players and sweepers (interchangeable sweeper) at the same time, which means they are able to sublimate 1 v 1 play by applying both zone and mixed zone systems, according to the tactical needs in each particular situation. Furthermore, it is important to exploit the technical skills of the goalkeeper so that he should often be involved in the game to clear and play the ball to his teammates or change the point of attack; in practice, the goalkeeper acts as the fourth back in the offensive scheme. It is extremely important for the three defenders to be particularly eclectic: apart from defending, they should also take an active part in setting up the offensive play and create - by means of their movements - the numerical advantage over the opposition both in midfield (in the area of the ball) and on attack.

In midfield there are three players forming a triangle, the top of which is turned towards the rear guard. The central midfield player should have a clear tactical sense and be able to maintain the balance between the different units of the team. Moreover, he must act as a central defensive player when the tactical situation is critical (in this case the number of the defenders rises to four again). The two other midfielders should work as filters and directly take part in the offensive play. In addition, there are two outside linkmen playing on the two flanks respectively (the figure of the linkman has been revived in very recent times: youth teams should play a crucial role in coaching these players): not only do they give their support on attack, but they should also be able to cover the team in the defensive phase. The offensive line consists of an attacking midfield player - who obviously has good offensive skills - and an attacker who acts as the reference point for the whole offensive scheme.

This kind of play implies that the coach can decide to apply various systems of play and make adjustments according to the situations occurring in the course of a match. In order to properly do that, the team must be able to make a series of well-organized movements while defending, on the basis of extremely precise directions. Their movements strictly depend on the position of the opponents' action:

- if the opposition attack centrally (see **diagram 35**), the team position in one single unit; the defensive rectangle consists of six players covering the central area in front of the goal;
- if the opposition attack from outside on the flanks (see **diagram 36**), the team makes the defensive diagonal by forming three defensive triangles.

The movements are obviously precise and well organized in the offensive phase too, (see **diagram 37**), to help the goalkeeper to kick or throw the ball and the defenders to set up the offensive play, if necessary.

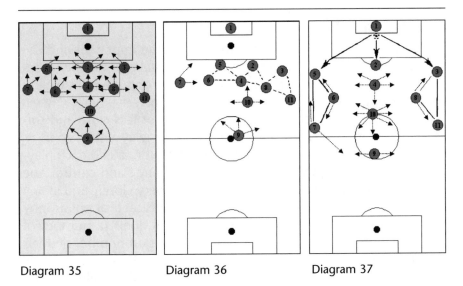

Diagram 35   Diagram 36   Diagram 37

The offensive play should combine well synchronized movements made by the team as a whole and the creativeness and the technical skills of each player (see **diagrams 38 and 39**). Finally, the team should offer suitable and effective cover both while trying to win the ball after a possible clearance and when quickly re-organizing the defensive arrangement.

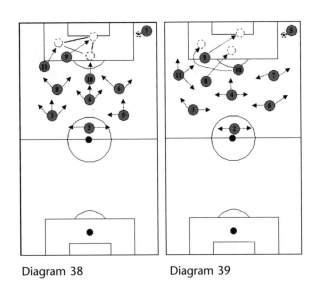

Diagram 38   Diagram 39

MIXED ZONE PLAY

This system of play combines the marking of the opponent and the covering of one specific zone. It is a great mistake to identify man-to-man marking with the close marking of the opponent, as well as zone marking with the remote control of the player.

As a matter of fact, marking can be more or less close and suffocating regardless of the fact that the team play either zone or man-to-man defense. In the case of man-to-man marking each player is previously assigned an opponent to challenge and control: the defender must follow and mark his opponent very closely and in any part of the field he is playing. According to this tactical philosophy the match should consist of several individual duels (a number of 1 v 1 situations), where the side winning the largest number of duels should theoretically win the match. But the match does not simply come to this, since plenty of other elements occur to influence the final score.

The concept of zone play - which has already been largely explained - identifies the area where a player is supposed to challenge his opponent any time the ball is played there. The player who was previously assigned the zone in question must mark that opponent, challenge him trying to win the ball from his feet and therefore act as a man-to-man marking player.

In man-to-man defense, the coach plays a crucial role in properly identifying and setting the right marking positions and roles. Each opponent, especially if he is very skillful and dangerous, should be committed by the ideal marking player preventing him from being the least decisive as possible in the game. In addition, the coach must be able to read the weaknesses and difficulties of his marking players during the match and make suitable adjustments, if necessary.

This play philosophy also has its weak points (like all other theories) which can be synthesized as follows:

- if the opponent systematically wins the duel which he is personally engaged in, he (theoretically) plays a decisive and crucial role for his team;
- the opponent - who is marked very closely - can create free space for the penetration of his teammates even though he does not win any personal duels, by simply moving all over the field; in this way, he definitely upsets the opposing defensive arrangement.

Furthermore, the sweeper plays a critical role in man-to-man marking, since the defensive line all need to adapt to his rhythm, personal features and skills.

Man-to-man marking is performed when the squad is in a defensive situation (that is when the opposition are in possession of the ball): at that moment, some players are supposed to immediately commit some specific opponents. Marking tactics is therefore the action of a player playing in a defensive situation. He is supposed to position - in relation to the position of the opponent he is responsible for marking - so as to easily challenge his opponent or successfully intercept the ball any time it is played to him.

The rules regulating man-to-man marking consider three fundamental elements:

- the position of the ball;
- the position of the opponent one is supposed to mark;
- the position of one's own goal.

Moreover, there are some main conditions concerning play organization; it is particularly important for the coach:

- to be fully aware of the physical, tactical and psychological possibilities and skills of his players;
- to know everything about the system of play he chooses for his team, including all its advantages and flaws;
- to have all the time he needs to coach the basic essential elements of that particular system of play;
- to coach his players to fit into that system of play (for instance: Argentina - where zone play has always been a strong tradition - shifted from zone defense to man-to-man marking during 1986 World Cup, while Germany changed from man-to-man to mixed zone play in the course of the same competition).

However, all the different systems of play share common general principles. Here are some of these basic features:

- always concentrate on the ball and be ready to be involved in the game;
- be ready to attack the ball without waiting for it to be played;
- help the teammate in possession by getting free from the opponent's marking, support him and cooperate (with the voice: man on, you are alone....);
- do not risk too much while defending (avoid dribbling, sideways passes....);

- be careful and accurate while marking the opponents (avoid wrong positions);
- the more the opponent approaches the goal, the closer the marking should be;
- never lose possession of the ball carelessly;
- look for the unmarked teammate, the free space and then play the ball on the path of the teammate's run;
- anticipate if possible, otherwise delay;
- never fall to the ground;
- play in a very creative manner, by making faking and sudden movements;
- create pressure and apply pressing strategy;
- always use positive and quick solutions (ball control aimed at one specific direction, one-touch play...).

As far as the defense (the base of the whole organization) is concerned, here are the main tactical principles:
- slow down the action or delay;
- reduce free spaces;
- maintain defensive balance;
- use defensive aggressiveness.

Finally, for the defensive organization to be really effective, it is fundamental to constantly and systematically apply all the four principles in any situation during the match.

Slowing down while defending: defenders always benefit from delaying the play and it is therefore helpful and reasonable for them to slow down the opposition's offensive scheme. This slowing down action can be successful only if the whole team cooperates to this purpose. The larger the number of players standing behind the ball, the more our defensive line will benefit.

If a player is in a 1 v 2 situation on some particular occasions - which means he must control two opponents at the same time and one of them is in possession of the ball - he must pretend to directly challenge and disorient the opponent in possession, thus slowing down the opposing play so as to allow his teammates to suitably reorganize.

Reducing free spaces: if creating free spaces is the main goal of the offensive play, it is therefore reasonable to believe that the defense are supposed to prevent the opponents from cutting their way towards the goal. If the defenders are taken by surprise because they have failed to properly slow down the opponents' offensive attack, there will undoubtedly be various defensive areas unguarded and uncovered that the opponents could freely exploit to easily penetrate towards the goal.

Reducing free spaces is therefore of critical importance, especially as the opposition are approaching our goal. Reducing free spaces far from our penalty area consequently means offering more protection and safety to our defensive unit.

Defensive balance: for the defense to carry out their task in the best and safest way possible, the defensive line should first of all outnumber the opposition playing on attack. There should be at least one defender more than the attackers. If the defenders are always on their guard and well-organized, they will undoubtedly prevent their opponents from upsetting the defensive arrangement, from outnumbering them or creating free spaces.

The defensive action is therefore successful if it ultimately helps the team to win the ball: this is the reason why the whole team has to work to this specific purpose and concentrate on the ball. Delaying, reducing free spaces, and maintaining the balance in the defensive line are the main essential principles for successfully achieving the defensive objective. However, its perfect final achievement is the practical challenge of the opponent (involving defensive aggressiveness), aimed at helping the defender to win the ball and control it.

THE IMPORTANCE OF THE DEFENSE

Consequently, as we have previously suggested, the main difference between the various systems of play directly results from the organization of the defensive line.

The main advantages of individual defense:
- each player is aware of and responsible for his own defensive role and task;
- the opponents can be marked according to their personal features;
- it enhances personal pride;
- it can be adjusted to any offensive system;

- it encourages the coach to make suitable changes and adjustments (like switching marking assignments, for instance).

The tasks of the defender:
- he has to properly position in relation to the position of his opponent, so that he can successfully commit his opponent (challenge, tackle, ball interception...) when he is about to receive the ball;
- he has to "feel" his goal at his back, without necessarily seeing it;
- he must be able to perceive any possible change at any moment during the match (if my eyes concentrate either on the ball or on my opponent exclusively, I make a big mistake);
- he must be able to cover, protect and support the whole defensive line.

The main features of the sweeper:
The player playing in this position must show intuition, tactical intelligence and awareness, and sense of positioning. Like the defender, he is supposed to:
- concentrate on the movement of the ball;
- commit the opponent who has previously beaten his marking teammate;
- clear or win any ball breaking through the defensive wall and arriving in a dangerous zone where the opposition can favorably shoot at goal;
- lead his teammates by directly speaking to them ("challenge, cover, don't foul, don't let him turn around....").

COMPARING THE DIFFERENT DEFENSIVE ARRANGEMENTS

Individual defense: it is based on man-to-man marking, regardless of the position of the opponent on the field. In this case, the defender bears full responsibility for one particular opponent (primary responsibility) and is supposed to constantly control him and prevent his movements. In this defensive organization:
- the position of the defender strictly depends on his direct opponent's position;
- the opponent is mainly left to lead the game and take the initiative;

- it is much more difficult to maintain the different lines in contact;
- players are scattered on the field (the group is less homogeneous), which offers the opposition more room, thus allowing them to play more freely and in depth;
- free spaces obviously favor counterattack (individual or team counterattack) and opposing attacking players can skillfully benefit from this favorable situation;
- each player is asked to be more aggressive, to relish body contact with his direct opponent and look for personal duels; moreover, he is asked to assume more responsibilities;
- the whole defense runs more risks, since each individual mistake is very dangerous, especially in the case of the sweeper;
- applying offside tactics is more difficult as is double teaming and pressing (partly, at least);
- the axis of play is vertical and is directed from the rear guard to the attacking line;
- directing playing actions is much easier.

Zone defense: the defender is supposed to mark the opponent in the area which he is responsible for and control the nearby zone. In this defensive arrangement:
- the position of the defender strictly depends on the position of the ball;
- there are more defenders in the area of the ball and it is therefore easier to put pressure on the opponents (get closer to them) and press them (they directly impose the rhythm of play);
- offensive pressing is much easier and defenders can therefore immediately win the ball and diversify the offensive maneuver;
- it is much easier to obstruct the opposition, cover and support some particular zones;
- it is easier to control, play the ball and maintain possession when the team are compact, so that the opponents can only move forward slowly;
- shifting to man-to-man marking needs a certain period of adjustment;
- it is much easier for players to shift from one situation to another and they can also be more creative and definitely surer;
- it favors players to position in line so as to make offside, double

teaming and pressing strategies much easier to apply;
- the axis of play is horizontal and the team are very close together;
- players have collective responsibilities.

COMPARING ROLES BY POSITIONING
IN INDIVIDUAL MARKING
Goalkeeper: normal.

Sweeper: he plays in a more withdrawn position at the back of the defense; he must play a decisive role and offer more covering protection (see **diagram 40**).

Defenders: they stand close to their respective opponents. They must be particularly careful when marking (see **diagram 41**).

Midfield players: they can be given more or less defensive or offensive tasks according to their own abilities and to the opponents' tactics.

Forwards: more isolated. They should look more for personal solutions than for team play. They are supported less by their teammates.

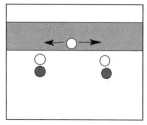

Diagram 40

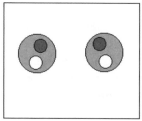

Diagram 41

IN ZONE MARKING
Goalkeeper: he must be trained to play far from the goal line and act as a second sweeper. He must pay more attention to the game and choose various solutions.

Sweeper: he plays closer to the defense. He should be more technical, quicker in his movements and much more attentive.

Defenders: they play farther from the opponents. They are supposed to control their area much more carefully but can more freely take part in setting up the offensive play.

Midfield players: they should be more skillful at controlling their zone than their opponents. They must be able to create free spaces and occupy them, making penetrating runs.

Forwards: they stand less isolated from their teammates. They should create more free spaces for their teammates and look for team solutions.

HISTORICAL HINTS

The main modifications occurring in the various systems of play since the origin of soccer have always mainly concerned the defensive arrangement. They have often been influenced by the changes in the laws of the game, but they especially result from the fact that "controlling free spaces" has gradually acquired an increasingly crucial importance. Actually, in the past only the defense (in the general sense) were responsible for preventing the opposition from creating and exploiting free zones.

In the systems of play commonly used at the beginning of the 20th century, the defensive lines were often forced (because of the nature of the system itself) to leave wide spaces for one or more opponents to exploit. This was the main consequence of the system of play, since little attention was focused on the defense and the concept of "free space" did not exist at all.

Free spaces are considerably reduced in the defensive lines of all the teams using zone systems (either 4-2-4 or 4-3-3 formations). As time went by, the problem of challenging attackers with exceptional technical and tactical skills gradually led many soccer schools to choose man-to-man marking or very close defensive systems. However, these defensive dispositions could not prevent the opposition from creating "free spaces" by means of movements without the ball and the spectacular nature of soccer was partially repressed to pursue the final successful result at all costs. At that point, people gradually began to understand that for the defensive line to effectively cover all the free spaces, the defenders needed to be much more aware of their important roles and concentrate their attention on their specific tasks, but always in close relation to all the other players on the team. The attention was therefore gradually shifted from individual actions to collective team play.

This new play philosophy combined with the new arrangement of players on the field favored the creation of new concepts, like that of Block (or Unit or Group) so as to further reduce free spaces to the opposing attacking players and to the primary sources of play as well. *Consequently*:

the midfield players and the forwards act and move increasingly closer to the defensive line (regardless of the system of play);

the defenders, who are much closer together and closer to the other units, push the team up and reduce the playing field both vertically and horizontally by applying offside tactics on some special occasions and calling for the whole team to properly press the opposition.

If the problem could not be solved by playing more players on defense or by changing several systems of play, pushing the team up was finally thought to be the right solution to the question. There is a simple consideration underlying all the various defensive tactical strategies: a team could dominate a match in terms of ball possession, but what is really important is the number of goals scored, since the final score decides the winner. This is the reason why the defenders should be ready to be involved in the offensive maneuver, since ball possession implies:

on attack: penetration - mobility - improvisation - creativeness;

on defense: concentration - slowing down and delaying - reducing spaces - balance - aggressiveness.

Winning possession of the ball is the main purpose of the whole team, not only in the defensive phase. If it is impossible to successfully and fully achieve this goal in some particular play situations, it becomes necessary to obstruct the opposition and prevent them from shooting at goal or creating any dangerous situation.

THE PSYCHOLOGICAL ATTRIBUTES OF THE DEFENDER
What kind of player is or should the defender be and which psychological attributes should he have to successfully play his role? What kind of soccer mentality should he have to prefer this position on the field and not to feel cheated out of a role which would

undoubtedly elect him the leader of the team (with the exception of some rare cases)?

The defender, therefore, need not be particularly creative, but should have clear team spirit and be a good organizer. This is how sports psychologists usually describe him. It is evident that each competition is characterized by the conflict between attacker and defender, which is often considered as a real duel, individual or collective, where the successful attacking player (or the offensive line in general) is always more obvious and usually creates greater excitement than the defender (or the defensive line in general).

Consequently, the defender must be a person "of great humility" to accept his role, since there is no defensive action - however exciting it may be - which can raise the same enthusiasm resulting from a goal.

In short, the best attributes of a defender are:
- humility
- spirit of self-sacrifice
- inclination to socialize
- weak disposition to become the leader of the group (with the exceptions of some rare cases)

THE FUTURE

It is extremely difficult to give precise directions as to the future of soccer, but we would like to suggest two specific topics on which we firmly believe coaches should really focus their attention and their work.

The first theme concerns the **system of play** and the arrangement of the players on the field, by assigning different specific roles and positions both in the same match and in the following competitions, while never forgetting that technical skills have always been and will always be of critical importance in soccer. This means applying an "elastic" and flexible play organization so that the team can adapt to any circumstance and solution. The coach can decide to modify his system of play not only when he is losing the match, but also to upset any situation of perfect balance, to create new problems for the opposition, to outnumber the opponents in some specific areas of the field and so forth... Obviously, this system of play will considerably test the psychological attributes of the player: concentration, attention, ability to quickly make a decision, ability to switch position and take up different roles in the course of the same match, etc..

Moreover, it is important to overcome the contrast between man-to-man and zone marking by sublimating the best features of each one of them and using them in the various systems of play: in this way, players are trained to shift from zone play to combined marking, to 1 v 1 situations all over the field and so forth according to the specific needs of the moment. This is possible thanks to the coach's tactical and strategic ability to read the match and to the work carried out during training sessions, which should help players to gradually get accustomed to this tactical approach to the opposition.

This approach is possible not only thanks to the substitutions made during the course of the game (the reserves can be an important solution), but especially thanks to the personal characteristics of some particular players, who are able to change roles and attitude, take different positions and master different situations during the same match. These players are usually referred to as "utility" players, which does not mean they can effectively fit and play in any position of the field, but they can, especially from the mental point of view, switch their role in the vertical mechanisms of the team, i.e. the outside back with the outside midfielder - the center half with the central defender - the offensive midfield player with the withdrawn striker and so forth...

Tactical adjustments: in a match where both sides are playing a 5-3-2 formation, the coach could decide to make the following adjustments:

- shift to a 3-4-1-2 arrangement: two defenders closely mark the two opposing forwards (man-to-man marking) and the third defender acts as a sweeper, otherwise the coach can choose a zone defense playing three defenders;
- the four midfield players position zonally, two stand centrally and two play on the flanks;
- one withdrawn striker plays far from the three opposing central backs and two outside forwards work wide open on the flanks;

  in this way, while playing on attack, they directly commit the two opposing outside defenders and completely leave the three central backs without any reference points.

This new arrangement (see **diagrams 42 and 43**) allows us to benefit from the above-mentioned situations and also helps us to outnumber the opposition in midfield. For this to be possible and really effective, the coach should make suitable adjustments as follows:
- the two outside backs play as outside midfield players;
- one midfield player acts as a withdrawn striker;
- the two forwards operate on the flanks.

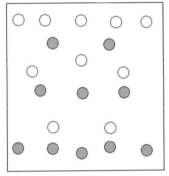

Diagram 42

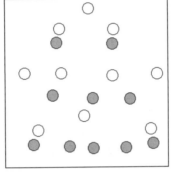

Diagram 43

The coach can choose the 4-4-2 formation as another possible solution:
- zone defense consisting of four players, one central or outside back playing in a more advanced position in midfield;
- zone midfield line consisting of four players;
- the two forwards inter-change their positions playing one behind the other, in a vertical line: in this way they offer the opposition one single reference point and force them to choose between either: 1) maintaining the same formation, thus forcing one midfielder to mark our forward in the defensive phase; or 2) playing four midfield players.

By making the above-mentioned tactical adjustments, we will easily outnumber the opposition both in midfield and on the wings (see **diagrams 44 and 45**).

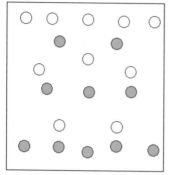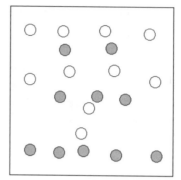

Diagram 44   Diagram 45

It is evident that there are a number of different tactical systems and adjustments (4-3-3 formation and so forth...), but the personal creativeness of the coach plays a crucial role in discovering and adapting them to his team.

TOTAL MAN-TO-MAN MARKING

Another possible solution the coach can apply during the course of the match is *total man-to-man marking*, regardless of the system of play he has previously chosen for his team. The physical and psychological condition of the players is of absolute importance in this play organization, since it creates nine or ten 1 v 1 situations on the playing field. This tactical strategy, if it can be defined in this way, was used by the former East German National Team exclusively some years ago. It requires great endurance and has never been particularly successful since it lacks (in our opinion) imagination, creativeness and flexibility - attributes of critical importance in soccer.

In some particular situations, when it is necessary to score to equalize, or restore the starting balance, this defensive attitude can change into covering pressing - this strategy can be successful only if it is used for a short period of time.

Covering pressing - we would like to suggest different examples:
*   the opposing goalkeeper is in possession of the ball, all the players move to their respective opponents, thus creating nine 1 v 1 situations. The least technically and tactically skillful opponent is left uncommitted (he is not supposed to be able to get free and take part in the offensive maneuver) so that the goalkeeper does not choose to directly play the ball to him and

prefers to kick the ball down field. One of our players is left uncommitted at midfield: this player, we could refer to him as the "ball-hunter" or "safety man", should run to win the ball wherever it falls. Moreover, apart from being particularly skillful in 1 v 1 situations, our defenders must know how to implement the offside tactics in the defensive phase (see **diagram 46**).

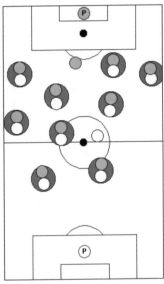

Diagram 46

- the goalkeeper does not kick the ball down field but passes it to the uncommitted player, who receives it turning his back to our goal. In this case, our players, standing near the area of the ball, should immediately move to press their opponents, while also carefully synchronizing their movements and involving our "safety man", the uncommitted player who is now involved in the marking. In this way, there are ten 1 v 1 situations on the field. Our defensive line must be ready to apply the offside trap in case something does not work proper- ly or if the opponent in possession of the ball gives a long pass when he is pressed closely. Like in the previous situation, the goalkeeper obviously acts as a sweeper or as an uncommitted player (see **diagram 47**). **Diagram 48** shows the same situationas above, but there are fewer players moving diagonally to press the opponents (diagonal covering pressing);

- the goalkeeper plays the ball to his teammate who has been left uncommitted intentionally; this player passes the ball sideways to the flank since none of his teammates is unguarded. In this situation, our marking player immediately gets close to his opponent who is now in possession (1 v 1), while the "ball-hunter" sprints to support his teammate and double team, this creates a 2 v 1 situation in the zone of the ball and should imme- diately win possession of the ball. For this tactical strategy to be really successful, all the other players must press their direct opponents (see **diagram 49**).

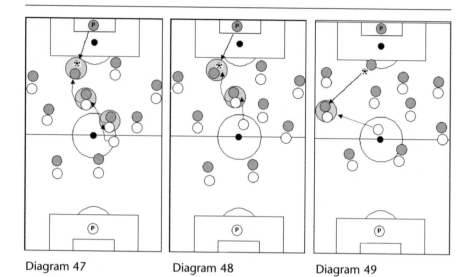

Diagram 47   Diagram 48   Diagram 49

A COMPLETE PLAYER

The second important theme (the first one concerned the system of play) focuses the attention on the "player" exclusively. Some distinguished experts directly investigating the problems of soccer - like Prunelli, Cabrini and others - have clearly underlined the fact that most people have always thought it necessary to coach the player in the most complete way as possible to help him to prepare for any situation he may face. In this way, the player has never had to think, choose, decide, propose or be responsible by himself, without being guided by someone else.

Consequently, the soccer player has never been completely free and particularly motivated to investigate, know, develop and harmonize all the features and skills which he is endowed with. On the contrary, for a coach to properly coach and educate a truly complete player, he has to work to develop each player's personality and mental qualities, to enhance his creativeness and stimulate his motivations, and help him to be ready to cooperate and offer his personal contribution to the group.

We know that our mind controls all our qualities and skills and cannot therefore be trained with the same systems we use to train our body. Our mind is alive when it feels completely free and is not threatened by anything, otherwise it withdraws in passive obedience and submission, which prevents any form of creativeness.

During the training sessions, the coach should create conditions of total freedom combined with situations of full responsibility in order to help his players to successfully develop their qualities.

Soccer players need a self critical attitude, knowledge and understanding, the desire to test themselves, the inclination to create and suggest something new, personal initiative, and the ability to pursue and achieve something without being guided by somebody else. These are the main qualities on which the coach should work to help the athlete become a truly complete player, keeping up with modern times and with the constant evolution characterizing soccer today.

As far as personal character is concerned, modern soccer needs a concrete, objective and rational protagonist who shows a reasonable capacity to direct and master his main resources and skills in the best way possible, free from any distressful interpretation of his role. Soccer players necessarily require creativeness, personal initiative, and freedom of thought and action, but are strictly bound to a controlled collective creation at the same time. This is the reason why the player should work hard not only to win during the game, but also to overcome his own weaknesses and constantly learn something more than he is directly coached so he can successfully prevail over his opponent and all the limitations which he is faced with.

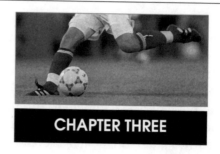

CHAPTER THREE

SHOOTING AT GOAL

COACHING PLAYERS TO SHOOT AT GOAL

Shooting at goal is the most exciting moment in the game. Any other technical element, any tactical strategy, any spectacular personal performance obviously has more or less importance in relation to whether the shot at goal is successful or not. The player who can approach the opposing goal and properly exploit any opportunity to shoot at goal automatically becomes a decisive element for his team, since these favorable opportunities very seldom occur in the course of a match.

The higher the number of players having these important skills, the more the team is likely to win the match. Like all the other skills, the ability to shoot at goal must be trained in a rational and constant manner. Not only has the good striker a powerful shot (that is the proper ratio between the explosive capacity of the muscles of his lower limbs and the shooting technique) and great accuracy (shooting skill and body balance), but he is also able to immediately assess the tactical situation and properly adapt to it.

As to preparatory physical training, it is fundamental to properly strengthen the muscles of the lower limbs - by means of explosive practice - while also combining mobility exercises to improve the hip movements. In this way, it is possible to considerably stimulate the hip joint and the whole thigh-pelvis region and further enhance the elasticity of the muscles directly connected to these joints.

There are no special rules concerning shooting technique, both as to the part of the foot used to make contact with the ball and to the body's position while shooting (non-kicking foot, maintaining the balance on the non-kicking foot, position of the arms, and so forth...): however, every coach should know and properly teach his players all these fundamentals.

There are plenty of exercises aimed at practicing shooting skills. Apart from dead-ball situations, most exercises are carried out with moving balls (rolling, bouncing, volleying and so on..) coming from different directions and at various speeds. Every coach showing great creativeness can conceive and plan many exercises to teach shooting technique: they could involve dribbling, playing a one-two with a teammate, playing team strategies and combining different technical and tactical elements. However, before starting shooting practice, it is advisable for the coach to clearly explain to his players how they should approach the ball to strike it. **It is fundamental for the player to avoid taking the right position too early and then waiting for the ball to arrive. Instead he needs to directly attack the ball as if he were meeting it too late, at the last second.**

THE FOUR DIFFERENT PHASES

This technical movement can be divided into four phases:

1) **attacking the ball:**
   the frequency of the steps on the playing field increases gradually; during the run-up phase the player is supposed to assess either the path of the moving ball or its position in case of a dead-ball situation, and carefully analyze everything around him (the opponents, the goalkeeper's movements, the specific area of the field...);

2) **position of the non-kicking foot and impact with the ball:**
   the non-kicking foot should be placed far enough to the side of the ball - but everything mostly depends on the morphological features of each player, his automatisms and on the shot he wants to take (instep shot, inner- or outer-instep kick);

3) **the contact between the foot and the ball (shooting movement):**
   when the foot makes contact with the ball, the ankle is extended and perfectly rigid, while the knee of the non kicking foot is bent:
   - **instep shot:** the toe must be pointing down very close to the ground; the foot makes contact with the ball through its horizontal mid-line;

70

- **inner-instep shot**: the toe must be pointing down and the foot comes across the ball from a side position, from inside to outside;
- **outer-instep shot**: the kicking foot is place inside the ball and the toe must be pointing towards the inside.

4) **restoring the starting balance position:**
after striking the ball, the player must immediately recover his starting balance - by using his arms and his trunk - so as to promptly follow the action.

EXERCISES

We are not going to dwell upon the description of individual shooting exercises based on either a steady or a moving ball, which can be practiced in different ways and in various positions using posts, cones, small goals and so forth..., but we would like to focus the attention on specific exercises involving two players at least.

Two-player practice:

1. The player starts 20 yards outside the penalty box, dribbles the ball and plays a wall pass with the coach - standing 10 yards outside the penalty area - and with one of his teammates at the edge of the box and shoots at goal. The two triangles can be performed on the same side or on the two different flanks. The shooter then becomes the teammate ready for the wall pass.

2. The player starts 20 yards outside the penalty area, he plays the ball to the coach who controls it and plays it back to him. The player receives the ball and passes it to his teammate standing at the edge of the penalty box. This player controls the ball and takes a shot at goal. In this case, the shooter makes a vertical run to meet the ball and shoots with the instep.

3. The player starts 20 yards outside the penalty box, he plays the ball to the coach who controls it and plays it back to him. The player in possession dribbles past the coach, plays a wall pass with his teammate at the edge of the penalty area and takes a shot at goal. It is possible to modify this exercise by asking the player to give a wall pass first and then dribble.

Variations of these exercises are possible: apart from dribbling the ball, the player can also toss it with his feet, or head it; it is also useful to vary the starting position and include various passing angles.

Two-team practice:

Two groups of players practice in two different 30 by 30 yards areas and goals, with two goalkeepers defending their respective goals.

1. One player in group A (in possession of the ball) makes a long pass to the teammate standing at the opposite end and then follows its path. The player in group B controls the ball, quickly dribbles towards the teammate who is approaching him, feints and lays the ball off to player A who shoots at goal. Then, they change positions (see **diagram 1**).

2. Player A passes to his teammate stand ing at the opposite end of the field and immediately follows the path of the ball; player B controls the ball, dribbles towards his teammate, feints and leaves him the ball. Player A dribbles the ball wide and crosses the ball to player B who shoots at goal.

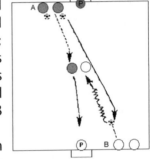

Diagram 1

3. The same situation as before, but when player B feints and leaves the ball for his teammate, player A controls it and dribbles back to the outside of the field and crosses for his teammate to shoot at goal (see **diagram 2**).

4. The same situation as above, but when player B makes a feinting movement and his teammate receives the ball, player A controls it moving right or left, turns and takes a shot at the goal which he started from.

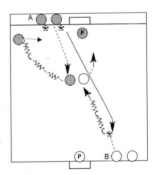

Diagram 2

5. The same situation as above, but when player B plays the ball to his teammate A, player B becomes a defender and promptly creates a 1 v 1 situation.

6. The same as above, but when player A gives a long pass to his teammate, player B either heads or kicks the ball towards A. Player A can either volley the ball or control it moving right or left to strike at goal. He can decide which goal he wants to shoot at.

7. This exercise involves another player, C, standing in the center. A plays the ball to B, who heads or kicks it back and moves to defend his goal from the attack by players A and C. This exercise can result in various solutions (2 v 1, 2 v 2, 3 v 2, 3 v 3), which are very similar to real game situations.

8. The coach takes part in this exercise: he is in possession of the ball in the middle of the field. Player B runs towards the opposite goal, receives the ball from the coach and shoots at goal. Then, he controls a ground pass or a lob from his teammate A - standing on the goal line - and strikes at goal again (see **diagram 3**). It is also possible to ask player B to dribble past the coach.

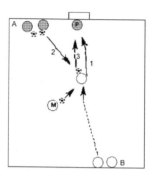

Diagram 3

Three groups and one goal (defended by the goalkeeper): The coach divides the players into three groups: two of them (B and C) have one ball each, while group A has no ball. The players in group B are standing in a central position 30 yards from the goal, the players in group A position on the side, while those in group C are near the corner flag.

1. A sprints towards the goal, receives a pass from player B directly in his path, and shoots at goal just before entering the penalty area. Then, player A positions so as to meet the cross from player C and heads or volleys the ball. After finishing the exercise, the three players switch their respective positions by moving clockwise (see **diagram 4**).

2. Player B sprints towards the penalty box and shoots at goal; then, he receives the cross from C and heads the ball, aiming it on the penetrating run of his teammate A, who shoots at goal.

3. The same situation as above, but as soon as player A receives the ball, he promptly engages in a 1 v 1 situation with player B, who immediately acts as a defender.

4. In this case, player A is in possession of the ball and positions on the flank on either side of the penalty area, or near the corner flag. Players B and C stand in a central position, without the ball, ready to perform a cross-over play as soon as their teammate crosses the ball, so that they can easily strike at goal (see **diagram 5**).

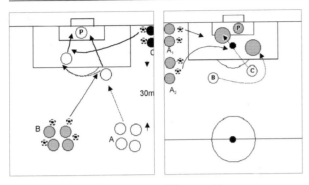

Diagram 4   Diagram 5

5. Player C, in possession of the ball, positions near the corner flag, while players A and B stand 5 yards apart (either vertically or horizontally) at the edge of the penalty box and play a ball between each other. When the coach gives the starting signal, player C gives an outswinging cross and players A and B abandon their ball to take part in the action: player A (the farthest from C) becomes the attacker while B acts as a defender to create a 1 v 1 situation for the final shot at goal (see **diagram 6**).

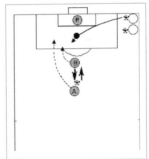

6. The same exercise as above, but when player B controls the ball, his teammate A gains possession of the ball, dribbles past him and shoots at goal. Then, play-   Diagram 6
er A positions to meet the cross by player C and strikes at goal again.

MORE SOLUTIONS

The coach can also suggest some exercises which considerably approach real game situations, to help his players to adapt to a number of different situations and further enhance their personal skills while dealing with various solutions.

In pairs:

1. Players A and B position 20 yards from the penalty area. Player A dribbles the ball straight ahead followed by his teammate B; before entering the penalty box, A moves sideways so as to leave

the ball for player B, who shoots at goal (defended by the goal-keeper).

2. In this exercise, player A dribbles the ball to the edge of the penalty box and chips the ball for his teammate B to volley at goal.

3. Players A and B head the ball up to the edge of the penalty box, where one of them controls the ball and plays it to his teammate who shoots at goal.

4. Players B and A stand 3 and 5 yards from the penalty area respectively and play the ball to each other without moving. Player B suddenly decides to leave the ball or kick it sideways. Player A sprints to the ball and shoots at goal before the ball enters the penalty area (see **diagram 7**).

5. The same exercise as above, but when player B controls the ball, his teammate A moves towards him for a 1 v 1, wins possession of the ball, beats his teammate and shoots at goal (see **diagram 8**).

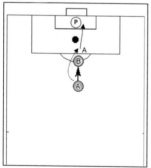

Diagram 7   Diagram 8

6. The same situation as above, but players A and B are asked to head the ball and when player B lets the ball bounce on the ground or kicks it sideways, his teammate A sprints to take a shot at goal.

7. The same as above, but when the ball lands on the ground and player B controls it, player A moves in for a 1 v 1, beats his teammate and shoots at goal.

All these exercises can be modified by asking the players to dribble the ball in different ways.

In groups of three players each:
1. Players A and B position outside the penalty area and pass to each other. Player C is standing behind his teammate A in a slightly diagonal position. As soon as player C decides to sprint forward, player A plays the ball to him so that he can shoot first time at goal (the goal is defended by the goalkeeper): the shot must be taken just before entering the penalty area (see **diagram 9**). Players A and B can pass the ball in various ways.
2. Players A and B pass the ball to each other; when B controls the ball, player A moves in for a 1 v 1, dribbles past his teammate and plays the ball to C (who was standing behind A, at the beginning) who is making a penetrating run to shoot at goal. Player C has to sprint on the side opposite to the area where player A has dribbled past his teammate B (see **diagram 10**).

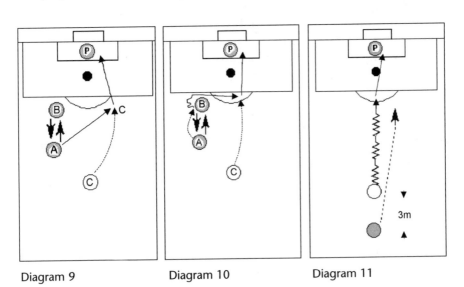

Diagram 9   Diagram 10   Diagram 11

SHIELDING THE BALL

The coach can also suggest specific exercises combining shooting skills and the ability to shield the ball for the final shot at goal. Skillful attacking players also need to be able to elude the opponent's marking and shield the ball from the challenge by the defender.

1 v 1 situation: the attacker in possession starts 20 yards from the penalty box. He is asked to dribble the ball at speed and take a shot before entering the penalty area, while also eluding the recovery movement of the defender starting 3 yards behind him. The attacking player must focus his attention on dribbling the ball, the goalkeeper's movements, the shot at goal, and the recovery action by the defender (see **diagram 11**).

2 v 1 situation: one player starts wide on the wing, he dribbles the ball to the goal line trying to elude the opponent's challenge (semi-passive defender - he starts from the central position about 15 yards from the touch line); he crosses to his teammate, who has started from the same line and is penetrating centrally to meet the cross and shoot at goal. The outside attacking player should concentrate on shielding the ball, spotting his unchallenged teammate and giving an accurate cross; the central attacking player particularly concentrates on timing his penetration, taking the best position and choosing the right way to shoot (see **diagram 12**).

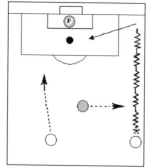

Diagram 12

2 v 1 situation: one attacking player starts 20 yards from the penalty box, dribbles the ball and takes a shot at goal before entering the penalty area, while also eluding the recovery runs by two defenders starting 3 yards behind him. The attacking player especially concentrates on dribbling the ball, the goalkeeper's movements, the accuracy of his shot, and the recovery runs of the two defenders on both sides (see **diagram 13**).

2 v 1 situation: two players start 20 yards from the penalty box: one of them dribbles the ball (he can dribble the ball by knocking it forward, for instance), while the other follows him. Once they approach the opponent standing at the edge of the penalty area, the player in possession stops the ball and sprints away getting free on the left, while his teammate runs onto the ball, beats the opponent on the right and shoots at goal. The unguarded player is ready to attack the ball in case there is a rebound off the goalkeeper (see **diagram 14**).

2 v 1 situation: one player positions on the flank in the attacking third of the field; he crosses to his teammate who is standing in a central position 5 yards from the penalty box. This player controls the ball and sprints to shoot at goal while also eluding the challenge

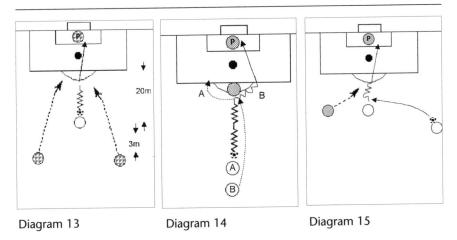

Diagram 13   Diagram 14   Diagram 15

by the defender who was standing 5 yards behind him (see **diagram 15**).

2 v 2 situation: one player moves on the wing in the attacking third, and crosses to his central teammate 5 yards from the penalty area. The central attacker promptly controls the ball, eludes the marking by two defenders coming from a distance of about 5 yards on either side, and shoots at goal. The attacker can strike the ball either in front of or behind the immediate defender, or lob the ball over him (see **diagram 16**).

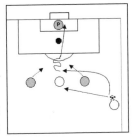

Diagram 16

2 v 2 situation: 2 players start from a central position 20 yards from the penalty box. One dribbles the ball while the other follows him. Once they approach two opponents standing at the edge of the penalty box, the attacker in possession stops the ball and sprints to the right, thus getting free of the opponent, while his teammate gains possession of the ball to create a 2 v 2 situation for the final shot at goal. The two defenders must be particularly skillful at marking their opponents very closely (theoretically, the back defender is responsible for attacking the opponent sprinting without the ball - see **diagram 17**).

3 v 3 situation: this exercise involves three attacking players and three defenders (one of

Diagram 17

them starts from an unfavorable position). Two attackers start from a position 20 yards from the penalty box, supported by their teammate, who is running unchallenged on the wing. They elude the challenge by the defenders (two of them commit the attackers from the front, while the third defender starts 5 yards behind the opponents) and quickly move to shoot at goal. The attackers shall specifically concentrate on shooting quickly and using the supporting penetration of their teammate on the wing either for the shot or for the cross. The two defenders are supposed to slow down the offensive build up, to help their teammate to recover quickly and properly organize the marking to prevent the opposition from shooting at goal (see **diagram 18**).

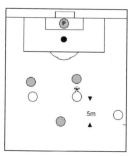

Diagram 18

"SITUATION" PRACTICE

The above-mentioned simple situations can be combined with more difficult and complex solutions, which increasingly approach real game situations.

2 v 2 situation: divide a 30 by 15 yard field into two squares, with two goals defended by their respective goalkeepers. One player on each team is allowed to defend (in the two halves of the field), while the two players in each group can take part in the offensive build up. This means a 2 v 1 situation on attack and a 1 v 2 situation in the defensive phase (see **diagram 19**).

2 v 2 situation: prolong the two side-lines of the penalty box up to 30 yards. In this marked area, the team in possession set up a 2 v 1 action, and try to quickly move to shoot at goal, while also eluding the offside trap as well as the recovery movement by the second defender starting from a position 10 yards behind them.

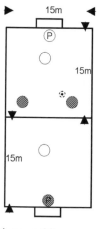

Diagram 19

The attacking players should especially concentrate to avoid being caught in the offside trap (see **diagram 20**).

2 v 2 situation + one all-round player: use a 30 by 30 yards field with two goals and two goalkeepers. The exercise involves a

2 v 2 situation, while the all-round player supports the team in possession of the ball, but can never shoot at goal. This exercise is aimed at improving one's ability to elude the opponent's marking near the goal (see **diagram 21**).

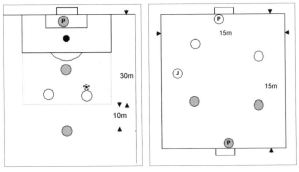

Diagram 20   Diagram 21

In order to further enrich specific shooting skills training, the coach can also suggest suitable tactical scheme exercises which considerably approach real game situations. Moreover, all the exercises can be either with or without defenders according to the final goal the coach wants to achieve.

TACTICAL SCHEME PRACTICE

Modern soccer - which is always in search of the best and constant improvement - cannot be based on "theoretical" principles exclusively (even though they are very useful). By means of tactical scheme practice every player should learn to think in the right way from the tactical point of view during the training session. The main principle underlying scheme-based training is to help every single player, and the team as a whole, to better adapt to real game situations directly on the playing field, while also improving physical and technical skills and team spirit.

Tactical scheme practice allows soccer players to realize that the phase of the training session especially focused on this important process directly leads to something unknown which they are going to discover. As a matter of fact, they should have a feeling that they always need to learn something new. Moreover, in light of much more general tactical training, this specific practice enhances the total skills of each player, while also helping him to properly perform his duties as a member of a team.

Two-player scheme practice

The exercises involving the participation of two players can be practiced by: attacking players, midfield players and defenders. In addition, they are also particularly useful to practice shooting skills.

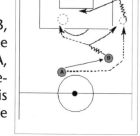

1. Player A passes the ball to his teammate B, who dribbles from outside towards the middle of the field and plays the ball to A, who is making an overlapping run to penetrate on the flank. Player A crosses to his teammate B, who shoots at goal (see **diagram 1**).

Diagram 1

2. Player A dribbles the ball inside and feints to let player B gain possession of the ball; B dribbles the ball outside and centers the ball for his teammate A to shoot at goal (see **diagram 2**).

3. Player A gives a pass to his teammate B, who dribbles the ball inside and plays it to A who is sprinting wide open on the flank. Player A crosses to B, who shoots at goal (see **diagram 3**).

4. Players A and B play the ball to each other while also moving forward; player A opens up by passing the ball to B, who is sprinting wide open on the wing. B crosses to A, who shoots at goal (see **diagram 4**).

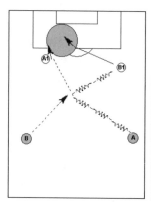

Diagram 2

Diagram 3

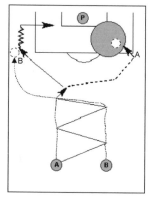

Diagram 4

Three player scheme practice
(with or without defenders).

A group consisting of three players can act as a single team unit in soccer. According to one of the main rules regulating team games, the player in possession of the ball should always choose between two different solutions (at least!) at his disposal. This is possible only if two teammates can position unchallenged to receive the pass: this situation is usually referred to as "triangle" or wall pass.

In a real play situation the triangle can be more or less "flat" in relation to the players' positions; it is important to remember that the worst solution directly results from three players standing on the same line (the triangle does not exist at all).

Diagram 5

1. Player A dribbles the ball, makes a wall pass with his teammate B and crosses to player C, who is sprinting centrally to shoot at goal (see **diagram 5**).
2. Player A dribbles the ball diagonally, performs a cross-over play with his teammate B, and makes a feinting movement to leave the ball for him. B dribbles the ball outside and crosses to player C, who is rapidly penetrating from behind (see **diagram 6**).
3. A plays the ball to B, who dribbles it outside and makes a feint to leave it to his teammate C. Player C dribbles the ball inside and passes to B, who sprints unchallenged on the wing and crosses for player A to shoot at goal (see **diagram 7**).
4. Player A passes the ball to B, who dribbles inside and plays the ball to his teammate C. C is rapidly making an overlapping run on the outside; he meets the pass from B and crosses to A and B, who have made cross-over movements so as to penetrate forward (see **diagram 8**).

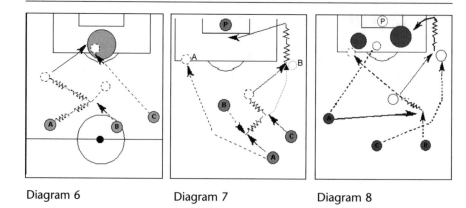

Diagram 6   Diagram 7   Diagram 8

5. Player A makes a wall pass with player B, dribbles the ball out side and gives a high cross to his teammate C. C heads the ball to B, who is penetrating forward to shoot at goal (see **diagram 9**).

6. Player A makes a wall pass with his teammate B - who is moving towards him - dribbles the ball forward and gives a long cross to B, who is sprinting wide open on the wing. B crosses the ball to players A and C who are moving forward after a cross-over play (see **diagram 10**).

7. A gives a long pass to player B on the wing. B dribbles the ball and makes a wall pass with his teammate C, while also moving towards the goal line. From this position he crosses to either A or C to shoot at goal (see **diagram 11**).

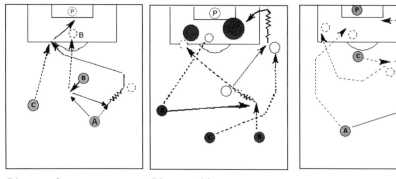

Diagram 9   Diagram 10   Diagram 11

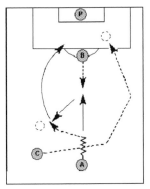

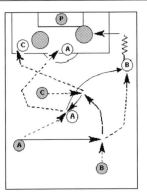

Diagram 12   Diagram 13

8. Player A performs a wall pass with B and crosses to his team-mate C, who has overlapped and moved into the penalty area (see **diagram 12**).

9. A plays the ball to B, who gives a pass to his teammate C who is quickly moving to meet the ball. C plays the ball back to A, who promptly crosses to B who is sprinting wide open on the wing. Player B crosses the ball towards A or C, who are approaching the goal after a quick cross-over movement (see **diagram 13**).

10. Player A plays the ball to B, who dribbles and gives a pass to C. C plays the ball to A on the wing, who crosses for either B or C to shoot at goal (they are standing to meet the ball on the near and far post respectively) (see **diagram 14**).

11. A makes a wall pass with B and passes the ball to player C, who plays it back to B. Player B passes to his teammate A on the wing, who crosses the ball for either B or C to shoot at goal (they position on the near and the far post respectively, or vice versa) (see **diagram 15**).

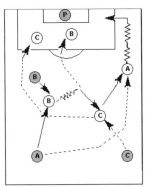

Diagram 14

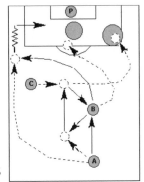

Diagram 15

12. Player A plays the ball to his teammate B, who gives a direct pass to C. C plays the ball back to A, who opens up the attack by making a long pass to B on the wing. Player B dribbles the ball forward and crosses for either A or C to shoot at goal (see **diagram 16**).

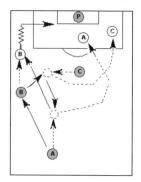

Diagram 16

Four player scheme practice
(with or without defenders).

The situation becomes more complete - and therefore more complex - when the attacking line is made up of four elements instead of three. This tactical arrangement is based on the creation of a quadrilateral, that is a group of four players moving in perfect synchrony and creating a number of different tactical combinations, solutions and relevant variations.

In this quadrilateral formation, the defensive cover is much stronger, more compact and well-balanced, while the offensive build up offers more favorable solutions for players to suddenly and successfully penetrate forward. In modern soccer, the quadrilateral can consist of 4 players playing different roles and can constantly break up and promptly form again during the course of the game, with different players taking part in the formation each time. Although the basic tactical arrangement does not change, the four players continuously alternate their positions and tasks. The quadrilateral is made up of four triangles and can appear as a more or less plane figure or even result in a rhombus.

1. Three midfield players and a forward. This exercise is for the forward penetration of two midfielders: one moves wide open on the wing, the other sprints centrally. Player A plays the ball to his teammate D (the attacking player who is moving back to meet the ball); D gives a pass to player B, who immediately gives a long cross-field pass to player A who is sprinting down the opposite flank. A dribbles the ball and crosses for either C or D to shoot at goal (see **diagram 17**).

2. The same situation as above, but player A plays the ball to C, who gives a direct pass to his teammate D. Player D opens up the action by playing the ball to B, who is sprinting forward on the wing and centers the ball towards A, C and D, who have promptly positioned to strike at goal (see **diagram 18**).

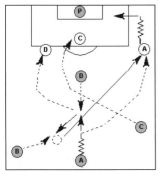

Diagram 17   Diagram 18

3. Three midfield players and an attacking forward. This exercise is for the central penetrating movement by one midfielder. Player A plays the ball to C, who pretends to give a pass to B and then passes the ball to his teammate D. D makes a wall pass with B and sprints inside to take a shot at goal. (The same solution can be chosen to support player C to shoot at goal) (see **diagram 19**).

4. Three midfield players and a forward. This exercise is aimed at helping one midfielder to penetrate wide open on the flank, while also favoring the other two midfield players to finalize the action by supporting the forward. Player B plays the ball to C, who dribbles back and gives a pass to his teammate A. A plays a long ball to B, who makes a wall pass with D, sprints up to the goal line and crosses for A, C or D to shoot at goal. Players A, C and D position so as to create a triangle inside the penalty box: in this way, there is a large area for them to meet the cross and shoot (see **diagram 20**).

5. Two midfielders and two attacking players. This exercise is aimed at supporting one forward to sprint unchallenged on the wing and give a cross to his teammates standing in the penalty box. Wall pass between A and B. B gives a long pass to his teammate C, who is sprinting wide open towards the goal line

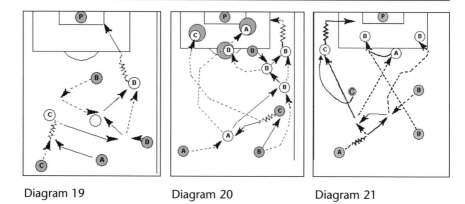

Diagram 19   Diagram 20   Diagram 21

and crosses the ball for his teammates to shoot at goal. The coach can suggest different solutions to finalize the offensive action, but remember that the attacking line should always position to create a triangle when the outside player makes the cross (see **diagram 21**).

6. Two midfielders and two attacking players. This exercise is aimed at helping the midfield player to penetrate on the wing and cross the ball to the penalty box. Player A passes the ball to B, who directly plays it back to his teammate D. D gives a long pass outside to A, who is running forward wide open on the wing and gives a final cross for the sudden penetration of his teammates (see **diagram 22**).

7. Two midfield players and two forwards. The attention is focused on the midfield player rapidly penetrating on the wing to cross the ball to the center of the penalty box. Player A plays the ball to C, who plays it back to his teammate B and sprints forward by making a cross-over run. Player B gives a long pass to D, who is sprinting unchallenged on the wing and crosses the ball towards his teammates (see **diagram 23**).

8. Two midfielders and two attacking players. This exercise is aimed at supporting one of the two forwards to sprint wide open on the wing and center the ball. Player A passes the ball to C, who makes a wall pass with his teammate A and then gives a long pass to the outside teammate B. B dribbles the ball on the flank up to the goal line and crosses towards the penalty area. There are several solutions for his teammates to shoot at goal (see **diagram 24**).

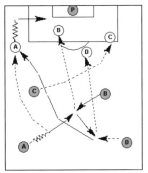
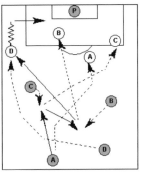

Diagram 22   Diagram 23   Diagram 24

9. Two midfielders and two attacking players (the two forwards are standing on the same vertical line). This exercise is aimed at helping one of the two forwards to penetrate centrally to shoot at goal. Player A plays the ball to D, who dribbles outside and plays it back to his teammate B. B gives a long central pass to C who takes a shot at goal (see **diagram 25**).

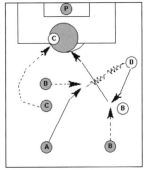

Diagram 25

10. Two midfield players and two forwards (the two attacking players are on the same vertical line). The attention is focused on the central penetration of one of the two midfielders to strike at goal. Player A gives a long pass to D, who dribbles outside and plays it back to his teammate B. B gives a long inside pass to A, who is penetrating centrally to shoot at goal (see **diagram 26**).

11. Two midfield players and two forwards. One midfielder is asked to penetrate on the wing so as to freely cross the ball to the penalty box. Wall pass between A and C. Player A gives a long cross to the forward run of his teammate B, who is sprinting wide open towards the goal line and crosses for his teammates to shoot at goal (see **diagram 27**).

12. Two midfielders and two attacking players. This exercise is aimed at supporting either one midfield player or one forward to penetrate unchallenged on the wing to give a cross to the penalty area. Player C passes the ball to A, who plays it back to his

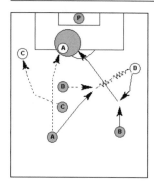
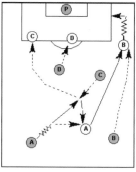
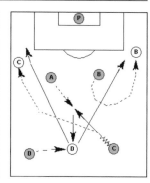

Diagram 26   Diagram 27   Diagram 28

teammate D. D can choose between two different solutions: he can give a long pass outside either to the midfield player C on the wing, or to the attacking teammate B sprinting on the opposite side. The player who receives the ball crosses to one of his teammates (see **diagram 28**).

Five player scheme practice
(with or without defenders).

A group of five players is very likely to create a number of different tactical formations and solutions and consequently allows every single player to take constantly different positions and play various roles. This also allows them to support each other in the best way possible, combining their complementary skills and therefore approaching what is usually referred to as "total" players in modern soccer.

1. Three midfield players and two forwards. The exercise is aimed at supporting one midfielder to move unchallenged in the central position and shoot at goal. Player A crosses to his teammate C, who dribbles wide open on the wing towards the goal line and is challenged by a real or an imaginary opponent. At this point, C immediately switches the direction of his run and plays the ball to B, who makes a wall pass with G and then shoots at goal. The attacking player F sprints wide open on

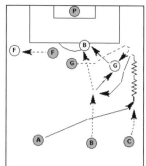

Diagram 29

the wing of to leave room for his teammate to penetrate forward (see **diagram 29**).

2. Three midfielders and two attacking players (the two forwards are standing on the same vertical line). The attention is focused on one midfielder sprinting unchallenged on the wing to cross the ball, while another penetrates in a central position to meet the cross and strike at goal. Player A plays the ball to G, who passes it back to his teammate B. B directly gives a long pass to F, who dribbles inside and gives a back pass to C. C plays the ball into the run of B, who is sprinting on the wing and crosses for F, G or A to shoot at goal (the three forwards position so as to create a triangle) (see **diagram 30**).

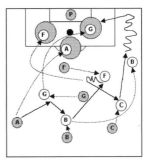

Diagram 30

3. Three midfield players with two forwards operate on the center-right side. Purpose: one midfield player makes an overlapping run, sprints unchallenged on the wing and crosses the ball for his midfield teammate to take a shot at goal. Player A plays the ball to B, who dribbles inside and gives a pass to C. C gives a long pass outside towards his teammate D, who is sprinting wide open towards the goal line. D crosses the ball for E, C or B to finish the action. Player A is standing in a covering position (see **diagram 31**).

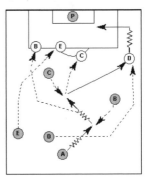

Diagram 31

4. Three midfield players and two forwards operating on the center-right side of the field. *Purpose*: two midfield players penetrate on attack and one of the two forwards sprints to cross the ball. Player A makes a wall pass with his teammate D and plays the ball to B. B dribbles inside and gives a back pass to his teammate E, who directly plays a long cross-field ball to player C sprinting unchallenged on the wing. C dribbles the ball towards the goal line and crosses for his teammates B, D or E to strike at goal. Player A stays in a covering position (see **diagram 32**).

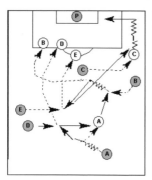
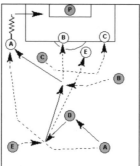

Diagram 32   Diagram 33

5. Three midfielders and two attacking players. This exercise is aimed at supporting one midfield player to penetrate on the flank to cross the ball, while the other sprints in a central position to finalize the offensive build up. Player A plays the ball to D, who passes it back to his teammate E. E gives a long central pass to B, who can either dribble the ball or play it directly into the run of his teammate A who is sprinting down the wing. A moves to the goal line and crosses for B, C or E to take a shot at goal. Players B, C and E can position in different ways to meet the cross from A. D stands in a covering position (see **diagram 33**).

6. Three midfield players with two forwards operating on the center-right side. Purpose: one attacking player sprints unchallenged on the wing to cross the ball, while two midfielders penetrate to receive the cross and shoot. Wall pass between A and E; A passes the ball forward to his teammate C, who plays it back to D. D gives a long pass outside to his teammate B, who is sprinting wide open on the wing towards the goal line to freely cross the ball for his teammates C, D or A to strike at goal. Player E stays in a covering position (see **diagram 34**).

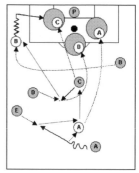

7. Three midfield players, with two forwards position wide open on the wings of the field. The attention is focused on one forward who moves quickly to cross the ball and on two midfield players who

Diagram 34

rapidly penetrate on attack. Player B passes the ball to A, who dribbles and then plays it back to C. C gives a long cross-field pass to his teammate D, who is sprinting unchallenged on the wing to cross the ball from the goal line. Players E, B and A position so as to meet the cross and strike at goal, while player C stays in a covering position (see **diagram 35**). The coach can suggest several variations for the offensive build up (players E, A and C penetrate on attack while B stands in a covering position and so on).

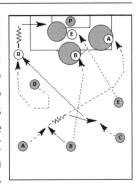
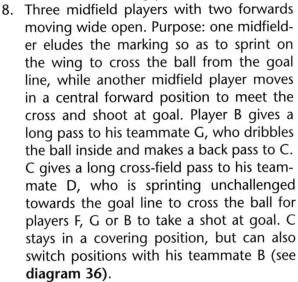

Diagram 35

8. Three midfield players with two forwards moving wide open. Purpose: one midfielder eludes the marking so as to sprint on the wing to cross the ball from the goal line, while another midfield player moves in a central forward position to meet the cross and shoot at goal. Player B gives a long pass to his teammate G, who dribbles the ball inside and makes a back pass to C. C gives a long cross-field pass to his teammate D, who is sprinting unchallenged towards the goal line to cross the ball for players F, G or B to take a shot at goal. C stays in a covering position, but can also switch positions with his teammate B (see **diagram 36**).

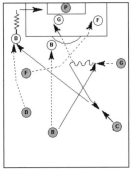

Diagram 36

9. Three midfielders and two attacking players. The attention is focused on the central penetrating movement by one of the midfielders to take a shot at goal. Player B dribbles the ball and plays it to G, who dribbles inside and gives a back pass to his teammate C. C makes a long central cross towards his teammate A, who shoots at goal (see **diagram 37**).

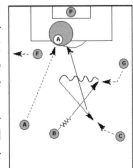

Diagram 37

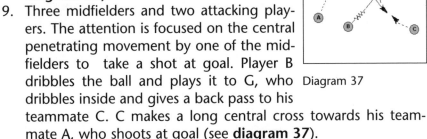

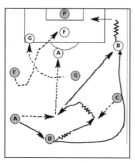 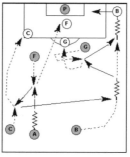 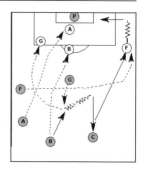

Diagram 38   Diagram 39   Diagram 40

10. Three midfield players and two forwards. This exercise is aimed at helping one midfielder to elude the marking and sprint unchallenged on the wing to cross the ball, while another midfield teammate penetrates forward to finalize the offensive action. Player A plays the ball to B, who dribbles it outside and gives a short pass to his teammate C. C dribbles the ball inside and passes it back to A. A runs to meet the ball and gives a long diagonal pass to B, who is sprinting wide open on the wing and makes a cross to the penalty box for his teammates F, G or A to shoot. C stays in a covering position (A and C can switch their positions: in this case, C penetrates forward on attack) (see **diagram 38**).

11. Three midfielders and two attacking players. This exercise is aimed at supporting one of the midfield players to sprint wide open on the wing to cross the ball from the goal line, while another midfield teammate penetrates in a central position to meet the cross and shoot at goal. Player A plays the ball vertically forward to F, who immediately plays it back to his teammate C. C gives a long cross-field pass to B, who is operating on the opposite flank. B makes a wall pass with G, dribbles the ball forward to the goal line and crosses for his teammates C, F or G to shoot at goal. A is standing in a covering position (see **diagram 39**).

12. Three midfield players and two forwards. Purpose: two midfielders penetrate forward into the penalty box to meet the cross from one of the forwards and take a shot at goal. Player B plays the ball forward to G, who dribbles outside and then passes it back to his teammate C. C gives a long pass outside to F, who

sprints forward dribbling the ball to the goal line and then cross-es for his teammates G, A or B to shoot. C stays in a back covering position (see **diagram 40**).

Seven player scheme practice (with or without defenders).
Increasing the number of players practicing on the playing field obviously means improving both supporting and covering play, while also increasingly approaching real game situations (applied tactics).

The seven players can combine in pairs and in groups of three, so as to create - directly on the playing field - particular movements which obviously result from the occasions and the situations occur-ring during the course of a match. The coach can gradually suggest specific exercises involving up to eleven players, to approach real game situations, or even organize a match where all the tactical arrangements previously practiced during training sessions can be implemented. This situation is usually referred to as a "shadow" match and specifically helps the coach to investigate and develop all the various elements concerning applied tactics.

1. Three central midfielders, two outside mid-field players and two forwards. *Purpose*: one midfielder sprints wide open on the wing to cross the ball, while another mid-field teammate eludes the marking to meet the cross and shoot. Player B dribbles the ball and gives a pass to F, who is moving towards him to meet the pass. F plays the ball back to C, who gives a long diagonal pass to D. Meanwhile, player D is sprinting forward on the wing thanks to the move-

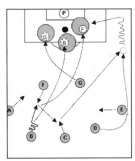

Diagram 41

   ment of his teammate E, who is moving towards the center of the pitch. D dribbles to the goal line and crosses for one of his teammates to shoot: F is standing on the near post, G on the far post and B in a central position. Players A, C and E stand in a covering position (see **diagram 41**).

2. Three central midfielders, two outside midfield players and two attackers take part in this exercise. *Purpose*: an outside midfield

player penetrates in a central position to take a shot at goal. Player C dribbles forward and gives a pass outside to E on the wing. E dribbles the ball inside and plays it back to D, who is moving in a supporting position. Player D gives a central penetrating pass to A, who is sprinting diagonally from the opposite side. Players F and G considerably favor the penetration of their teammate A by moving wide, thus creating free space in the middle. Player B, C and D maintain their covering positions (see **diagram 42**).

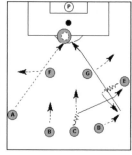

Diagram 42

Eleven player scheme practice
(Shadow game)

1. The goalkeeper distributes the ball to a central back, who promptly sets up the offensive action which develops through specific movements by the whole team (see **diagram 43**) and is achieved through a particular tactical formation on attack (see **diagram 44**). Player 2 crosses, centering the ball to his teammates 11, 10 and 9, who position to create a triangle. Players 3, 8 and 7 build up a supporting defensive line, while players 6, 5 and 4 position to create the second defensive line (the back line).

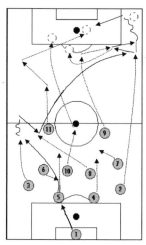

Diagram 43

2. The goalkeeper releases the ball to an outside defender who immediately starts the offensive build up. The attack develops through specific movements by all the players on the team (see **diagram 45**) and is achieved with the tactical arrangement you can see in **diagram 46**. Player 6 is wide open near the goal line and crosses the ball to his teammates 11, 8 and 9, who position to create a triangle of attack in front of the goal. Players 10

Diagram 44

and 7 make up the first supporting defensive line, while players 2, 4, 5 and 3 form the second defensive unit.

This kind of tactical scheme practice can also be used as pre-match warm up. The coach sets up a shadow game by playing the starting eleven and another goalkeeper, who positions in the center circle to defend a goal

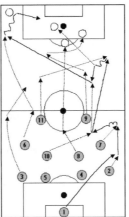

Diagram 45

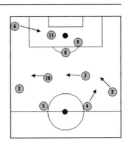

Diagram 46

made up of two upright posts. The coach asks his players to build up various offensive actions which should all be achieved with a shot at one of the two goals (it is fundamental for the players to perform the tactical formations previously practiced during training sessions). After the shot, the goalkeeper gains possession of the ball and can choose between two different solutions:

- distributing the ball to one of his teammates so that he can start the offensive build up (see **diagram 47**);
- kicking or throwing the ball directly to the opposite goalkeeper, to force the whole team to promptly withdraw to build the defensive line (see **diagram 48**).

When a player is moving forward to shoot, at least two teammates should follow and support the maneuver, to be ready to immediately exploit any possible mistake or clearing pass by the goalkeeper (see **diagram 49**).

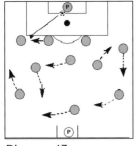

Diagram 47

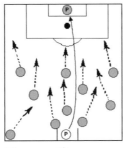

Diagram 48

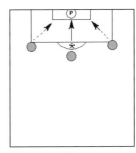

Diagram 49

On the other hand, if a player suddenly freezes the game by stopping the ball in some particular area of the playing field (the outside flanks):

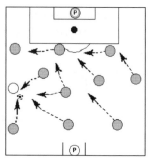

Diagram 50

- the whole team should press the area of the ball and promptly build up the defensive covering line (see **diagram 50**);
- the whole team should press the area of the ball, win possession of the ball and quickly start the offensive build up in the opposite direction.

Coaching notes:

The two symbols show the correct positions of the players when getting ready to shoot: if the player does not stand inside the shaded area, this means he could not practice the tactical arrangement properly.

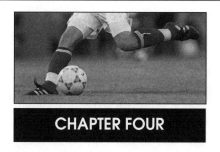

CHAPTER FOUR

TRAINING YOUR MIND

THE IMPORTANCE OF THE TRANSITION

When analyzing all the different phases of a match, it is possible to observe sudden changes in the "emphasis" when the possession of the ball shifts from one team to the other. Practically, a match is made up of two distinct phases of play, the offensive and the defensive build up, and while shifting from one phase to the other every player undertakes different tasks. There is an important "moment" of transition dividing these two phases. In practice, modern soccer is mainly focused on ball possession: when the opposition have possession of the ball, the whole team should try to retrieve it, otherwise everybody should play to take the ball up to (or inside) the opposing goal.

The distinction between defending and attacking players in this kind of play (or model of play) is no longer as clear as it was before. Nobody should stand inactive, including the goalkeeper (who immediately becomes the first attacking player in many cases); everybody should take part in the action, both during the offensive build up (retaining possession of the ball and shooting at goal) and during the defensive phase (regaining possession). While it is possible and advisable to properly train these two moments by means of technical and tactical practice, schemes, standard situations and so forth..., the "transition" especially requires mental training.

In order to help soccer players understand how useful it is to instantaneously change from attacking players (possession play) to first defenders (lose and retrieve possession of the ball), and vice versa, we are going to show you some exercises which will help players perform this delicate phase of play in the right way and with the necessary immediacy. These exercises should be used principally in youth sectors, where the ability "to memorize" is definitely higher and where the young are particularly receptive.

Moreover, these exercises are also useful for developing other abilities which are of critical importance both for the "cultural" richness of every single player and for general play development (pressing, double teaming, help, support, recovery action, diagonal play, strong and weak side formation and so forth...). For the same purpose, the coach can also suggest tactical scheme practice (involving a few players, definite lines or groups of players, or the whole team in a shadow match), carried out either with or without opposition.

Today, only 10% of all the goals are scored after tactical actions, while nearly 50% directly result from an anticipation action (interception) or from a possible mistake by the opposition (bad pass and so on...). In practice, goals are usually scored after regaining possession of the ball both actively (organization of the defensive phase by the whole team) and passively (technical error by an opponent while passing, throwing the ball in...).

Therefore, the ability to rapidly and properly (both at the technical and tactical level) control the mental passage from the defensive phase to the offensive build up, and vice versa, is becoming increasingly important for the final success of a match. Restarting continuously is not really profitable: what is more important is the ability to understand, choose, assess and develop an offensive action (the most effective one possible), intended as a collective movement (the players should all be prone and ready to participate, to offer a great variety of choices and solutions), where rapidity (directly connected to a change in the mental attitude of the player) is fundamental for the positive outcome. In practice, technical movement and tactical choice should combine with intuition.

In this context, it is particularly important for each player to turn his attention to the spaces and the opportunities created by his own teammates, so as to promptly and accurately develop the whole action. Restarting by dribbling the ball and maintaining possession, in order to exploit a probable superiority in numbers, is undoubtedly one of the possible solutions. But this is not the best one - assessing the speed of the player in possession and of the player recovering his position without the ball - compared to an offensive build up implying an immediate end-to-end movement, by means of a through pass, in a well-organized maneuver where all the players promptly attack the space towards the opposing goal. As to the transition from the offensive phase to the defensive one, the whole team should show the same important ability to "release the mental switch", which allows each player to take his best position with the right concentration and in the shortest time possible.

Being able to change one's attitude very rapidly implies a number of benefits while reorganizing the defensive line, in order not to be overtaken by the opposition's attack. The ability to slow down the opponents' ploy (by means of a suitable arrangement on the playing field) allows inattentive teammates to recover lost time - especially when the team is outnumbered by the opposition.

Since the ball continuously passes from one squad to the other, all the exercises a coach can suggest directly train this transition phase. This fundamental skill should also be improved separately, with suitable specific exercises aimed at applying it properly - for further details consider the exercises shown below.

EXERCISES

1. The players are divided into two groups, each one with a ball: the first group is positioned in the center circle, the other beyond the goal line, in the area between the penalty box and the corner area. One player starts from the halfway line, dribbles the ball towards the coach standing at the edge of the penalty area, stops the ball, dribbles past the coach and takes a shot at goal. Then, he immediately sprints outside to challenge the player starting from the goal line, to direct his movements. He acts as a marking player - although it is passive marking - and therefore has to follow the opponent and seal off space (see **diagram 1**).

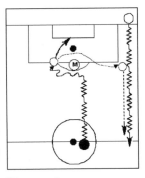

Diagram 1

2. The players are divided into two groups (A and B): the first group has possession of the ball and positions in the center circle, while the other positions beyond the goal line without the ball. One player of group A dribbles the ball towards the goal

area, while one player of group B starts from the goal line and positions to meet the pass from his teammate. Player A approaches the coach standing at the edge of the penalty area and makes a wall-pass with B. When player A is played the ball back, B immediately sprints to challenge him and prevents him from shooting at goal, thus creating a 1 v 1 situation (see **diagram 2a**). After taking a shot at goal A becomes the defender, while B acts as an attacker. The goalkeeper throws the ball to B, who is sprinting unchallenged on the wing. A follows him up to the halfway line (1 v 1 situation to drive the opponent and seal off space) (see **diagram 2b**).

Diagram2a

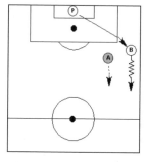

Diagram2b

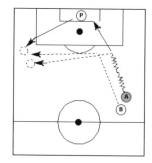

Diagram3

3. Transition from attack to defense involving a 1 v 1 situation: player A, who can start from various positions, dribbles the ball forward, eludes the opponent's marking and takes a shot at goal. Player B starts 5 yards behind player A, (the starting position can vary: the player can lie on the ground, stand with his back to the opponent...) follows him and tries to prevent him from shooting. Then, the goalkeeper releases the ball to B, who is running wide open on the opposite wing. A, who is now a defender, presses the opponent and drives him backward, forcing him to dribble the ball up to the halfway line (see **diagram 3**).

4. Transition: attack with a triangle, and defense with a 2 v 1 situation. Player A starts 20 yards from the penalty box, in a sideways position on the center-right, dribbles the ball, makes a wall-pass with player B - who is standing at the edge of the

penalty box, and finally shoots before entering the area. Meanwhile, player C starts 5 yards behind his teammate A, makes an overlapping run and sprints unchallenged on the wing (see **diagram 4a**).

After the shot at goal by player A, the goalkeeper plays the ball to either B or C, who are sprinting wide open on the two wings, A is supposed to drive the player in possession by directly controlling him and exerting pressure up to the halfway line, while also concentrating on the movements on the weak side. Moreover, he has to prevent the player in possession from making a cross-field pass, by defending in a 1 v 2 situation (see **diagram 4b**). If B dribbles up to the halfway line, and player A cannot mark him properly, and therefore allows him make a cross-field pass to his teammate C, now player A must try to recover his covering position on player C, who dribbles the ball forward to strike at goal, by playing in a 2 v 1 situation (marking and recovery movement in a 2 v 1 situation) (see **diagram 4c**).

Diagram 4a   Diagram 4b   Diagram 4c

5. Transition: offensive phase with a triangle and defense in a 2 v 2 situation. Players A and B stand 5 yards apart on one wing near the halfway line; they make a wall-pass while also moving towards player D, who is running to meet the ball. A gives a pass to D, who directly plays the ball back to B. B gives an inward pass to his teammate C, who is penetrating on the opposite side from the halfway line. In this way, the players create a 2 v 2 situation on attack for the final shot at goal (C and B are the attacking players, while A and D are the defenders - see **diagram 5a**). As soon as the offensive action is achieved, players A and D

immediately sprint on the wings to set up the offensive build up, while players B and C immediately change into defenders. The goalkeeper throws the ball to A; player B presses him and directly follows him, while player C defends the weak side, by controlling the movements of D. Players B and C can double team the player in possession (A) in the middle of the field (successfully perceiving the positions on attack and defense in a 2 v 2 situation) (see **diagram 5b**).

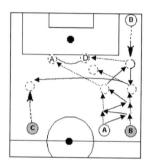

Diagram 5a   Diagram 5b

6. Transition: attack with a triangle and defense by pressing on the strong side and supporting on the weak side. Player A starts at an angle 20 yards from the penalty box; he dribbles the ball forward and attacks supported by his teammate B, moving on the opposite side. Players C and D (defenders) position about 5 yards from the penalty area in relation to their respective opponents. A dribbles the ball, makes a wall-pass with C and takes a shot at goal before entering the penalty area (see **diagram 6a**). The goalkeeper distributes the ball outside to D, who is moving wide open on the wing. Player B presses him and drives him up to the halfway line, while waiting for his teammate A (who was defending the weak side) to double team the opponent (2 v 2 defense and double teaming in the middle of the field) (see **diagram 6b**). If the defenders cannot double team properly, player D is free to give a cross-field pass to his teammate C on the opposite wing of the field, so that players A and B must immediately position in a new covering position.

Diagram 6a   Diagram 6b

7. Transition and attack-defense involving a 2 v 2 situation. Players A, B, C and D start from the halfway line and carry out a specific tactical scheme creating a shot at goal (see **diagram 7a**). If player C gives the last pass and D is responsible for shooting, the transition develops in this way: players A and B become the forwards and sprint unchallenged on the wings, while players C and D position to defend their area. The goalkeeper plays the ball to A and player C presses him up to the halfway line, while D helps his teammate to defend the weak side. When the player in possession is near the halfway line, the two defenders double team the opponent in possession (awareness of the defending and attacking positions in a 2 v 2 situation) (see **diagram 7b**). If double teaming is unsuccessful and player A can give a cross-field pass to his unchallenged teammate B sprinting on the opposite side, C and D must restore the 2 v 2 defense again. Player D marks B, who is in possession of the ball, while C

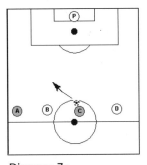

Diagram 7a   Diagram 7b

supports and defends the weak side (see **diagram 7c**). Players A and B try to get closer to the goal to shoot, while C and D are supposed to prevent the opponents from shooting at goal (see **diagram 7d**).

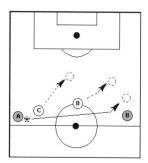
Diagram 7c

Diagram 7d

8. Transition from attack to defense with a 2 v 3 situation: this tactical scheme involves 5 players in the build up to the shot at goal. The situation directly results from the same sequence as the previous exercise: after the attacking player shoots at goal, the goalkeeper distributes the ball outside to player A, who is moving wide open on one wing, while player B is supporting the offensive build up on the other side. Player C follows A (in possession of the ball) very closely by pressing him; player D retreats very rapidly after striking at goal, moves up to the halfway line and double teams the player in possession if necessary. Player D supports the defensive maneuver, while also controlling the weak side (see **diagram 8a**). A eludes the marking by C and D and gives a cross-field square pass to B, who is operating on the opposite wing. Player E immediately sprints to drive and press B, while player C moves inward to defend the critical central area and is always ready to double team the player in possession. Player D supports the action and defends the weak side from any possible penetration by A (see **diagram 8b**).

9. 3 v 3 situation with supporting play, anticipation, double teaming and rotation: 6 players start from the middle of the field to develop a shot at goal by applying specific tactical schemes. After shooting, players A, B and C become the attacking players, while D, E and F are the defenders. The goalkeeper releases the

ball to A, who immediately gives a cross-field square pass to his teammate B, standing at the edge of the penalty box on the other side of the field, while player C immediately sprints unchallenged on the same flank as A. B dribbles the ball forward while the opponent F tries to press and drive him. D, who was marking A at the beginning, now makes a diagonal movement to support his teammate on the strong side and double team the player in possession near the halfway line if necessary. E (responsible for marking C) withdraws diagonally in a covering position (see **diagram 9a**). If player D moves to double team the opponent at midfield, E positions in a central area to help support the defense on the weak side (see **diagram 9b**).

Diagram 8a

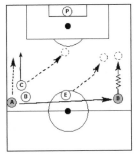

Diagram 8b

Diagram 9a

Diagram 9b

Shadow games: as we have briefly explained in the above paragraphs, the coach can gradually suggest different exercises involving an increasingly larger number of players, to create various situations characterized by numerical equality, superiority or inferiority (4 v 3 - 5 v 5 - 6 v 5 - 7 v 7...); in this way, training practice progressively approaches real game situations where the eleven players are all involved in tactical schemes (see the shadow game, for instance).

10. Mark a 50 by 50 yards area in the middle of the playing field, where the eleven players position themselves in regard to their tactical formation (system of play). The players freely move on the pitch by making two-touch passes, while always maintaining their shape, distances and their positions. As soon as the coach calls a player, the team abandons the ball and the offensive build up, and immediately adopts their defensive positions. The teammate in possession is considered as a reference point (assuming he is pressing the opponent in possession of the ball) and all the other players are supposed to make the best defensive movements in relation to their positions on the field (diagonal play, defending both the weak and the strong side, double teaming, and so forth...see **diagram 10**). This exercise clearly shows the principle of transition. The players, who are mentally prone to set up the offensive maneuver, are forced to immediately abandon this tactical formation to adopt the defensive structure, to prevent the opposition from suddenly penetrating forward, slowing down their play, and quickly setting up the defensive line.

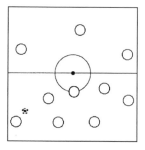

Diagram 10

11. The same situation as above, but when the coach gives the starting signal the player in possession of the ball immediately becomes the defensive reference element, with that player winning the ball.

12. The same situation as above, but when the coach throws or kicks another ball into the playing field, the player who wins possession of the second ball immediately becomes the new defensive reference player. When immediately shifting from the offensive phase to the defensive one, the players should all be ready to

move diagonally as a compact unit from the weak to the strong side, to re-build the defensive line. Rapidly changing one's mental attitude is of critical importance for players to immediately shift from ball possession to total defense.

13. In the offensive half of the field, the team moves maintaining possession of the ball and keeping their distances and positions. When the coach releases a second ball on the playing field, the players must all change their tactical behavior and immediately apply free, but well-organized, tactical arrangements to approach the goal and shoot. This exercise is aimed at helping players to gradually become aware of the transition action, train the possession phase, and suitably develop the offensive build up in the shortest time possible.

14. The team position in regard to their tactical system of play: the players are asked to make specific defensive movements in strict relation to some particular goals. When the coach releases a second ball on the playing field, the players must all change their tactical behavior and immediately shift from a defensive formation to the finalization of the offensive build up by means of special attacking strategies.

Opposed games: conditioned games specifically focused on the final phase of the transition learning process. For players to properly improve their skills while restarting the offensive build up or to completely eliminate the weaknesses on defense, they should be given specific training practices stimulating them to immediately react at a mental level. This is only possible if the player experiences these particular situations during training sessions. By constantly improving his technical and tactical skills he is trained to successfully deal with different solutions and master several situations.

1. Procedure: use a 50 by 50 yard field with two goals and two goalkeepers; eight-a-side conditioned game with two-touch play. Any time the ball moves outside the field (shot at goal, throw-in, corner kick....), the coach releases another ball in the same area to the team he prefers, and that team is responsible for restarting the game (see **diagram 11**).

2. Procedure: mark a 50 by 50 yard field, with two goals and two goalkeepers; eight-a-side conditioned game with two-touch play. The coach gives a special signal and releases another ball

into the field. The players must immediately abandon the ball they are playing with and restart the game with the new ball without interrupting the action. During the course of the game, the coach can freely whistle a set play situation in any area of the field (even in favor of the team who are not in possession of the ball at that moment). The defending players must immediately re-position to properly manage the new situation.

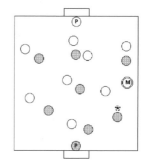

Diagram 11

3. Procedure: use a 50 by 50 yard field, with two goals, two goalkeepers and 4 small-sized portable goals lying sideways. Seven-a-side conditioned game + 2 players who always play on the team in possession of the ball (in practice this is a 9 v 7 situation). The team in possession are forced to strike at goal after making 5 to 7 passes (the two 'offense' players are also allowed to take a shot at goal). If they cannot finish the attack, the coach introduces another ball on the playing field (in any area of the pitch), giving it to the defending team. The game develops involving a new 9 v 7 situation (see **diagram 12**).

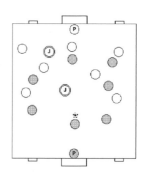

Diagram 12

4. Procedure: use a 60 by 50 yard field with two goals and two goalkeepers; nine-a-side conditioned game with two-touch play. The team losing possession of the ball (by interception, bad pass, tackled, etc.) are outnumbered by the opposition: 6 v 9 situation. Three players (who are previously selected and change every 5 minutes) must leave the game and immediately sprint to touch the opposition's goal line; then, they can immediately recover their positions to support their teammates to restore the equality in numbers (see **diagram 13**) This exercise, which also involves strenuous physical work, is aimed at coaching:

• the team which is temporarily outnumbered to properly

organize to delay the opposition's play while waiting for their teammates to recover their positions and re-build their defensive line;

- the team which has temporarily outnumbered the opposition to search for an early shot at goal.

5. Procedure: mark a 70 by 50 yard field, with two goals and two goalkeepers; 10-a-side conditioned game with two-touch play and five balls spread on the pitch. When the coach calls one player (of the team who are not in possession of the ball), this player quickly wins possession of the closest ball and restarts the game (see **diagram 14**). The coach can also set up some other small-sized portable goals (targets) on the playing field in relation to the specific aims of this particular exercise (defending the ball in a central position, defending the wings....).

6. Procedure: use a 70 by 50 yard field; the two teams defend one goal (with one goalkeeper) and the relative goal line; 10 v 8 situation in a conditioned game. When the team outnumbering the opposition wins possession of the ball, the players immediately move unchallenged towards the goal to strike at goal: their offensive build up develops according to the tactical formation and the number of passes the coach has previously decided. After shooting at goal, the coach plays a ball to the squad in numerical inferiority (in any area of the field) and they immediately dribble it beyond the goal line to score one point, while the larger opposition try to challenge and win possession of the ball (see **diagram 15**).

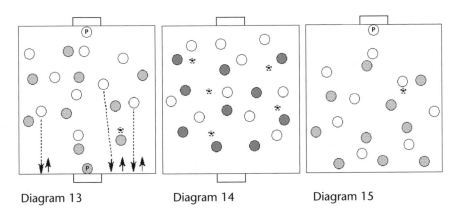

Diagram 13   Diagram 14   Diagram 15

7. Shadow game using the whole field; the team positioned in a defensive arrangement (the players are pushed up in their half). The coach plays the ball: first to the forwards, then to the midfield players and finally to the defenders. Immediate attack for the shot at goal (either free or conditioned by the coach's suggestions). The players must all move in a very compact way (never pushing up too much on attack, covering all the zones of the playing field, and so forth...). Some cones show the starting defensive position of the team. After shooting, the players immediately retreat in their covering positions, to build the starting defensive line by moving diagonally (see **diagram 16**).

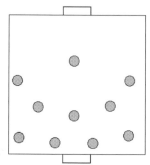

Diagram 16

8. Eight-a-side conditioned game in a 50 by 60 yard field; two-touch play. Place 9 small-sized goals on the pitch (the goal can also consist of two flags standing 1.5 yards apart). The two sides play and when the coach introduces another ball (in the area of the play action, by suggesting who is going to gain possession of the ball) the players immediately set up their defensive and offensive lines to face the new play situation. The team restarting the game have to make three consecutive passes before taking a shot at goal. A goal is scored only if the ball is played through the posts to reach another player (see **diagram 17**).

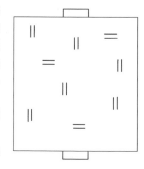

Diagram 17

9. The 11 players are positioned on the field according to their tactical system of play, but the different lines are wearing shirts of different colors. The ball must always be played to a different color and the players constantly move to approach, and shoot, at goal. This exercise forces the players to immediately switch their positions so that they are all involved in the offensive build up (see **diagram 18**). The same exercise can also be practiced by assigning each vertical line shirts of different

colors (the team is divided in vertical groups: right, central and left line). In a team playing the 4-3-3 tactical system: the outside lines are made up of the left or right outside back, the left or right outside midfield player and the left or right link, while the central line consists of the two central backs, the central midfield player and the forward.

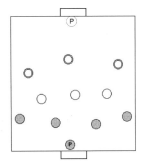

Diagram 18

PSYCHO-TECHNIQUE AND PSYCHO-TACTICS

The "Encyclopedia of Sports" defines training as: "The physiological process by which the person enhances his or her motor skills, his or her capacity for physical or mental work, and his or her resistance to fatigue, by practicing physical exercise constantly and regularly".

This definition is undoubtedly right, but modern soccer training is definitely much more complex as it involves much wider themes and principles and could therefore be defined as follows: "Sport training is a large combination of actions and educational teaching experiences allowing the athlete to sublimate his or her physical, psychological, technical, tactical and character attributes in order to enhance his or her performance during the competition. Physical exercise should be carefully organized to gradually increase in quality, quantity and intensity: in this way, increasingly heavy training loads considerably stimulate any possible hyper-compensation physiological process".

Consequently, the final outcome of physical practice directly results from the sublimation of physical skills (strength - speed - acceleration - quickness - endurance - power - agility...) combined together with psychological attributes (like technical and tactical features - will - motivation - adaptation spirit - creativeness...). As a matter of fact, there is no effective training if these two components are not combined together.

One aspect can obviously prevail over the other while practicing various exercises, but they are both necessary to properly and successfully develop the training process, since modern soccer involves intermittent high speed practice, combining both action and thought. This is the reason why all the different training plans cannot be separate moments, but directly result from a much more general "collage".

But what is the right key to effective learning?

Modern soccer could be defined as an "open" sport discipline which, unlike all the other "closed" disciplines characterized by repetitive and stereotyped movements, requires suitable motor skills directly conditioned by external and emotional conditions, which considerably influence the performance at any particular moment. Skillful players know what they are supposed to do in a particular situation, and how they should act. They usually prefer tactical organization to technical skills: as a matter of fact, top-class players often use very simple movements to get spectacular results, which clearly shows that understanding, selecting, and properly assessing the situation and the technical movement is more important then merely performing the specific movement.

The tactical movement directly results from the ability to properly respond to new and always different situations, while also properly assessing the final outcome in a critical and accurate manner. This constant conscious analysis of the cause and the final outcome creates the tactical skill.

The following phase focuses on the progressive stabilization of this important skill, to make the response increasingly steady, accurate and prompt. When searching for a new methodology for coaching soccer, it is first of all necessary to properly select and investigate all the parameters which strictly combine to create the technical movement; know all the different existing methods which could help to improve the new one and help players to gradually become aware of the new situation. It is possible to distinguish 4 main phases in this important process: **observation, understanding, choice and performance.**

The first phase (observation): is strictly influenced by memory, attention, the general atmosphere, and the mental attitude with which one is looking around. As a matter of fact, it is proven that those who observe and fear they cannot understand hardly understand what is happening; on the contrary, those who observe confidently, with a positive and loose formation, can successfully analyze and understand the situation. This is the reason why it is fundamental to "observe" not only with one's eyes, but also with one's mind, always with a very confident attitude. We should not be conditioned for fear of failure, and we should think we are observing something with which we are perfectly familiar.

The second phase (understanding and identification): is influenced by past experiences, memory and the ability to "abstract". These attributes allow the athlete to identify particular situations he has never experienced before; these unknown situations are the result of real life experiences combined with accurate discussions stimulating deep investigation and reflection, so that practical experience is finally translated into "theoretical principles".

The third phase (choice): can be introduced only if the situation is perfectly understood; this phase implies a final decision and it is therefore fundamental to choose what to do. The choice can be influenced by the following parameters:

- memory of similar past experiences;
- more or less deep emotion brought about by the situation;
- expectation of either the success or the failure of one's choice;
- motivation;
- competitiveness (constant attribute);
- aggressiveness (contingent reaction feature);
- awareness of one's skills or weaknesses as to applied technique.

Any tactical movement is the result of all these elements.

The fourth phase (the final gesture - performance): corresponds to the motor reaction, which is inevitably influenced by acquired skills (automatism), coordination (ability to adapt to varying situations by means of very quick adjustments), one's mental formation (stressed, emotional, strict... mental condition), the opposition's behavior (challenge, tackle...) and by one's physical condition (fatigue, inaccurate and clumsy movements and so forth).

These four phases (perception of the situation and identification - mental investigation and solution of the problem - selection of the tactical movement - motor performance) should obviously be trained for an extended period of time. For this process to be really effective:

- exercise should be constant and intense;
- the coach should suggest specific and proper exercises;
- the attention should be focused on the movement being accurate.

As a matter of fact, all these factors considerably increase the level of the technical and tactical movement.

For athletes to successfully and considerably improve their technical and tactical skills, the coach should use suitable coaching methods and plans which help to develop all the different phases of the training process simultaneously, while also respecting their individual importance. The coaching methods commonly used up to now favor the systematic improvement of the motor skills, but often neglect the perception and creativeness side, which is too often suggested at best on a theoretical level by the coach.

Both psycho-technique and psycho-tactics are a helpful answer to the constant need for a new global and analytical coaching method, which favors the complete development of the athlete from all the different points of view. Their effectiveness is based on three main principles:

- the educational ability of the coach, who should suggest rather than demand the exercise by assigning each player specific tasks, to attract the athletes' attention to very few particular details at a time and wait for them to solve the problem by themselves without anticipating the solution;
- the enthusiasm of the players, who should be particularly receptive to everything that is suggested;
- a stimulating atmosphere during training sessions; the coach should work to create harmonious, constructive dialogue and never act in a repressive manner.

Moreover, don't forget that:

- the coach should always be able to justify his suggestions which should also strengthen the relationship between the athletes;
- it is very important to discuss one's feelings and be ready to share one's experiences with the other members of the team.

Only in this way is it possible to improve - from the neurological point of view - one's awareness (be perfectly aware of what one is doing and why) as well as automatic replies to external stimuli.

By developing a new awareness of what is happening around you it is possible to achieve the final goal, that is immediately referring one's motor reactions to one's automatic activity. The player who constantly practices this exercise unconsciously stimulates his perceptive faculty which allows him to gradually become aware of his body, (either when he is standing motionless or when he is moving) and of external information concerning space and time in relation both to himself and to the people around him. Only after enhancing this critical sensibility can the athlete recognize his own automatisms and eventually work to modify them.

The exercises the coach suggests should always be quite simple, since they should never raise unpleasant reactions (such as refusing to compete, inaccuracy, and so forth), while also stimulating a critical approach. Each exercise should include:

- a phase in which experience results from continuous attempts (praxis) to solve the problems arising from the situation;
- a phase especially dedicated to analysis, communication, mutual exchange and dialogue to share one's experiences;
- an investigation phase to accurately define the elements by which one can further improve the solution.

By combining together all the various suggestions - which can often be very similar - it is much easier to further improve the learning of all the principles underlying the interpretation of the different situations. As a matter of fact, constantly repeating the same principles inevitably helps the athlete to internalize and memorize them, so that they can be easily used on other occasions. In this way, the player enhances his own learning process and stores useful concepts allowing him to solve several motor problems, which definitely improves his capacity to immediately understand and select. These abilities are the basic principles for the final creation of any tactical movement.

All these phases include possible mistakes, which should be felt as positive experiences, since they help the athlete to realize that his inaccurate performance needs suitable adjustments. Only with this awareness can the player also accept other people's mistakes with more understanding, and, consequently, the whole group are much more consolidated.

Psycho-technique and psycho-tactics are fully exploited in soccer practice. But remember that each exercise should include a "discovery" phase, an "experience" moment (praxis) and finally the "choice", which should always be directed and never imposed from outside.

Psycho-technique and psycho-tactics: these words are used to define the ability to make any intentional, conscious, and justified movement. This is possible only by creating particular situations which should be fully experienced by the athlete to specifically improve the "combination" between everything occurring in his mind (psycho) and his moving body (kinetics). This important combination helps the mind to perceive the information the body receives through its perceptive receptors, process all these sensations, think a suitable response to the particular moment and carry out - through the body - a number of movements in relation to what that particular situation is asking for.

There are four main stages which are of critical importance to properly develop the awareness and learning process:

perceptive phase - experiencing one's own body, accurately listening to it, perceiving it in relation to space, time, other people and to any training tool (this is the ability to "consciously" collect external information);

processing phase - analyzing the problem, elaborating a suitable response while also considering the information the body has received and past experiences;

verification and adjustment phase - assessing the effectiveness of the motor response to the situation and making suitable adjustments if necessary;

"abstraction" phase - speculating the essence of the practical situation, to properly react in other similar situations.

EXERCISES

At the beginning, the coach should suggest exercises without the ball so that the attention is focused on the movement exclusively to achieve the final goal. Moreover, he should explain nothing at all in order to let the players interpret what they have been asked to do. After some minutes, the coach should stop the players and ask them to explain what they have been trying to do in relation to his former request. Each player gives his own explanation and his personal experience will undoubtedly be useful for the others. This short discussion is of critical importance - especially at the first stages of training practice - since each player feels as if he has created something of his own or realizes he has lived the same experiences as his teammates and this undoubtedly enhances his feeling to be part of a larger group.

The difficulty of each exercise is proportional to the age and abilities of the athlete. The first exercises we are going to show you in the following paragraphs could be useful to implement this new coaching method to youth players or could be used as a sort of educational approach for adults who have never practiced this kind of exercise.

The real value of this practice does not lie in the automatic performance of each movement, but in the perfect understanding and interpretation by each player (in a very personal manner), while never forgetting the final goal one wants to achieve.

As we have previously underlined, the way in which the coach approaches his players is of crucial importance in this context. He should suggest and never demand specific tasks to the athletes, in order to focus the attention on very few specific details at a time. This coaching method is aimed at helping players to gradually achieve the final goal, that is referring motor response to automatic activity.

Only when the player becomes aware of his own automatisms can he work to modify them. Each exercise should focus on one single specific goal at a time and the athlete should concentrate on approaching the exercise in the best possible way. We are now going to follow the development of a very simple exercise in all its different phases.

Position in space: the coach only shows the space limits in which the players have to work and the way to occupy that area (walking, running, dribbling the ball) and tells them nothing else, to stimulate his players to freely interpret the exercise. Then, he can freeze the exercise and pose some particular questions which could help them understand the basic rules for the exercise they are practicing, without offering any solution, while also:
• stimulating the athletes to experience new theories to check their real effectiveness;
• stimulating the creativeness of each player in a very harmonious and relaxed atmosphere.

Here are the main considerations which should directly result from this exercise:
• it is fundamental to occupy free spaces;
• it is necessary to maintain suitable distances between players and from the goal line;

- never move outside the playing field;
- the teammates can never touch each other.

The proper tactical behavior includes:
- running in different ways and in different directions (stop, accelerate, recovery movement, withdrawal...);
- constantly keeping the whole field and one's teammates under control;
- anticipating and attacking possible free spaces resulting from the movements of one's teammates (this is very important because it implies not only observation but also anticipation skills).

Variations on the same exercise:
- gradually sealing off free spaces;
- increasing running speed;
- running, dribbling the ball (this is very helpful since it stimulates the players to increase their peripheral vision).

If the coach wants to stimulate his players' concentration, he can suggest the following variations:
- increase running speed when the opponent makes a change of pace and strengthen his play (this usually leads players to look at each other in an astonished way);
- when one player stops, the others stop too;
- when one player approaches another one, all the other players position themselves in pairs and keep on practicing the exercise to achieve the final goal (each player has his personal solution for moving in relation to what he sees and understands, but he cannot separate from his partner and therefore must immediately assess the behavior of the teammate and adapt to his solution if he thinks this is the best one);
- play the ball to each other;
- move to gather around one player (nobody tells the others or shows which teammate); in this situation the attention is focused on how the players interpret what is happening around them, on their adaptation and receptiveness;
- create different groups of 3, 4 or 5 players each;
- abandon the ball in one's possession and sprint to touch - one

at a time - all the others or move around each one of them;
- abandon the balls and move outside the marked area; then run back into the field to take the same position or another one;
- conditioned game with one ball less than the number of players positioned on the playing field (run to occupy free spaces; when the coach gives the starting signal the players all sprint to gain possession of a ball - one of them moves without a ball).

Elimination game: the coach can suggest this exercise only when his players have clearly shown they can successfully position themselves to occupy free spaces. Procedure: two teams; one group plays by handling and throwing a tennis ball, while the other uses a soccer ball. Each team tries to eliminate the opponents in the shortest time possible by touching them with the hand (one of them at a time). There is only one player who can eliminate the opposition: the player who is in possession of the tennis ball at that moment. For this reason, the teammates of this player should endeavor to pass the ball to the teammate who is standing in the best position to eliminate the opponent. The opposition must move away in order not to be touched; however, they can defend and save themselves by handling the ball. The players should therefore play to pass the ball to the teammate in difficulty. The group who succeed in eliminating the opposition in the shortest time possible win the game. Suggestion: never search for personal solutions (1 v 1 situations), but look for the cooperation and the support of teammates, by applying "tactical strategies".

Practice without the ball

1. Divide the team into groups of 4 players; the players position themselves to create a square and run without changing their shape and maintaining their distances (it is better to change the player responsible for directing the movements of the square from time to time).
   Variations: when the coach gives the starting signal, the guiding players of each square mutually exchange their positions or the three other members of each group take another position inside the square or in another group.
2. The same exercise as above, but each group is made up of either three players forming a triangle, or five players forming a line.

3. The players are divided into two groups (they are wearing shirts of two different colors): when the coach gives the signal, the players belonging to one group immediately position to mark the players on the other group (1 v 1 situations).
4. Different groups with the same number of players run and position in a particular area (each player can sprint and change the group, provided that the number of members in each group remains unchanged). This exercise shows how the players can mutually switch their positions as it usually happens during the course of a match.

Practice with the ball

The accurate performance of the technical skill is of critical importance in these exercises.

Individual work:
1. The players dribble the ball in a marked area and perform a series of controls (stops) acting as if their teammates were the opposition (concentrate on free spaces, direction of the control of the ball, and so forth...).
2. Bounce the ball on the ground, throw it backward over the head and control the ball in different ways: concentrate on the movements like in the previous exercise.
3. Bounce the ball on the ground, throw it backward, listen for it to bounce and turn around to catch it at full speed, while also focusing the attention on the same aspects as in the previous exercises.
4. Bounce the ball on the ground and control it in various ways; dribble the ball around beating the other teammates as if they were the opposition (guided control towards the teammates and dribble past them).

Work in pairs or in groups:
1. One ball for each pair, position to seal off spaces by throwing the ball and not letting it fall to the ground (each player moves by himself, but always keeps his eyes on his partner).
2. Two teams with two balls: position to occupy the area and play the ball (one-touch play).

3. Four teams with four balls (repeat the previous exercise, but remember that in this case the players should concentrate on positioning rather than on their group - this should prevent the groups from getting closer to make the exercise much simpler, without taking care of effectively positioning on the field and occupying free spaces).

4. All the players in the group pass the ball to each other by directly throwing it (one-touch play). When a player sprints outside the marked area, the ball must be played to him immediately and all the other players follow him as soon as he receives the ball.

5. Two teams with one ball. The coach previously decides the pairs who are going to challenge each other and when a member of a team sprints to receive the ball out of the marked area, the marking player who was previously assigned to him sprints to follow and mark him very closely. As soon as the player receives the ball, all the others sprint outside to create a number of 1 v 1 situations.

6. The players stand 2 or 3 yards apart and play the ball by heading it to each other. When a player heads the ball past his teammate, the teammate immediately turns around and gains possession of the ball by volleying it or controlling it on the ground (a series of guided controls).
   Variation: the player who has previously headed the ball past his teammate is responsible for regaining possession of it.

7. Two players are facing each other and play the ball by giving one touch passes. From time to time, one of them lets the ball go by and the other immediately sprints to retrieve it.
   Variations: the player who let the ball go by is responsible for retrieving it; the players can lob the ball instead of passing it on the ground.

8. Two players give a series of volley passes without letting the ball fall on the ground; when a player intentionally lets the ball bounce, the teammate immediately sprints to regain possession, controls the ball, and dribbles past the other player.

9. Two groups. All the players in the first group handle one ball and position themselves in a marked playing field; while the members of the second squad have to move very quickly searching for an opponent handling the ball and making technical

movements (volleying the ball, heading it and so forth...).

10. Divide the players in pairs with one ball per pair. The players position in two different squares: one is 20 by 20 yards and the other is 10 by 10 yards. The players dribble the ball by giving a series of passes in the large square; when they enter the small area together with their partners, they dribble the ball, beat their teammates and then play the ball to them.

11. Use the same squares as in the previous exercise, but in this case each player has one ball. When the coach gives the signal, the pairs move from the small square to the large one and vice versa, by changing their pace and the way they control the ball (for instance: small square = ball possession and dribble; large square = heading passes).

Targeted training

We are now going to show you a group of exercises which could be used specifically to train cerebral analyzers and the peripheral vision and stimulate quick reflexes.

1. Three players position on the field: A and B are facing each other standing 5 yards apart, while C positions behind B to mark him. Player A is in possession of the ball and passes it to B who assesses his opponent's marking and therefore dribbles in the opposite direction. The players can also volley or head the ball: this causes B to stop and control the ball (guided control) to elude the opponent's marking (see **diagram 1**).

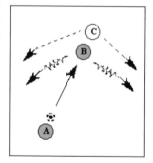

Diagram 1

2. Four players. A and B are standing 5 yards apart facing each other; D and E position on the two sides, at a distance of about 3 yards from B; C is standing in a marking position behind B at the start, but can move freely to mark either D or E. A always plays the ball to a teammate who is not marked by the opponent C (see **diagram 2**).

3. Four teammates and two opponents. A and B are facing each other, while C and D position on the two sides. The two opponents E and F start 3 yards behind C and D respectively (according to their marking positions), and force player A to always pass

the ball to an unmarked teammate. E and F can also mark player B (see **diagram 3**).

4. Three teammates and one opponent. Players A and B play the ball by giving a series of direct passes and when their teammate C - who is standing behind B and marked by D - sprints unchallenged on the right or the left side, A immediately plays the ball to him. Otherwise, if the opponent follows him, players A and B go on playing the ball with ground passes, lobs or heading passes (see **diagram 4**).

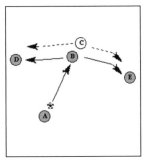 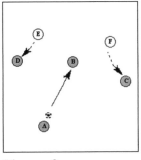 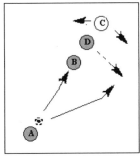

Diagram 2   Diagram 3   Diagram 4

5. Four teammates and two opponents. Players A and B play the ball to each other and when C and D - who are standing behind B together with their respective marking opponents - sprint unchallenged on the right and left sides, A immediately plays the ball to the player who is not guarded by his marking opponent. If both the teammates are marked, A and B keep on playing the ball (see **diagrams 5a - b -c**).

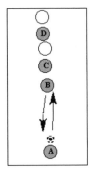 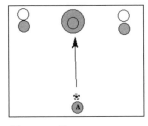 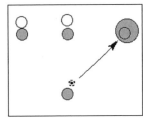

Diagram 5b   Diagram 5c

Diagram 5a

6. The same exercise as above, but there is just one marking player who has to immediately decide which opponent he is going to follow closely (see **diagrams 6a - b - c**).

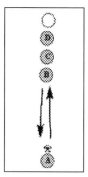

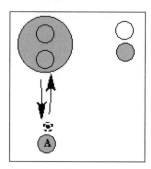

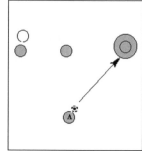

Diagram 6a

Diagram 6b

Diagram 6c

7. Four teammates. Players A and B play the ball by giving direct passes (one-touch play); B has to play the ball to C or D provided that they are not turned around with their backs to him (see **diagrams 7a - b - c - d**).

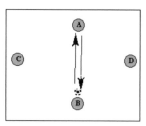

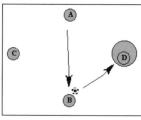

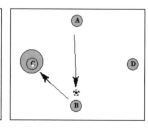

Diagram 7a

Diagram 7b

Diagram 7c

8. The same exercise as above, but in this case there is an opponent who decides the player he is going to mark each time, according to the situation. Players C and D play in the same way as in the previous exercise. Since the marking player controls a different

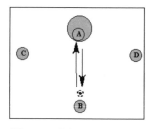

Diagram 7d

opponent each time, the direction of the action constantly changes (see **diagrams 8a - b - c**).

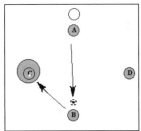
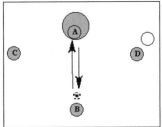
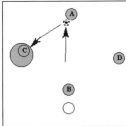

Diagram 8a   Diagram 8b   Diagram 8c

9. Four teammates and three opponents: Players A and B play the ball and are always the center of the action. This exercise is very similar to the previous one but includes *some variations*: if B is challenged by an opponent, he has to play the ball to the opposite side but only if his teammate is unmarked and is looking at him; otherwise, he plays the ball back to A. If B is marked by two opponents, he has to give a pass to his unmarked teammate, provided that he is not turned around with his back to him. Player A's defender is also free to mark whoever he wants (see **Diagrams 9a - b - c - d**).

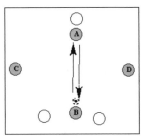
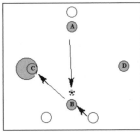
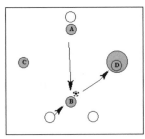

Diagram 9a   Diagram 9b   Diagram 9c

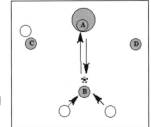

Diagram 9d

10. Two teammates and three opponents. Players A and B play the ball; if A is challenged by one or two opponents, he has to play the ball back to his teammate B. If B is also pressed by another opponent, A has to find other solutions and choose the most suitable way to shield the ball (see **diagrams 10a - b - c - d**).

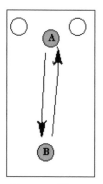
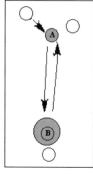
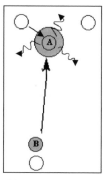
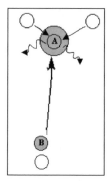

Diagram 10a   Diagram 10b   Diagram 10c   Diagram 10d

PSYCHO-KINETICS FOR DEFENDERS

Psycho-kinetics can also be included in tactical-scheme training practice and applied for each different unit on the team. This coaching method is aimed at enhancing quick reflexes (prompt reaction to the play situations), while also stimulating the search for the best tactical solution.

In the exercises we are now going to show you, the game always starts with the goalkeeper releasing the ball to set up the offensive action. These exercises include five teammates and four opponents; the opposition plays both actively and passively without preventing the development of the game. It is advisable to work on vertical lines to focus the attention on the players operating either on the left or the right side at a time. Don't forget that each exercise is supposed to consist of three important phases: the discovery, the experience and the final choice which should be directed but never imposed from outside.

1. Two defenders (one central and one outside back) and three midfield players (one outside and two central midfielders) position on the field according to their usual tactical system of play. The goalkeeper throws the ball to the outside back, who is

sprinting wide open on the wing to start the offensive build up, but is immediately pressed by an opponent forcing him to find a solution. The outside midfield teammate approaches the defender, but is followed very closely by another opponent. One of the two central midfielders sprints outside on the wing, in the position of his outside teammate, but is immediately marked by his opponent. The other central midfielder pretends to move forward, changes direction, eludes the opponent's marking and approaches the player in possession to receive the ball (see **diagram 11**).

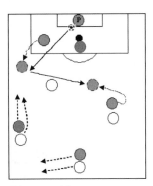

Diagram 11

2. The same exercise as above, but the outside back plays the ball to the outside midfield teammate who is approaching him on the wing, after successfully eluding the opponent's marking. All the other teammates are marked by their respective opponents (see **diagram 12**).

3. The same exercise as above, but the outside back plays the ball to the central midfielder who is sprinting wide open on the wing, to take the position his outside teammate has previously vacated(see **diagram 13**).

Diagram 12

4. The same exercise as above, but the outside back gives a pass to the central defender who has positioned to support the defensive line as all the other teammates are marked by their opponents. The outside back can also decide to play the ball to the goalkeeper (see **diagram 14**).

5. The same exercise as above, but the outside back plays the ball to the central defender, who is moving forward to exploit the space cleared by the movements of the two central midfield players committing their direct opponents in other positions (see **diagram 15**).

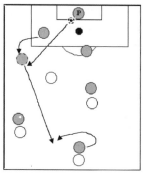
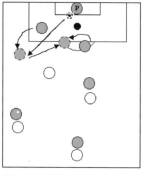
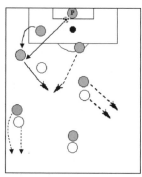

Diagram 13   Diagram 14   Diagram 15

PSYCHO-KINETICS FOR OUTSIDE MIDFIELD PLAYERS

These exercises include: one outside midfield player, supported by one central midfielder or one central midfielder and one forward; the opposition can defend them both actively and passively.

1. The central midfield player plays the ball to his outside teammate, who is placed in the attacking third of the field or near the penalty box. The outside midfielder can freely turn around to attack his opponent, dribble the ball past him and cross or give a through pass (see **diagram 16**).

2. The central midfield player plays the ball to his outside teammate near the halfway line. The outside midfielder can freely dribble the ball inside to clear the space for his teammate to penetrate on the wing and give a pass to his teammate who is standing in a better position (see **diagram 17**).

3. The central midfielder plays the ball to his outside teammate. The outside midfielder is immediately pressed by his opponent and therefore plays the ball directly back to the unchallenged teammate (see **diagram 18**).

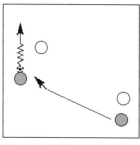
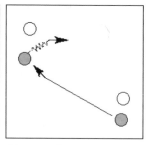
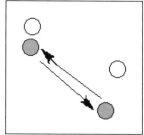

Diagram 16   Diagram 17   Diagram 18

4. The ball is played by the central midfield player to his outside teammate. The outside midfielder is pressed by his opponent and cannot play the ball back to his teammate as he is followed very closely by another opponent. For this reason, he has to shield the ball and dribbles it inside to the middle of the field (see **diagram 19**).

5. The same exercise as above, but the outside midfield player dribbles the ball back to retreat in a back position (see **diagram 20**).

6. The same exercise as above, but the outside midfielder gives a one-touch pass to the forward who is sprinting in a supporting position behind him (see **diagram 21**).

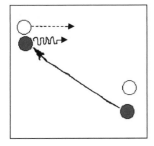 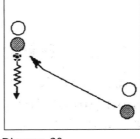 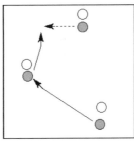

Diagram 19   Diagram 20   Diagram 21

PSYCHO-KINETICS FOR CROSSING THE BALL

4 v 2 situation. The marking players can play both actively and passively. The attacking team fields two players on the wing near the goal line and two attackers who are marked at the edge of the penalty area.

1. The two teammates standing near the goal line pass the ball to each other and are ready to cross the ball as soon as one of the two forwards can freely enter the penalty box (passive marking) to take a shot at goal. If the attacker cannot elude the opponent's marking (active opposition), the two teammates keep on playing the ball to each other. When the

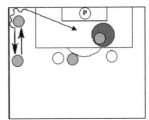

Diagram 22

player standing with his back to the goal line realizes that the forward is sprinting unmarked into the penalty area, he lets the ball go by and crosses for his teammate to shoot at goal (see **diagram 22**). Otherwise, when the other outside player spots the unchallenged forward sprinting forward, he dribbles the ball forward, beats his immediate teammate and crosses the ball for the attacker to strike at goal (see **diagram 23**).

Diagram 23

PSYCHO-KINETICS FOR CENTRAL MIDFIELD PLAYERS

Two central and two outside midfield players take part in this exercise. The two central midfielders play the ball to their two outside teammates who are pressed and marked (either actively or passively) by their respective opponents.

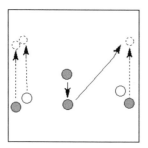 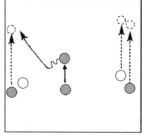 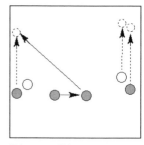

Diagram 24   Diagram 25   Diagram 26

1. When the outside player succeeds in getting free of the opponent's marking, the central teammate immediately gives a long outside pass to him (see **diagrams 24 and 25**); otherwise, if the player on the wing of the field cannot sprint unchallenged, the teammates keep on playing the ball to each other both vertically and horizontally until the outside player manages to elude the opponent's marking (see **diagrams 26 and 27**).

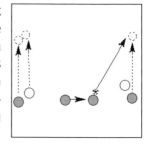

Diagram 27

2. Apart from the 4 midfield players, the exercise can also include some other teammates (and their relative opposition), to create a number of real game situations. For instance, when introducing an attacking player, the game could develop in this way: one central midfielder plays the ball to the forward who is immediately pressed by his opponent and therefore gives a direct pass back to the other center half. This player assesses the situation and makes a long outside pass to the outside midfield teammate, who is sprinting wide open on the wing (see **diagram 28**).

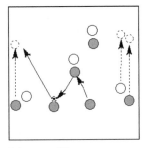

Diagram 28

Psycho-kinetics for crossing the ball and shooting

1. Two forwards position 10 yards from the penalty box facing each other on a vertical line and play the ball to each other. Two outside players (they can be either defenders or midfield players according to the tactical system of play) position on the two wings at a distance of 5 yards behind the two forwards; they try to elude the opponents' marking and sprint forward to cross the ball.

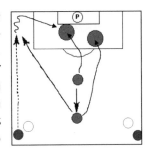

Diagram 29

The first one who can sprint unchallenged immediately receives the ball from the central teammate and makes a long cross to the two attackers, who are standing on the near and the far post (see **diagram 29**).

Psycho-kinetics for shooting at goal

These exercises are aimed at improving the movements to elude the marking, as well as passing (assist) and shooting (the forwards) skills and strategies.

1. Players A and B position vertically to face each other outside the

penalty area and play the ball. Players C and D position sideways 5 yards behind the two attackers and are marked either actively or passively by their respective opponents. When either C or D sprints forward, thus eluding the opponent's marking, player A immediately gives a pass for his teammate to take a shot at goal before entering the penalty box. If neither C nor D can sprint unchallenged to the goal, players A and B go on playing the ball (see **diagram 30**).

2. The same exercise as above, but the coach can also include some variations. For instance: if players C and D are marked very closely by their respective opponents, A dribbles the ball forward, beats his teammate B and strikes at goal. Otherwise, player B lets the ball roll past him and then turns to shoot at goal.

3. The same exercise as above, but players A and B are asked to play the ball by heading or volleying it.

4. The same exercise as above, but all the players position in a horizontal line at the edge of the penalty area, either opposed or unopposed (see **diagram 31**).

Diagram 30

Diagram 31

Psycho-kinetics for attacking players

One forward and two midfield teammates, with three opponents playing actively or passively. The attacking forward should play by adjusting his movements to his opponent's play.

1. The forward eludes the opponent's marking, moves to meet the player in possession, receives the ball, turns and engages in a 1 v 1 situation with the defender, who has meanwhile recovered his marking position (see **diagram 32**).

2. The forward moves to approach the teammate in possession, receives the ball and immediately plays it back to the unmarked teammate, since he is pressed very closely by his opponent (see **diagram 33**).

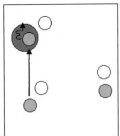

Diagram 32

3. The forward moves to meet the ball from his teammate in possession. As he is pressed by his opponent and there is no unmarked teammate to play the ball to, the attacker shields the ball sideways or backwards, while waiting for his teammates to sprint wide open and clear the space for him to freely move forward (see **diagram 34**).

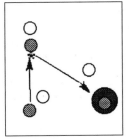
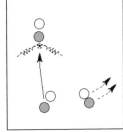

Diagram 33   Diagram 34

It is possible to vary these exercises by asking the players to sprint sideways wide open on the wings, while also maintaining the tactical solution and behavior (see **diagrams 35 a - b -c**).

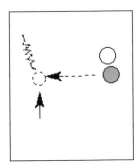
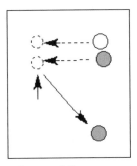
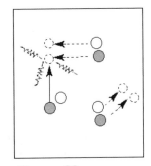

Diagram 35a   Diagram 35b   Diagram 35c

4. Extend one of the two penalty boxes by making it 10 yards longer. 3 groups (wearing shirts of three different colors) position inside this area; three players and one ball for each group (see **diagram 36**).

Diagram 36

The exercise develops as follows:
- one or two-touch play; when the coach calls one of the three colors, the player in posses- sion on that particular team immediately shoots at goal without entering the penalty box;
- the teammates play the ball to each other; when the coach calls one color and introduces another ball into the playing area, the players without the ball on that particular team immediately sprint to win possession of the new ball and quickly strike at goal without entering the penalty box;
- the three teams move without the ball to properly seal off free spaces; when the coach calls one color and introduces the ball into the playing area, one of the players on that particular team sprints to win possession of the ball and gives a direct pass to one of his teammates, who immediately shoots from outside the penalty area. In this exercise, the passer shall especially concentrate on timing and directing the pass.

TEAM PRACTICE

These exercises combine together all the situations we have been showing up to now and should be suggested only in a later stage during the coaching-learning process, when players have reached a good technical and tactical level. They are aimed at effectively training the player's physical and athletic skills, while also enhancing his psychological approach to the situation. In modern soccer, practical performance and abstract thinking necessarily combine together to eventually shape the athlete.

1. Two teams made up of 6 players each positioned in a 30 by 30 yard square. One ball for each couple of players. The game develops as follows:
- dribble the ball and, when the coach gives the signal, give a quick pass to a teammate;
- volley or head the ball and, when the coach gives the stop

signal, immediately play the ball to a teammate;

- dribble the ball and when a teammate sprints outside the square, immediately play the ball to him, by giving either a short or a long cross;
- the same exercise as above, but the player volleys or heads the ball and then controls it to give a pass or a cross to his teammate;
- dribble the ball and, when the coach gives the signal, play the ball to a teammate and follow the path of the pass, immediately creating a 1 v 1 situation;
- the same as above, but at the beginning the player volleys or heads the ball.

Purpose: position to properly occupy the space, peripheral vision, quick reflexes (prompt reaction), applied technique and so forth... **(see diagram 37)**.

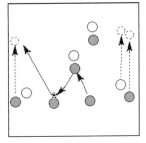

Diagram 37

2. Two teams made up of 6 players each positioned in a 30 by 30 square field. One ball for each team. They practice as follows:

- play the ball to teammates with one touch passes;
- dribble the ball very quickly to a teammate, with sudden changes of pace, and give a pass to him;
- wall pass with a teammate who immediately sprints to the player in possession and pass to another teammate;
- pass to a teammate, who quickly sprints unchallenged;
- pass to a teammate, who immediately runs unchallenged out of the square.

Purpose: position to properly occupy the available space, peripheral vision, help and support to one's teammate, applied technique (see **diagram 38**).

3. Two teams made up of 6 players each positioned in a 30 by 30 yard square; 1 ball (two-touch play). The exercise develops as follows:

- pass the ball in sequence (from one team to the other);
- wall pass with a teammate (one teammate at least should always

support the action by approaching the player in possession) and pass in sequence;

- a series of passes in sequence; after each pass, the other players attack the player who is receiving the ball; this player immediately makes a wall pass with another teammate (at least two partners should always position to support the player in possession) in order to elude the opponent's marking and then re-starts the series of passes in sequence (to one of the players on the other team).

Purpose: occupy the available space, color vision, transition from attack to defense and vice versa, support to a teammate, applied technique and so forth... (see **diagram 39**).

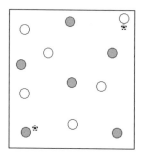 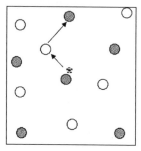

Diagram 38   Diagram 39

4. Two groups of 6 players each position in a 30 by 30 yard square; one ball. It is advisable to practice this exercise by handling and throwing the ball at the beginning, instead of kicking it. The exercise develops as follows:

- pass in sequence and attack the receiver to force him to turn and play the ball to his supporting teammate. The supporting player then gives a lateral pass to the teammate who is sprinting unchallenged (see **diagram 40**);

- when a player is in possession of the ball, his immediate teammate sprints unchallenged in deep (by making a through cut), while another teammate approaches him to perform a triangle. After the wall pass, the player in possession re-starts the series of passes in sequence (to another color).

Purpose: exploit free spaces, color vision, transition, help and support to one's teammate, gain space forward and so on...

5. Four teams of 4 players each position in a square field 30 x 30 yards; 1 ball for each group. The game develops as follows:

- occupy free spaces and pass the ball to another teammate wearing a shirt of the same color (one or two-touch play); if the ball is played to a player wearing a shirt of a different color, this player directly passes the ball back (one-touch play);
- position to occupy the available space; wall pass with a different color and pass to one of the teammates;
- combine the two previous exercises, but when the coach gives the signal, the players immediately sprint in four different directions so that each group is gathered in a different corner of the square; they continue to pass the ball to each other;
- the same exercise as above, but four players of 4 different colors gather in each corner of the field.

Purpose: positioning, occupy free spaces, peripheral vision, color vision, prompt perception and quick reflexes, applied technique and so on... (see **diagram 41**).

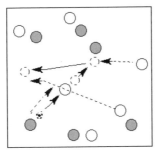 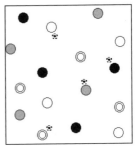

Diagram 40   Diagram 41

6. Use one half of the playing field; two teams position along the goal lines with one ball. The team in possession throws the ball to the opposite group; they receive the ball and immediately set up the attack by playing the ball with the hands (rugby-like game), while also moving forward to cross the opposite goal line and score one point. The defending team must intercept the ball and touch the player in possession to immediately start another offensive build up. The same exercise can also be practiced with the players using both their hands and feet or their feet exclusively.

Purpose: position to occupy the available space on attack, pass to the unchallenged teammate, avoid contact with the opposition, vision of play and so forth... (see **diagram 42**).

7. Two teams of 6 and 9 players respectively position on a square field 30 x 30 yards. The team in numerical superiority dribbles the ball and plays a series of passes to the unopposed team-mates. The players who are marked very closely by their respective opponents must stand in their position without moving (marking positions continuously change to create new play solutions, there are always 2 possible passes if the unmarked teammates practice the exercise properly and are not covered by any teammate or opponent). The same exercise can be carried out in an 8 v 6 situation; in this case there is always one possible solution (just one unmarked teammate).

Purpose: prompt reaction, peripheral vision, marking skills and ability to elude the opponent's marking, applied technique, ability to sprint unmarked and approach the player in possession to meet the ball... (see **diagram 43**).

8. Two groups of three players each position in a 20 by 15 yard field; 1 ball for each group. Each team plays the ball by giving a series of passes; when the coach gives the signal, the two players without the ball act as opposition and double team the player in possession. This results in two 2 v 1 situations.

Purpose: quick reflexes in the transition phase, prompt double teaming, accurate choice of double teaming positions and so forth... (see **diagram 44**).

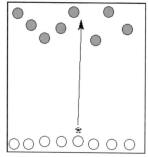 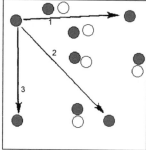 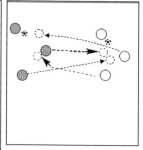

Diagram 42   Diagram 43   Diagram 44

9. Two teams of 6 players each position in a 25 yard square field; one ball. The two groups play the ball with their hands to defend the goal line. The players cannot run while also handling the ball and every time the ball falls to the ground the other team wins possession. For a point to be scored, the ball must be played to the teammate standing on the goal line. The same exercise can be practiced by kicking the ball instead of throwing it (two-touch play).

Purpose: ability to elude the marking and sprint unopposed, timing the penetrating movements.... (see **diagram 45**).

10. 4 v 2 situation in a 15 yard square; 2 balls. The four players in possession play the balls by giving two-touch passes, while the opponents try to win possession of the two balls (it is enough to touch the players in possession to gain possession). The player who makes the last bad pass directly presses the defending team together with his teammate to try to retrieve the ball.

Purpose: applied technique, attention focused on different balls and so forth.... (see **diagram 46**).

•   Two teams of 4 players each play in two 10 yard square areas; one ball. 4 v 2 situation in each area, but the players change continuously. The team in possession of the ball plays 4 v 2, using two-touch passes to maintain possession inside their own square. The two opponents try to win the ball and dribble or cross it to their two teammates in the other square. They follow the ball into the other square and this results in a new 4 v 2 situation.

Purpose: applied technique, aggressive play to retrieve possession of the ball, peripheral vision, transition and so on.... (see **diagram 47**).

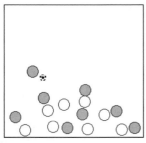
Diagram 45

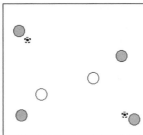
Diagram 46

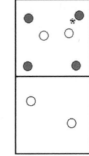
Diagram 47

CHAPTER FIVE

PRESSING, OFFSIDE, SCREENS, FEINTS AND SET PLAYS

PRESSING, OFFSIDE AND COUNTER-MEASURES

The effectiveness of some tactical strategies like offside and pressing is the result of more and more scientific, geometrical and accurate training. Their relationship depends on the fact that the offside strategy - although it is mostly defensive - can also become an offensive tactic if it is simultaneously combined with pressing. For this reason, these two tactical movements are interdependent in many cases, and the success of one of them often results in the proper performance of the other. We are now going to show you a series of "initial" exercises aimed at coaching and learning pressing, offside and their counter-measures.

EXERCISES

1. Seven players position along the halfway line, everyone with a ball. Another seven players spread along the line of the penalty area. The player in possession kicks the ball to the player directly facing him, who heads or kicks it back and immediately sprints forward. The player who first struck the ball moves into the position of the player who played it back.

2. The players position in pairs at the edge of the penalty area. The goalkeeper kicks the ball to the center of the field and one pair sprints to gain possession of the ball. The player who first wins possession becomes the forward and the other the defender, they play 1 v 1 and shoot at goal. This exercise can be modified

by increasing the number of players to create a coaching pro-gression from 2 v 2 up to 6 v 6.

3. The players are divided into two teams, both arranged at the edge of the same penalty box. The goalkeeper distributes the ball to the midfield. Both teams attack the ball, which must be touched by the forwards first. Once the attacking players gain possession of the ball, they immediately begin the offensive build up to approach the goal and shoot.

4. Four players (2 for each team) position at the edge of the penalty area, and a fifth player is standing in the center circle. The goalkeeper kicks the ball to the midfield. The pair gaining possession of the ball immediately starts the offensive action to shoot at goal, with the support of the midfield player (3 v 2 situation). The defending team can apply the offside tactics since they are outnumbered by the opposition.

5. Two teams (5 to 7 players each) arranged within the penalty area (forwards v defenders). The players take a series of corner kicks and throw-ins; if the ball is cleared back, the attacking players immediately sprint to win possession. The defenders press them and, once the game is resumed, they can apply the offside trap.

6. Two teams: one group positions within the penalty box and the other in the center circle. The goalkeeper distributes the ball and the players standing in the penalty area immediately sprint forward. After rounding a post placed in a central position at a distance of 20 yards, they quickly position to oppose the opposition's attack.

Countermeasures to pressing and offside: every team should prepare their own countermeasures to oppose the opposition's pressing and offside tactics effectively. This is of critical importance because in modern soccer the more training is carried out focusing particular attention on what could happen during a match, the more effective that team becomes. The experiences the player lives during training sessions help him to stimulate a series of automatic responses allowing him to oppose the opposition's play. We are now going to show you a number of situations every coach should practice by arranging his players on the field and using semi-passive defenders.

1. A player wins possession of the ball after a pass back by one of his opponents; he tries to break through the opposing defense alone by dribbling the ball or kicking it over the defensive line. This exercise is difficult to practice, since most teams systematically resort to tactical fouls.

2. A player regains possession of the ball in a wing position after a back pass by one of the opponents. Once he gets the ball, he immediately makes a cross-field through pass (one-touch play or before being pressed by the opposition) to beat the opposing defenders and supports the forward penetration of his teammate from a back position. The other teammates immediately retreat to avoid being caught offside (even if it is a passive trap) when the opponents move forward (see **diagrams 1 - 2 - 3 - 4**).

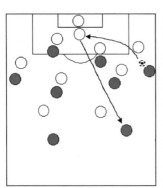

Diagram 1

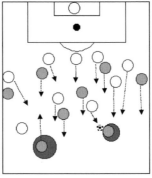

Diagram 2

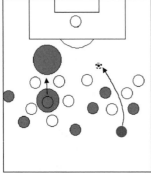

Diagram 3

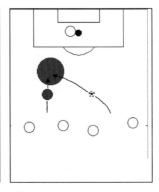

Diagram 4

3. The offensive build up mostly develops in a central position. One player controls the ball cleared by one of his opponents and turns around with his back to both his teammates and the opposition, who are moving forward. He plays the ball to one of his teammates standing in front of him and sprints forward to meet the back pass by his teammate; he should concentrate on not being caught offside (see **diagrams 5 - 6 - 7 - 8**).

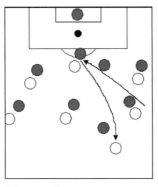

Diagram 5

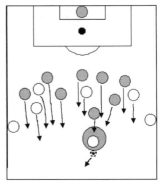

Diagram 6

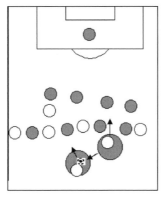

Diagram 7

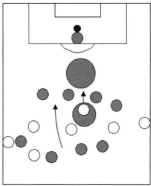

Diagram 8

4. A player wins possession of the ball either on the right or left wing after an opponent has cleared the shot resulting from a corner kick (the player is moving on the same side where the corner kick was taken). He delays to wait for the teammate who took the corner to immediately approach him for a give-and-go. This movement allows the player at the edge of the penalty box to sprint unchallenged to the goal.

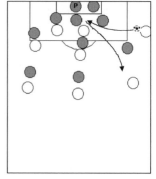

Diagram 9

5. A player wins possession of the ball on the wing after one of the opponents has cleared the shot resulting from a dead-ball situation. The player in possession plays the ball to a central unmarked teammate, who immediately opens up the action on the opposite wing for the sudden penetration of another teammate (see **diagrams 9 - 10 - 11 - 12**).

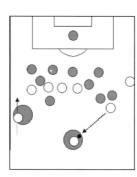
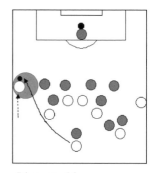

Diagram 10   Diagram 11   Diagram 12

6. A player gains possession of the ball after a back pass by one of the opponents and gives a mid-height pass to his teammate who is running back towards him in order to avoid being caught offside. The player moving back lets the ball go by, past the opposing defenders, for the forward penetration of the teammate who made the pass.

SCREENS AND FEINTS

When observing basketball games, it is very easy to understand the importance of screens in a sport where players are constantly looking for free spaces to shoot in a very small court. The playing field, the laws of the game and, consequently, the way in which players can use screening tactics are completely different in soccer. The player who gives a pass to the teammate who is sprinting unopposed plays a crucial role in the game since his pass is very likely to be inaccurate, especially considering that the pass is often made from a considerable distance. Moreover, soccer laws do not allow the same screen movements as in basketball, and the player screening his opponent must pay particular attention not to commit a foul.

In addition, the screen should only be performed a few times during the course of a match and at set plays in particular, taking care not to screen the same opponent if possible, otherwise the opponent could get accustomed to anticipating one's movements and therefore react roughly. For this reason, the player performing the screen should be ready to sacrifice himself for his teammates, while also restraining - like in the case of an attacking player - his natural instinct to move forward to shoot at goal.

Screens and feints: what are they?

In practice, screens and feints are particular movements aimed at helping a teammate to elude the opponent's marking and move more freely, while also supporting him to sprint unopposed or shoot at goal, by directly screening his immediate opponent who is putting pressure on him. Therefore, by means of screening tactics a player can break off the pressure and the marking of the opposing defender on one of his teammates.

Both screens and feints have the same purpose, but also show a fundamental difference: when performing the screen the player stands nearly motionless in front of his opponent (static position), while the feint is made by moving players. Consequently, feinting movements are more difficult to perform, since the two partners must perfectly time their action and show absolute coordination.

Furthermore, the feint can be made at any moment during the match, and its success directly results from the intuition and instincts of the players involved, while the screen is much more likely to be successful and effective in dead-ball situations.

Different kinds of screens

Before accurately analyzing how the screen should be performed, it is first necessary to underline that choosing one particular kind of screen rather than another directly depends on the position of the defender to be screened. The screen can be made:

in front - when there is enough room between the attacker and the relative defender; the player performing the screen positions between the two players, in front of the opponent and turns his back to the teammate, to help him play more easily and freely. This kind of screen is very difficult to perform (see **diagram 1**).

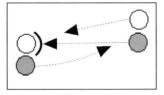

Diagram 1

on the left or the right side - if there is not enough room to exploit between the teammate and his immediate opponent, the player performing the screen positions on the side of the defender, to prevent him from properly following the movements of the teammate he is marking (see **diagram 2**).

behind - when the player performing the screen positions behind the defender who is marking his teammate (see **diagram 3**);

blind - when the player performing the screen comes from a position that the defender cannot see and control, and stands at his back (see **diagram 4**).

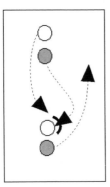

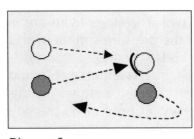

Diagram 3

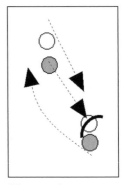

Diagram 2

Diagram 4

PRACTICE

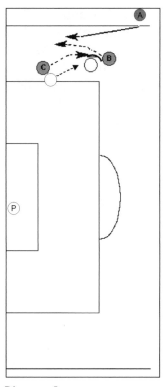

1. Screen at throw-in to free one of the teammates. Player A takes the throw-in aiming the ball to teammate B, who is sprinting forward on the wing to cross the ball. Player C moves to perform the screen on the marking opponent of his teammate B (see **diagram 5**).

2. Screen from the front to free the teammate in the penalty box. Player B continues the action described in exercise 1 and makes a cross for his teammate D, exactly when he manages to sprint unopposed thanks to the screen performed by E. The player performing the screen cannot stand passively, but immediately follows his opponent and takes a suitable position. Player B decides where he is going to aim the ball in relation to the position of the covering defenders. The two attackers move to screen the opposition and help their teammate D to sprint unopposed to the near post (situation in **diagram 6**) or exchange their roles and screen the opposition to help E get free from the marking and meet the pass (**diagram 7**). In this case the covering defender positions to prevent any forward movement by the opposition to the near post.

Diagram 5

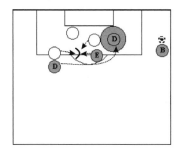

Diagram 6

3. Inside screen at throw-in to free one of the forwards in the central area. Player A has to work to play the ball

to his teammate B, as soon as he manages to sprint unopposed inside thanks to the screen performed by C. There are various solutions for the team to finish the attack: player B either dribbles the ball into the penalty box and shoots or takes a direct shot at goal; otherwise, D succeeds in eluding his defender thanks to the screen performed by his teammate E and sprints to meet a pass by his teammate B (see **diagram 8**).

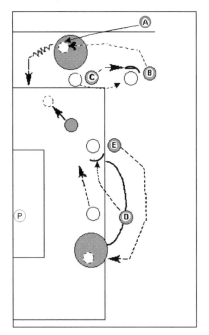

Diagram 7

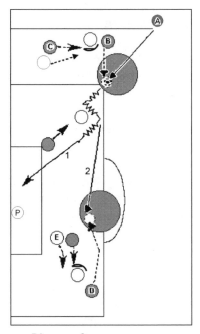

Diagram 8

4. Screen to free one of the forwards to meet a cross from the wing. Player A is in possession of the ball in an outside position in the attacking third of the field; he makes a cross to the middle of the penalty box as soon as his teammate B manages to sprint unmarked on the opposite side of the area by exploiting the screen performed by C. In practice, while C is screening the opponent, player B gets free by making a semi-rotation movement. This tactical scheme can be used when the opposition - playing zonally - commits their two center backs to the two attacking players (see **diagram 9**).

5. Screen to free one of the forwards to meet the central through pass. Player A starts from a central position in the attacking third of the field and immediately plays the ball forward to his teammate B as soon as B manages to elude the marking by exploiting the screen by his teammate C. In practice, the two forwards move to the

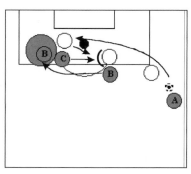

Diagram 9

center of the penalty box and, when they are close together, one performs the screen on his teammate's defender, while the other can sprint unchallenged to receive the through pass by A (see **diagram 10**). As was previously underlined, the two attacking players should specifically concentrate on the position of the covering defender and move accordingly.

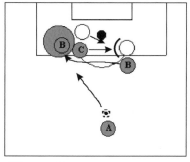

Diagram 10

6. Screen to support the teammate who is approaching the player in possession. Player A pretends to move to the player in possession, suddenly changes direction and performs a screen on the opponent who is marking B very closely. B can now sprint unchallenged to the player in possession; he receives the ball from his teammate and immediately turns to run to the opposing goal (see **diagram 11**).

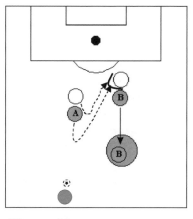

Diagram 11

7. Screen to free one of the forwards coming from the center-right or center-left. Player A pretends to move to the teammate in

possession to make a wall pass, but suddenly changes his direction and runs to screen the defender marking B. B can therefore get free from the marking and either approaches the player in possession to make a wall pass (which is much easier since he is unopposed), or penetrates into the free space to meet a through pass by the teammate in possession (see **diagram 12**).

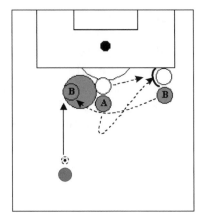

Diagram 12

FEINTS

Unlike screen tactics, feints are performed while the player is moving, either with or without the ball. This involves a number of problems because the player needs to combine the perfect synchronization of his movements and the timing of the movement together with a passive attitude (releasing the ball at the right time) and an active one (controlling or passing the ball), which should be perfectly coordinated to avoid making a bad cut (running into one's opponent, losing the ball and so forth...). There are three different kinds of feint, which can be explained as follows:

- feint to support the teammate dribbling the ball outside: player A dribbles the ball inside, crosses his teammate B, leaves him the ball by shielding it from the immediate opponent, while also screening the run of the opponent who is marking his teammate (see **diagram 13**);
- feint to support the teammate dribbling the ball inside (see **diagram 14**);
- feint to help another teammate meet the ball; the player moves to the ball played by one of his teammates, pretends to control it and lets it roll by (between his feet or sideways) to another teammate who controls the ball, thus deceiving both his own marking opponent and that of the partner receiving the ball.

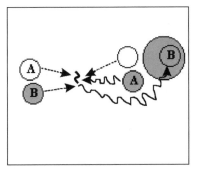

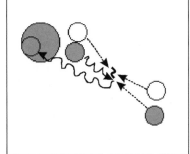

Diagram 13   Diagram 14

SET PLAYS

It is proven that most of the goals scored during soccer matches directly result from set play movements or from actions immediately developing from dead-ball situations. Therefore, the large number of set play situations gives every team the opportunity to influence the final score if they are able to exploit these situations in the best possible way. The success considerably depends on the players' ability and promptitude while dealing with these favorable opportunities.

Every coach should develop his own coaching method as to various set play situations. We usually suggest dividing the playing field into two zones:

defense and midfield zone: in this area it is particularly important to focus the attention not only on real set plays, but also on the goalkeeper distributing the ball (with his feet or, especially, with the hands) to set up the offensive action and on goal kicks. The balls coming from these areas could be considerably dangerous if they are played very quickly, in depth and with accuracy. In modern soccer, "time and space" are key and it is therefore fundamental to specifically concentrate on the accuracy and the speed of the passes in this zone of the field.

attack zone: set play situations in this area of the field are of critical importance in view of the final score. This is due to the great balance between the different teams in modern soccer, to the evolution of the various systems of play, to the performance of some very skillful players and to the ability of many teams to adopt a number of alternative tactical solutions.

The main attributes for players and coaches to be successful

Team organization: there should always be a leader in the team who is responsible for assessing and choosing the best solution in relation to the tactical situation, the position of the ball and the opposition's arrangement.

Surprise and alternative solutions: it is always advisable to practice different tactical solutions to oppose any possible defensive formation by the opposition. It is often difficult to anticipate and oppose all the possible solutions even for the most cautious defensive lines. In this way, the team can "frighten" and upset the opposition by changing their tactical formation every time.

Exploit the opponents' weaknesses: it is very important to successfully understand and exploit all the opponents' weaknesses, like badly-set defensive walls, bad defensive positioning, attackers forced to play as defenders, players standing in the defensive wall who fear the ball, inaccuracy, lapses of concentration and so forth...

Exploit the skills of one's own players: the coach should be able to get the best out of his players. If there is a particularly skillful shooter on the team, the other teammates should play to support him and give him the opportunity to shoot at goal: for instance, by defending his shot at goal with a double wall (the goalkeeper cannot see the ball), by screening the opponent or the opponents who try to prevent him from shooting, by playing suitable defensive tactics and so on...

Avoid lack of concentration during the first and the last minutes of the competition: players are very likely to experience a sort of "psychological relaxation" at the beginning and especially in the last minutes of the match; they usually think that the match has not started yet or is already over, and therefore do not properly concentrate on set play situations.

Firm belief that a goal is going to be scored: it is very important to "believe" and therefore be absolutely certain of the success of the direct shot at goal, as well as of the implementation of those "familiar" tactical formations which directly result from hard training or specific preparation for the match.

In short, although we cannot exclude the most immediate and simple solutions to exploit all the opponents' possible mistakes or the shooting skills of some of our players, all the possible set play solutions should be regularly practiced during training sessions to stimulate the greatest accuracy, the perfect synchronization, and agility in every movement.

Moreover, the player who takes a corner or a free kick shall time and combine his performance together with his teammates' movements (both active and passive), so that he properly plays the ball in the position where it is going to be met. Any dead-ball situation should start with the shooting player giving a particular signal; this signal should also be changed to prevent the opposition from perceiving and understanding it.

PRACTICE

We are now going to show you some tactical schemes concerning all the different set play situations; they are nothing more than simple suggestions for the coach to work on, to suitably adjust and adapt them to the characteristics and the needs of his own formation. Obviously, each team should organize and constantly practice their own tactical schemes, which should also be modified during the course of the season, to avoid being recognized by the opponents, who could then adopt suitable countermeasures to oppose them. Since set plays are becoming increasingly fundamental in modern soccer, specific training for dealing with these situations is key.

Corner kicks: when a corner kick is being taken, the players standing in the penalty area often move confusedly by getting in each other's way and hindering each other; in some other cases, the players all move to the near post, while the ball is aimed at the far post; or too many players gather at the edge of the penalty box and position badly so that they are easily overtaken by the opponent's counterattack if the ball is cleared out. This directly depends on the fact that both the single player (who takes the corner kick) and the whole team (those who should receive the ball or maintain the balance of the team) have not practiced properly. Here are some well-organized solutions to alleviate these problems.

1. Player A is standing on the goal line near the goal; when his teammate E taking the corner kick gives the signal, A moves forward to the center of the penalty area in order to:
   - extend the path of the ball;
   - prevent the opposition from clearing the ball out;

He pretends to challenge and meet the ball to confuse them.

His teammates position in a diagonal line outside the goal area and move simultaneously (when E gives the signal): B sprints to the near post, C penetrates in a central position and D to the far post; they should always take care of maintaining their diagonal formation, which allows them to attack in any position in the goal area. Player F positions inside the penalty area, ready to move in case the ball bounces out or in case his teammate E cannot aim the ball properly. The movement made by A and the penetration of his teammates must be perfectly synchronized. E must take an inswinging flat corner kick: if he takes the corner from the right side, he kicks the ball with the left foot and vice versa (see **diagram 1**).

2. The position of the opposing unmarked player L is particularly important, since it clearly shows the area where the ball should be played. This opponent is standing in a central position or in front of the far post; the player taking the corner kick should aim the ball to the teammate on the near post to exploit the covering weakness in the opposing defense. Player C makes faking and diverting movements to attract the attention of the opponent defending the corner of the goal area: in this way, he clears the space for one of his teammates to penetrate forward. A pretends to move to the zone of the ball, turns around and performs a screen on the defender marking B, so that B can freely penetrate to the goal mouth. Player D is ready to meet the ball in case it is cleared out or in case the path of the corner kick is inaccurate. F should drive his marker near the covering opponent in order to prevent him from challenging quite so easily (see **diagram 2**).

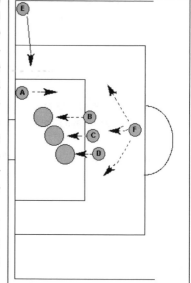

Diagram 1

3. Player A makes a cross-over movement with his teammate B and performs an active screen (he does not stand motionless) on his teammate's marking defender; then he positions near the goal to attack any possible pass back. Meanwhile, player C makes the same movement as his teammate A, to help D sprint unopposed to the center of the goal mouth. Player E should aim the ball to D or B and must concentrate on:
   - kicking the ball so that it passes over the opponent standing at the corner of the goal area: in this way, he cannot intercept it;
   - timing his movement so that it is perfectly synchronized with the movements of his teammates (see **diagram 3**).

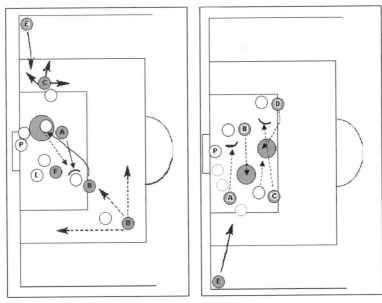

Diagram 2   Diagram 3

4. Player F moves to his teammate E who is about to take the corner kick and pretends to play the ball to his teammate: in this way, he forces his marking opponent and the opponent defending the corner of the goal area to follow him. Actually, the two opponents should prevent players F and E from creating a 2 v 2 situation at the edge of the goal area. A and C position

within the goal area and immediately sprint outside directly followed by their respective defenders; while players B and D - standing outside the goal area - penetrate to the near and the far post to seal off the spaces cleared by the movements of their teammates. E makes an inswinging flat cross aiming the ball at one of the two shaded zones (see **diagram 4**). Player G must be ready to attack the ball in case it is cleared out or if the teammate takes a bad corner kick.

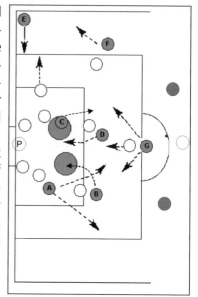

Diagram 4

5. Player A approaches his teammate E and makes a wall-pass; player B pretends to move to the ball, sprints back, runs by the screen performed by his teammate C who is committing his opponent, and moves unopposed to the far corner of the goal area, where his teammate E is aiming the ball. Player D makes some faking movements to drive his immediate opponent to the unmarked opponent standing in the middle of the goal area; in this way, the opponent cannot move to attack the ball. E makes an inswinging cross; otherwise, if he makes an outswinging cross, the triangle with his teammate A is inverted in the opposite direction (see **diagram 5**).

6. Players A and B position on the penalty spot; then, A sprints forward to the ball, while B moves back to screen the defender marking C: in this way, C can penetrate unopposed into the free space in the middle of the penalty box. F moves outside on the wing, while D is ready to move in any direction and to prevent the goalkeeper from leaving his line by disturbing his movements. Player E takes an outswinging corner kick: this means that if he is taking the corner from the left, he kicks the ball with his left-foot (see **diagram 6**).

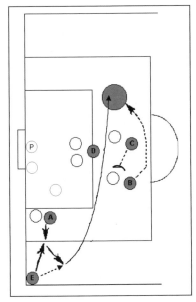

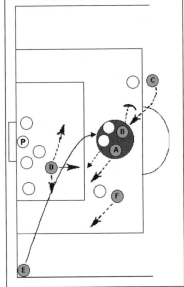

Diagram 5   Diagram 6

Free kicks: as was previously underlined in the corner kick para-graph, the team cannot exclusively trust the skills of individual play-ers to take free kicks, but should practice suitable tactical move-ments involving all the players, especially:

- when the position of the ball is not so favorable for a direct shot at goal;
- to support the teammate kicking the ball by disturbing the opposition;
- to open the defensive wall;
- to make faking movements to help another teammate sprint unmarked from the free kick zone and shoot or cross the ball;
- to create alternative solutions in order to help teammates move unmarked into favorable shooting positions;
- to disturb the goalkeeper's movement and prevent him from properly assessing the zone where the ball is going to be kicked.
1. From a nearly central position, 25 yards from the goal: player A lifts the ball for B, who passes to his teammate C by lobbing the ball forward over the defensive wall. C is standing in front of the wall, pretends to move to the ball, turns, runs by the wall, posi-tions to meet the pass, controls the ball and shoots at goal (he

should pay attention not to be caught offside). This tactical scheme can be applied only when there is no covering defender standing on the side of the defensive wall (see **diagram 7**).

2. Free kick from a central position far from the penalty box. Player B pretends to move to his teammate A, who gives a long diagonal pass to C. C controls the ball by exploiting the feint by his teammate B (see **diagram 8**), and can directly:

- give a pass for the forward penetration of B, who sprints unopposed into the penalty box after making the feint;
- lob the ball to E or D, who start from the edge of the penalty area and suddenly penetrate forward trying to overcome their defenders;
- players E or D can take a direct shot at goal or give a pass back to B to strike at goal.

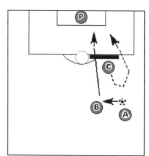

Diagram 7   Diagram 8

3. Free kick from a side position outside the penalty box. Players C and D position to disturb the defensive wall while also preventing the goalkeeper from clearly controlling the situation. D sprints off the wall, spins, and runs into the penalty box in the space cleared by his teammates E and F. A lays the ball off to B, who makes a faking movement and lobs the ball to the free zone for his teammate D to shoot at goal. If D is marked closely and cannot shoot at goal, E moves to screen the defender marking F, so that F can now sprint unchallenged and position to shoot at goal (see **diagram 9**).

4. Free kick from a side position outside the penalty box. Players A, B and C position near the ball. B runs over the ball and tries to sprint unchallenged on the side of the penalty area. C moves to

screen the opponent who is supposed to run to the ball. Player D screens the opponent marking E. Meanwhile A gives a diagonal pass to E, who is penetrating unmarked in a central position (see **diagram 10**).

5. Free kick from a side position outside the penalty area: this tactical formation should be used when there is no covering defender in the center of the penalty box. A plays the ball to C, who controls it and lays a pass off to his teammate B. B pretends to take a shot at goal and makes a one-touch diagonal pass to D, who is approaching his teammate after making a diverting movement. D plays the ball directly back to C, who sprints forward and shoots at goal (see **diagram 11**).

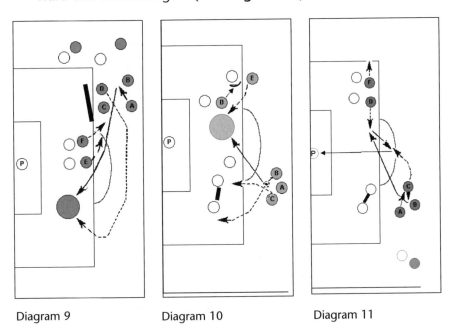

Diagram 9   Diagram 10   Diagram 11

Throw-in: the player responsible for taking the throw-in is often in great difficulty, since none of his teammates effectively come to him to receive the ball. Moreover, very few teams fully exploit the potential of throw-ins, which - on attack, in particular - could become something like a cross if they have players who can make very long accurate throws. This technical movement should be practiced following a special coaching progression from the very early stages of youth soccer.

The player should personally experience the effectiveness of his own technical movement, by taking the throw-in from a stationary position at the beginning - standing with his legs both close together and wide apart - and then with a very short run-up. The coach should gradually help the player to understand the differences between a throw-in taken while standing with one's legs wide open or with one leg behind the other. In the end, the player will be coached how to combine and coordinate the run-up and the technical movement, while also focusing the attention on the last steps: the player should actually take care that his supporting foot positions in front of the other to convey the greatest power to the ball, through the proper movement of his trunk. The player should be coached how to assess the power he should convey to the throw, so that the ball will land in the receiving area. Obviously, the coach cannot neglect the receiving phase and should therefore coach his players how to move to elude the opponents' marking and meet the ball.

1. Throw-in from a position near the penalty area (it should be taken only when there is a player who is able to throw the ball over a long distance and a skillful header to receive it). Player B pretends to move to meet the ball and then suddenly changes his running direction. C sprints to his teammate A and heads the ball: either, to one of his teammates D or E who are penetrating centrally to the far post, or to B who is penetrating into the penalty box from a side position (see **diagram 12**).

2. Throw-in in the attacking third of the field. Players C and B make a cross-over movement; A throws the ball to his teammate C who is sprinting unmarked inside. C can choose between two possible solutions: if he is not pressed by a defender, he dribbles the ball into the penalty box and shoots; otherwise, he gives a long diagonal pass to the far corner of the goal area to his teammate D, who makes a diverting cut and immediately penetrates forward to the far post (see **diagram 13**).

Diagram 12   Diagram 13

3. Throw-in from a position near the goal line. Player A exploits the cross-over movement made by his teammates B and C and plays the ball to C, who immediately plays it back. A makes an inswinging flat cross to his teammates E and D, who elude their opponents' marking and penetrate to the near and the far post respectively. F starts from the penalty spot and positions to meet any possible clearance. Players E, D and F gather around the penalty spot and disturb the opposing marking backs to prevent their movements (see **diagram 14**).

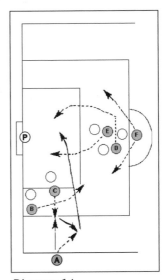

Diagram 14

DEFENSIVE SITUATION

Since set play situations are becoming increasingly important in modern soccer, properly covering the defensive area is obviously key.

As soon as a free kick, a corner, a throw-in... is awarded, the defense (the whole team) should pay particular attention not to be overtaken by the opposition. The players should all "retreat" and be ready to restore the defensive balance or to immediately change their mental attitude (if they win possession of the ball) to set up the counterattack, which could be very dangerous since it is completely unexpected.

The defensive wall should be an "insurmountable bulwark" and setting the wall in the best way possible is therefore of critical importance. Moreover, we usually suggest a different arrangement of the defensive wall and the relative movements, with a 3 + 2 formation. This formation allows the players to "cover" both sides of the goal (the two posts), while also allowing the goalkeeper to stand in a more central position.

CHAPTER SIX

COACHING TODAY

Memorizing an agility skill or movement is completely different from being able to move in a skillful manner in any situation. The soccer player needs to combine his intelligence together with practical sense rather than developing an exclusively logical approach, since increasingly high rhythms in modern soccer force the athlete to react and choose instinctively. However, his choices should always result from the wide range of possible solutions he has been experiencing during training sessions. This is why training should always simulate real game situations, to help the athlete to get accustomed to dealing with them.

The ideal practice intended to improve players' technical and tactical skills cannot be planned, prioritized, and fit into any background, circumstance, age group and agility level. Every coach should work on his team by trusting his specific knowledge and creativeness, since only he is in close contact with his players and can therefore accurately assess their skills, their potentialities, priorities and psychological reactions to what he has been suggesting and asking them. This is why we thought it necessary to show a wide range of drills, so that the coach can select those which best fit his purpose. The coach himself should adapt them to his own situation, in relation to the goals and the objectives he wants to achieve. By means of specific practice, the new applied coaching method should enhance:
- creativeness while making agility movements;
- the ability to anticipate the opponent's intents;
- the ability to immediately anticipate the intents of one's own teammates;
- supple mind;

- the ability to be fully involved in the team group;
- emotional approach (experience and approach the competition with total awareness and consider the training session in relation to the match);
- the ability to take the initiative;
- moral values and motivations.

The constant changes in the play situation, the differences between individual and team performance, the complexity of play organization as well as the evolution of all the elements influencing both individual and collective performance in modern soccer should help us to understand that practice is key, since it is the focal point of the player's training process, both in terms of "selection" (tactical movement) and "performance" (technical movement) - not to mention physical skills and psychological attributes, which are also of critical importance.

The complex nature of soccer implies an increasingly close relationship between matches and training sessions. Practice, in all its different forms and structures, should give the player the opportunity to transfer everything which has been explained to him and everything he has experienced during the match: therefore, the athlete is not involved in the training session as a purely passive element directly depending on the coach (the sole prophet) and his coaching plans, but takes part as an active subject who is perfectly able to understand what he is doing.

Meanwhile, the coach should offer his players the greatest amount of information and experiences as possible to stimulate their decision making processes and their ability to use them properly. For this to be possible, the player should develop fundamental resources helping him to successfully cope with various situations and solve all the technical, tactical, physical and psychological problems which he is constantly faced with in modern soccer (since this is a discipline involving constant movement).

Wide knowledge resulting from all the experiences the player lives during training sessions; it is the key to successfully solving all the problems which the player is constantly faced with during matches.

Awareness of what he is supposed to do in all the various circumstances; this is an evident sign of a successful performance.

The conscious ability to react to the situation properly; the solutions experienced while practicing definitely enhance the team performance.

In practice, what really characterizes a normal, poor or good soccer player is not his position on the playing field, but his ability to adapt (by making the most suitable choices) to the various technical and tactical situations, both in the defensive phase and in the offensive build up, as well as his individual skills which can considerably enhance the team performance.

The gradual development of decision making processes during training helps the player to form a wide range of possible solutions so that he can immediately find a good response to the largest number of situations which he is inevitably involved in (in a game based on constant changes). The player can therefore play in a very creative and constructive manner, by choosing the most applicable approach in any situation.

Consequently, practice should offer the athlete:

- a special analysis of the athletic performance as a whole to stimulate a complete training process;
- a number of possible situations, more or less complex, to create constantly new experiences which need to be lived directly, investigated, understood and internalized. Only in this way can the player develop all the skills and methods necessary to face them in the best way possible during the match (he obviously needs to learn how to recognize these situations to deal with them successfully).
- complex situations allowing him to improve his personal skills and everything concerning play situations;
- special training plans aimed at sublimating technical, tactical and strategic abilities, while also exploiting their creativeness and effectiveness completely.

By means of regular training, the player gets accustomed to instinctively dealing with all the difficulties of a competition (this inborn attribute is of critical importance and should never be overlooked), while also making reasonable, intentional and well-organized choices. This is possible only if the athlete is able to analyze, process and understand the real meanings of all the various elements in the competition to offer an optimum personal performance in the collective background of the team performance.

The coach cannot expect his players to have a special technical and tactical approach to the match if it has never been accurately trained or even introduced during practice sessions. Remember that the learning process can be refined only through constant imitation and active experience and that verbalization is just one of the components of the educational process. It is absolutely absurd to believe that the words of our "leader" are enough to achieve our goals and win. The coach should:

- offer individual players or the team as a whole the opportunity to improve their learning process;
- be particularly skillful at reading all the information he receives to react accordingly;
- assign his players special tasks which go beyond the reality they already know in order to stimulate his players to search for new and suitable solutions.

Each training session should:

- be approached in a constructive manner;
- have high qualitative levels;
- enhance creativeness and imagination;
- stimulate the players to work and not waste time;
- be approached enthusiastically by successfully involving both the athletes and the coaches.

"Soccer theory" should be expressed through well-aimed practice and the suggestions offered during training sessions should always refer to real situations occurring in matches. Every exercise the coach suggests should allow the player to deal with a real game situation, both in its details and as a whole, so that he can gradually get used to interpreting and immediately reacting to the complexity of the game.

Each exercise should be based on a specific "theme" the players should develop and practice (with different possible situations and solutions): with the help of their coach, with the good mental approach and in the technical and tactical context they are going to experience in the match.

PRACTICE

Practicing special exercises using the whole field is not always helpful during training sessions. This is why, in some cases, it is much better to mark out small areas of the playing field to reproduce specific situations commonly encountered during the course of a match. Such tools or strategies as small-sized goals, the line, well-organized ball possession and so forth, are the ideal supports helping the coach to focus the attention on the particular purpose of each technical and tactical session by offering his players specific goals to achieve.

Small-sized portable goals

They are particularly helpful to identify the positions (the zones of the field) where the attacking action should especially concentrate, or (in the defensive phase) to identify which are the most important areas to defend in relation to the next opponent and their system of play. Consequently, while planning a week's training, the coach should take two key factors into proper account:

- his own system of play, both on attack and defense;
- the play formation and the individual skills of the opposition, to properly practice opposing them in the most effective way as possible.

All the exercises we are going to show you in the next pages involve two teams, one playing one's own tactical system, and the other playing the opponents' formation. In some cases you are given further explanations if necessary.

While using small-sized portable goals it is also possible to clearly see and assess the final outcome of each action (goal for or against) and correct all the mistakes made by individual players or larger team lines.

Training one's concentration: single episodes play a key role in modern soccer. It often happens that a well-organized and trained team dominates the match and is eventually defeated, because one single player (or a team line) cannot effectively handle and solve one particular situation. Using small-sized portable goals during training sessions allows us to:

- anticipate dangerous situations which could occur during the match and "force" the player to defend one specific position on the playing field (the position where the small goal is placed);
- coach the players how to press or double team in some special areas of the playing field;
- coach the outside players to defend the wings by exploiting specific reference points;

- coach the defensive line to respect and control the areas of the field they are assigned (while also allowing them to help and support their teammates in the close areas).

The players should understand that defending does not mean protecting the goal area exclusively, but the defensive build up can be effectively carried out in any area of the playing field:

- to favor the transition from defense to attack (re-starting play);
- to immediately disturb the opponents (pressing and so on...) while also preventing them from setting up dangerous offensive actions.

The exercises using small goals are also useful for players to properly practice attacking in the positions where they could exploit their next opponent's "weaknesses".

Practicing a number of different offensive and defensive solutions during training sessions also stimulates the players to concentrate so that they can prevent frequent lapses of concentration during the course of a match.

Moreover, since the athletes are responsible for defending several positions, they will undoubtedly develop a stronger team spirit because their success directly depends on effective mutual help and support.

How to use small-sized goals:

- they should never be **defended** by the goalkeeper (unless the coach wants to use larger goals to practice special exercises and achieve specific goals);
- the size of the playing field should be decided in direct relation to the number of players involved in the drill and to the distances between the various team lines, since they should reproduce real game situations;
- each exercise should correspond to a special **tactical purpose**, unless the coach decides to use the goals and the exercise to help his players relieve psychological tensions (the exercise can therefore be suggested as a pleasure game);
- all the exercises should always be practiced at top **intensity**: consequently, the coach should always consider this aspect while setting up his training plans;
- the coach should always explain the exercises and the goals he wants to achieve very accurately by exploiting recovery periods.

By justifying all the solutions he is suggesting, the coach can considerably stimulate his players' concentration and motivation.

PRACTICE

1. 4 v 4 situation in a 40 by 20 yard playing field divided into two equal parts, with two small-sized goals; two-touch play. If the team wins possession of the ball in the offensive half of the field and scores a goal the team is awarded two points (see **diagram 1**).

2. The same as above, but if the team loses the ball in the offensive half of the field, they must immediately withdraw into their own defensive area before defending the attack.

3. 2 v 2 situation on a 40 by 20 yard playing field divided in two equal parts, with four small-sized goals; the players can position in any area of the field. Three-touch play during the offensive build up and two-touch play in the defensive phase. The team winning possession of the ball in the offensive half can immediately outnumber the opposition in that zone by supporting the forward penetration of one of the teammates (3 v 2 situation). If the team wins possession in the defensive area, the numbers of both defending and attacking players remains unchanged (2 v 2 situation) (see **diagram 2**).

4. 4 v 4 situation on a 40 by 30 yard playing field divided into three parts with four small-sized goals; the two side areas are 10 yards wide, while the central zone is 20 yards wide. When the team regains possession of the ball, they immediately create a 4 v 2 situation because two players on the squad losing the ball immediately retreat to the last defensive area. This exercise is particularly useful to coach the players (in the four-player defense) how to elude the challenge by the two pressing forwards. The two pressing attacking players should however slow down the opponents' offensive build up even when outnumbered and cooperate with their teammates when they withdraw into their defensive area (see **diagram 3**).

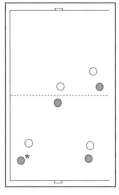
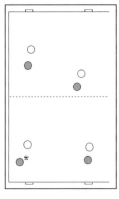
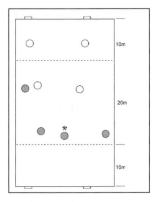

Diagram 1   Diagram 2   Diagram 3

5. Six-a-side game on a 40 by 25 yard playing field divided into 4 equal areas with 4 small-sized goals; two-touch play with both teams playing their own tactical system (for instance, a zone team should field: 2 center backs, 2 central midfield players and 2 forwards, or 2 outside backs, 1 central and 2 outside midfield players and 1 attacker). The game should develop progressively, which means that it is possible to cross one playing area at a time, but the team must always position on the field to occupy 3 adjoining areas at most (see **diagram 4**).

6. Six-a-side game on a 40 by 30 yard playing field; two-touch and the goal is awarded only if the shooting player directly kicks the ball first-time. Place four small-sized portable goals·10 yards off the end lines facing the outside zone of the playing area (see **diagram 5**).

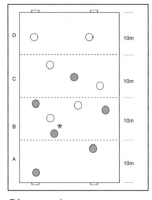
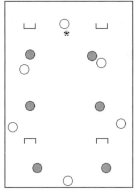

Diagram 4   Diagram 5

7. Eight-a-side game on a 50 by 40 yard field divided into three equal parts with 4 small-sized goals placed along the two lines dividing the three playing areas facing the two end lines. Two-touch play and the goal is awarded only if the ball is kicked directly first-time by the shooter and none of his teammates are standing in his defensive zone (see **diagram 6**).

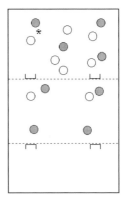

Diagram 6

8. Eight-a-side game on a 40 by 30 yard playing field divided in two equal parts, with 8 small-sized portable goals placed on the four sides of the pitch; two-touch play or different conditioned play for each one of the teams. Each team defends the 4 goals placed on the sides of their own defensive half by positioning according to their own tactical formation (see **diagram 7**).

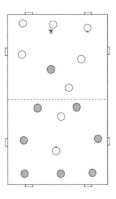

Diagram 7

9. The same as above, but: two-touch conditioned play in the defensive zone and free play in the offensive one. When the team wins possession of the ball in it's offensive area, the goal is worth two points.

10. 7 v 9 situation on a 40 by 50 yard playing field, with 4 portable goals placed along one end line; mark out a line parallel to the end line and at a distance of 15 yards in the playing area. Free game; the teams play their own tactical systems. The team in numerical superiority defends the end line where there are no goals, trying to prevent the opposition from dribbling the ball over that line. On attack, the team can shoot at goal only from a position less then 15 yards from the goal (that is only when they cross over the dotted line), by playing one-touch. This exercise particularly focuses on the outnumbered team (specific training for the group in numerical inferiority), who play their usual tactical formation, while the 9 player squad should play their next opponents' tactical system. The 7 player team play two-touch; for one point to be awarded, they must dribble the ball over the opposing end line (see **diagram 8**).

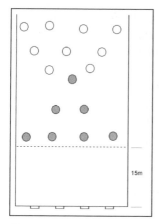

Diagram 8

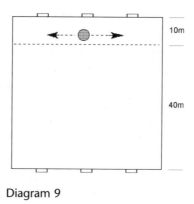

Diagram 9

11. 9 v 8 situation on a 50 by 50 yard playing field with 6 small-sized goals (three on each end line); the field is divided in two different parts: one is 10 by 50 yards and the other is 40 by 50 yards. Two-touch play or different conditioned play for the two sides. One player on the team in numerical superiority always moves in the smaller area and cannot operate out of it: he tries to prevent any opponent entering that area from shooting at goal (in this way, he creates a 1 v 1 situation). When his team is in possession of the ball, the player standing in the small area cannot be challenged if the ball is played to him: he can freely set up the action without being pressed by any opponent. This player can be asked to play in a different way from his teammates (different conditioned game). The coach can also field the goalkeeper in this area of the field, so that he gradually gets accustomed to playing as a sweeper-keeper (see **diagram 9**).

12. Nine-a-side conditioned game on a 70 by 50 yard field; Mark out two lines (parallel to the end lines) touching the center circle; 8 small-sized goals placed along the end lines (four on each side). The two teams position according to their own tactical system and their next opponents' tactical formation. Three-touch play in the two playing areas and one-touch play in the central zone (see **diagram 10**).

13. Ten-a-side conditioned game (two-touch play) on a 65 by 50 yard playing field divided into three parts: the central area is 15 yards wide with 6 small-sized goals (if the teams play either

4-3-3 or 4-4-2 formations) or 8 (if the team plays a 5-3-2 tactical system). If the team wins possession of the ball in the central zone of the field, they cannot move to the opposite goal, but must play the ball back into their defensive area. The player who receives the pass makes a direct pass into the offensive area. The game develops as usual if the team gains possession in the other two playing zones (see **diagram 11**).

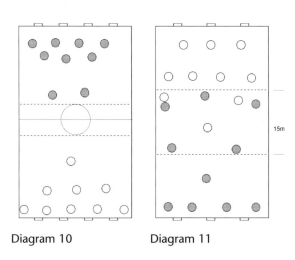

Diagram 10   Diagram 11

14. Ten-a-side conditioned game on a 65 by 40 yard playing field divided into three parts (the central area is 25 yards wide), with 7 small-sized goals (4 placed along one end line and three along the opposite line). The teams position according to their own tactical arrangement: the team playing either the 4-3-3 or 4-4-2 system defend the three goals, while the squad playing 5-3-2 formation defend the four opposite goals. At the beginning: 4 v 2 and 5 v 3 situations in the defensive zones and 3 v 3 situation in the central area. When the defenders (on both teams) are in possession, they must always dribble the ball (three-touch play) over the lines marking their own playing zones in order to outnumber the opposition at midfield (where they cannot be followed by the opposing attacking players). Two-touch play in midfield: in this area of the field the players can either immediately start the offensive build up or dribble and play the ball to maintain possession (1 point is awarded after 10 consecutive

passes). Free play in the offensive area: in this zone the players create a 3 v 4 or 4 v 5 situation for the forward penetration of one midfield teammate; the midfielder can enter this zone either dribbling the ball or penetrating when the ball is played there (see **diagram 12**). This exercise can be modified as follows:

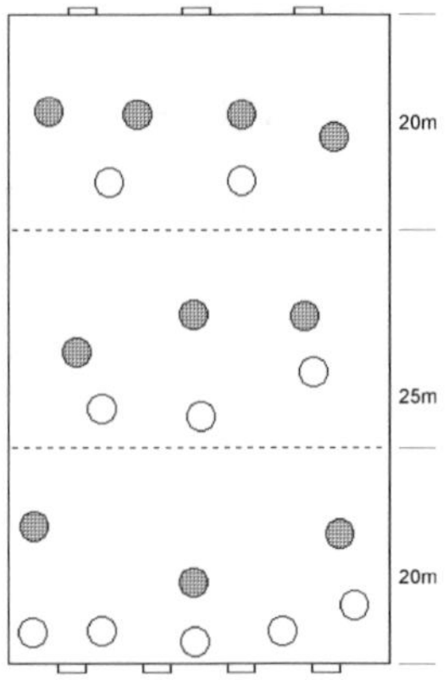

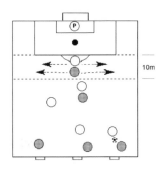

Diagram 12

* the players are not forced to dribble the ball through the midfield zone, but can directly chip it over by making a long pass to the offensive or defensive areas;
* when the team regains possession of the ball, they make an accurate pass allowing them to immediately move out of the defensive area;
* when the team regains possession of the ball, they must make three consecutive passes before moving out of that area.

Regular and small-sized goals

15. One half of the field is divided into three parts: the first part is the penalty box (including the wings), the second is 10 yards wide, while the third one covers the remaining area. Five-a-side conditioned game: the teams position according to their usual tactical formation (for instance: 4 midfield players and 1 forward or 1 forward, 2 outside links and 2 central midfielders); one team defends the regular goal - protected by the goalkeeper - while the other squad defends the three small-sized goals placed along the halfway line. The team attacking the regular goal tries to play the ball to it's forward, standing in the central zone (10 yards wide); the attacker shields the ball from his marking opponent, while waiting for 2 teammates

Diagram 13

to penetrate forward to create a 3 v 3 situation on attack. The other team can score by shooting at one of the three small-sized goals (see **diagram 13**).

16. Mark out a 50 by 50 yard playing field divided in two equal parts, with 1 regular goal (defended by the goalkeeper) and 2 small-sized goals (6 yards wide) placed along the halfway line. 6 v 8 situation (or 7 v 9 or 8 v 10 - the teams play their usual tactical system) + 1 two-way player (another goalkeeper) standing in the center circle. The team in numerical inferiority defends the two small-sized goals and the regular goal by playing three-touch passes. The team outnumbering the opposition also defends the two small-sized goals as well as the ball played to the player standing in the center circle, and play by giving two-touch passes. The 6 players are awarded one point if they dribble the ball beyond the two portable goals or if they give a long direct pass to the two-way player after crossing the line dividing the two areas of the field. The 8 players are awarded one point by shooting in the regular goal; they are awarded two points if their attack also develops by passing through the two small goals (see **diagram 14**).

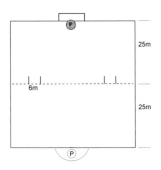

Diagram 14

17. Seven-a-side conditioned game on a 40 by 40 yard playing field vertically divided in two parts, with 2 regular goals (defended by the goalkeepers) and 4 small-sized goals. Two-touch play. The game develops with two 3 v 3 situations with the support of the two utility players, who can move freely. The teams position according to their usual tactical formation. For instance: in the case of a 5-3-2 formation, the team plays 2 defenders, 1 outside and 1 central back, plus 1 midfield player in the two zones; the utility player can act as a central back or a central midfielder (see **diagram 15**).

18. Seven-a-side or eight-a-side conditioned game in one half of the field, divided in two parts, with one regular goal and two small-sized goals placed on the right and the left along the same goal line; two goalkeepers: one defends the regular goal and the

other stands in the center circle. Two-touch play or different conditioned play for the two sides. One team defends the regular goal and the small-sized goals and is awarded one point when it scores or gives a pass to the goalkeeper standing in the center circle after making 5 consecutive passes in the defensive zone. The goalkeeper immediately distributes the ball, by kicking or fisting it back. If the ball lands into the offensive area, the team taking the shot can choose between two possible solutions: either they press beyond the mid-way line (pressing + offside tactics) or they position on the same line to defend. When the ball directly lands in the defensive zone, the team immediatey tries to regain possession. The opposition must shoot either at the regular goal or at the two small-sized goals (see **diagram 16**).

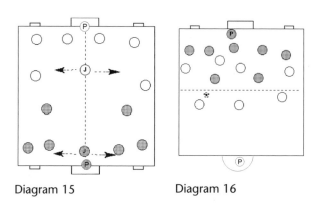

Diagram 15   Diagram 16

9. Mark out a 60 by 40 yard playing field divided into 3 parts: starting from the goal line, the first area is 20 long, the second is 10 yards and the third is 30 yards. One regular goal (in the 20 yards zone) defended by the goalkeeper and three small-sized goals placed on the opposite side. 8 v 7 situation with the teams applying their usual tactical formation. 5 v 5 situation and two-touch play in the largest area; the attacking players endeavor to shoot at one of the 3 small goals, while the defenders try to give through passes to their forwards whenever this is possible. The ball can be played or passed through the central area, but none

of the players can position there. In the 20-yard zone: 3 v 2 situation - the two attackers can play freely and try to shoot at goal, while the 3 defenders are obliged to give two-touch passes to play the ball to their attacking teammates (see **diagram 17**).

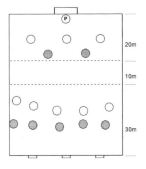

Diagram 17

Possible variations:

- 3 v 3 situation in the offensive area: one teammate is allowed to penetrate through the neutral zone and sprint forward on attack;
- when the team playing with three defenders is in possession of the ball, one of these players can move into the neutral zone to support the offensive build up;
- when the team attacking the regular goal is in possession of the ball (one of the two forwards is in possession), one of the 5 defenders can run into the neutral area to support the offensive action and shoot at goal (from a position within the neutral area).

20. 8 v 7 situation on a 70 by 50 yard playing field including the halfway line; one regular goal (defended by the goalkeeper) and 4 small-sized goals. Our team is the 7-player side: they position according to their usual tactical system of play; they must defend the 4 small goals and shoot at the regular goal: the goal is awarded only if all the players are standing beyond the halfway line. The opposition (8 players) must shoot at one of the four small goals, but a goal is awarded only if all the players are standing beyond the halfway line. Two-touch play or different conditioned play for the two sides (see **diagram 18**).

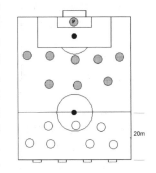

Diagram 18

21. Eight-a-side conditioned game on a 50 by 50 yard playing field divided into 3 equal parts, with 2 regular goals (defended by the two respective goalkeepers) and 4 small-sized goals placed on the right and left sides of each goal. Two-touch play. For a

goal to be awarded, the players must shoot at the regular goal by heading or volleying the ball, while there is no restriction as to the shots at the small goals. The two teams must always leave one of the three areas unoccupied (see **diagram 19**).

Diagram 19

Possible variations:

- apply the offside tactics;
- when the goalkeeper distributes the ball, the players must all move out of the defensive area;
- the goalkeeper can distribute the ball only into the defensive zone.

22. Eight-a-side conditioned game (two-touch play) on a 50 by 50 yard playing field, with a regular goal defended by the goalkeeper and two small-sized goals placed on its right and left side. Place some balls on the other side of the field, behind the end line. When the team attacking the regular goal and the small-sized goals lose possession of the ball and the opponents can make three consecutive passes, all the players imme-diately sprint to touch the goal line (where the goals are placed) and build the defensive line. The opposition (in possession) abandon the ball, sprint to the end line, take another ball and start another offensive action (see **diagram 20**).

Diagram 20

23. Eight-a-side conditioned game (two-touch play) on a 50 by 50 yard playing field divided by two vertical lines (which form two 10-yard wide side flanks) and one horizontal line (dividing the field in two equal parts). Two regular goals (defended by the two respective goalkeepers) and 4 small-sized goals. The teams play their usual tactical system. The players can give three pass-es at most in each one of the 6 playing areas, otherwise the team loses possession of the ball (see **diagram 21**). *Variation*: conditioned play (number of passes) different for each playing area.

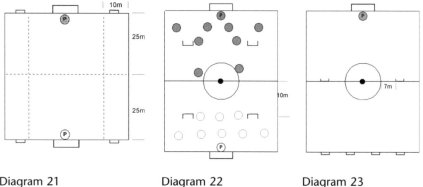

| Diagram 21 | Diagram 22 | Diagram 23 |

24. Mark out a 70 by 50 yard playing field, divided in two equal parts by the halfway line, with 2 regular goals (defended by the two respective goalkeepers) and 4 small-sized goals, placed 10 yards from the halfway line (two in each area) facing the regular ones. Eight-a-side (or nine-a-side or ten-a-side) conditioned game: two-touch play or differently conditioned play (2 passes in the defensive phase and 3 in the offensive one - or direct shot at the regular goal and free shots at the small goals). The teams defend one regular goal and the 2 small-sized goals placed in their offensive half of the field (see **diagram 22**).

25. Mark out a 70 by 50 yard playing field, divided in two equal parts by the halfway line; 1 regular goal (defended by the goalkeeper) and 6 small-sized goals: 2 on the halfway line and 4 placed on the end line. 9 v 8 situation (or 10 v 9); two-touch play or conditioned play different for each team. The team outnumbering the opposition defends the large goal and can shoot at each one of the small-sized goals; the team in numerical inferiority defends the small goals and attacks the regular one (see **diagram 23**).

26. Nine-a-side conditioned game (two-touch play) on a 65 by 50 yard playing field, divided in two equal parts by the halfway line; one regular goal (defended by the goalkeeper) and 4 small-sized goals (the number of portable goals varies from 3 to 5 in relation to the number of defenders our next opponents are going to field). The team defending the regular goal is in possession of the ball: they must give 3 consecutive passes before making a

pass to the attacking teammate who is standing in the center circle. The forward cannot be challenged and pressed when controlling the ball and his teammates must all position to counterattack immediately. The other team plays as usual and tries to score by shooting at the regular goal. The two teams can play different conditioned tactics (different number of consecutive passes) (see **diagram 24**).

27. Nine-a-side conditioned game on a 60 by 50 yard playing field, divided by 2 vertical lines (which form two 10-yard-wide side flanks) and one horizontal line dividing the central lane exclusively. Two regular goals (defended by their respective goalkeepers) and 4 small-sized goals. One-touch play in the 2 side areas, two-touch play in the defensive central zone and three-touch play in the offensive one. The coach can also vary the number of passes according to the purpose of the exercise (see **diagram 25**).

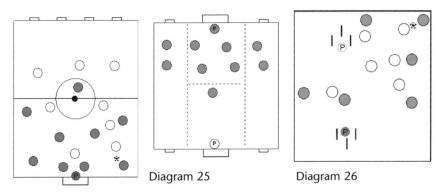

Diagram 25   Diagram 26

Diagram 24

Upright slalom posts and small-sized goals

28. Six-a-side conditioned game (two-touch play) on a 40 by 40 yard playing field, with three-sided goals 6 yards wide, placed at a distance of around 8 yards from the end line. A goal is awarded only if the player takes a direct shot. The goalkeeper defends the three-sided goals, corresponding to the three sides of the triangle made with the three upright posts (see **diagram 26**).

29. 8 v 7 situation on a 40 by 50 yard playing field divided in two

equal parts by the halfway line, with one goal placed inside the center circle and defended by the goalkeeper. Seven-a-side conditioned game (two-touch play) outside the center circle. Both teams can shoot at goal (from any position), provided they are outside the center circle. However, one of the players on the team in numerical superiority positions inside the center circle and his teammates should work to play the ball to him. When the player receives a pass from his

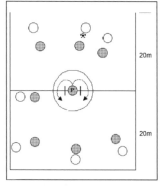

Diagram 27

teammates, he tries to shoot at goal by giving two-touch passes. *One possible variation*: two players stand in the center circle, to create a 1 v 1 situation (see **diagram 27**).

30. Eight-a-side conditioned game (two-touch play) on a 50 by 50 yard playing field. Place 9 1.5 yard wide small-sized goals in the playing area (there should always be one goal more than the number of players on a team). A goal is awarded when the ball passes through one of the goals and is controlled by one of the teammates. One point is also awarded when a team makes 10 consecutive passes (see **diagram 28**).

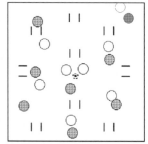

Diagram 28

31. Eight-a-side conditioned game (two-touch play) on a 50 by 50 yard playing field, divided in two equal parts by the halfway line; four six yard wide goals placed inside the center circle and defended by two goalkeepers. The teams can shoot at any of the goals, but a point is awarded only if the player takes a direct shot from outside the center circle. When one team wins possession of the ball, they must make at least three consecutive passes before shooting (see **diagram 29**).

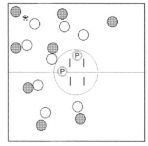

Diagram 29

32. Eight-a-side conditioned game (two-touch play) on a 40 by 50 yard playing field divided in two equal parts by the halfway line; one goal placed inside the center circle and defended by 2 goal-keepers. The two teams can shoot only from their respective halves. The goalkeepers can take part in the action by controlling back passes by their teammates and distributing the ball only with the feet (two-touch play). When one goalkeeper releases the ball to re-start the game, the other goal-keeper can pressure him provided he does not cross the halfway line (see **diagram 30**).

33. Eight-a-side conditioned game on a 50 by 50 yard playing field, divided in 2 equal parts by the halfway line. One three-sided goal (six yards wide) defended by the goalkeeper and 4 small-sized goals placed in the corners of the playing area 10 yards off the touch lines facing the end lines. A goal at the three-side goal is awarded only if the striker takes a direct shot from outside the center circle. Two-touch play to shoot at any of the small-sized goals (see **diagram 31**).

34. Eight-a-side conditioned game (two-touch play) on a 50 by 50 yard playing field, divided in two equal parts by the halfway line; one goal inside the center circle and defended by two goalkeepers and 4 small-sized goals placed in the four corners of the playing area 10 yards from the touch lines facing the halfway line. Each team defends the side of the goal facing it's own half of the field and 2 small goals. A goal is awarded only if it results from a direct shot (see **diagram 32**).

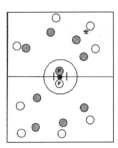

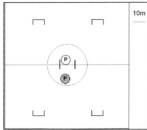

Diagram 30   Diagram 31   Diagram 32

Lines and goals

The team (or the players taking part in the exercise) play their usual tactical system and position accordingly. The players are responsible for defending one line, which means a much larger area than the usual 7 yard wide goal; therefore, they need to:

- improve their positioning skills;
- considerably exploit their intuition;
- refine their abilities to "read" all the different situations which they are usually faced with.

Obviously, the length of the line the team is asked to defend directly depends on the players' individual skills as well as on the mutual understanding between the different lines and the group as a whole. Consequently, the coach should gradually widen the area to defend, by extending the line and increasing the size of the playing surface.

35. Four-a-side (or five-a-side) game on a 40-yard-wide square field; one regular goal (defended by the goalkeeper) and two 10-yard-long horizontal lines parallel to the goal line and at a distance of 5 yards from it. The teams play their usual tactical systems (for instance: 1 forward, 1 central and 2 outside midfield players, or 2 forwards and 2 midfielders). One team attacks the goal, but one of the players is constantly standing between the two lines (playmaker - he is responsible for setting up the action). In this way, the attacking team is outnumbered by the opposition. For one point to be awarded, the opponents must dribble the ball beyond the two lines. *One possible variation*: restore a situation of numerical equality when defending the two lines (see **diagram 33**).

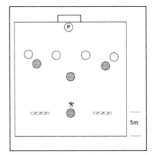

Diagram 33

36. Four-a-side game on a 30 yard wide square field, divided into 4 vertical zones; each team defends their goal line. Defensive phase: the players standing in zone A defend the area and support their teammates in zone B. The players positioned in zone B can help those in zones A and C; the players in zone C support the teammates in zones B and D, while the players in zone D help those playing in zone C. All the defending players must

strictly observe these rules and make diagonal, square, and triangle defensive movements. The attacking players, on the contrary, can move freely, but when they lose the ball, they immediately play according to the above-mentioned rules, using diagonal covering movements in particular. There are *several possible variations*: for instance, the coach could also introduce 2 small-sized goals in the two side areas of the field, or can award one point only if the players cross the end lines in the two flank zones, or could introduce three small-sized goals (2 on the sides and 1 in a central position) (see **diagram 34**).

37. Mark out a 50 yard wide square field, divided in two equal parts by the halfway line; 6 v 4 (or 8 v 6) situation to defend the center circle. The team in numerical inferiority prevents the opposition from dribbling the ball into the center circle by moving around the circle to defend it (they cannot cross into the circle). The defending team can be awarded one point if they manage to dribble the ball out of the playing area. The attacking team can only dribble the ball into the center circle: shots taken over the circle and passes given through it are not allowed (see **diagram 35**).

38. Divide a 50 yard wide square field in two equal parts; 6 v 7 situation with 2 goalkeepers (one defends the regular goal, while the other is standing inside the center circle behind the line marking the playing area). Two-touch play or different conditioned play for the two sides, playing their usual tactical systems. The team in numerical inferiority (on which the attention is focused) defends the regular goal, while the team in numerical superiority prevents the opposition from heading the ball to

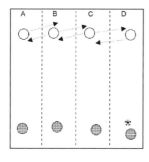

Diagram 34

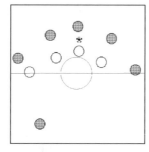

Diagram 35

the goalkeeper standing in the center circle. The pass is good only if it results from a direct shot taken from the offen sive half of the field (see **diagram 36**).

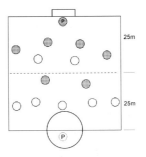

Diagram 36

39. Divide a 50 yard wide square field in two equal parts; 8 v 7 situation and two-touch play or different conditioned play for each one of the two teams. The team in numerical inferiority defends the regular goal, while the opposition defends the other end line. The team attacking the goal is awarded one point if it scores after winning possession of the ball in the defensive zone and two points if the ball was won in the offensive area. The team in numerical inferiority is awarded one point if it dribbles the ball behind the line after winning possession in the offensive zone; otherwise, if it gains possession of the ball in the defensive zone, it must make five consecutive passes before shooting at goal.

40. Eight-a-side conditioned game (two or three-touch play) in a 50 yard wide playing area. One point is awarded if the ball is headed over the end line. A goal is awarded only if it results from a direct pass. *One possible variation*: the teams play the ball with the hands for the same purposes, but the player in possession has to immediately throw the ball to one of his teammates before being touched by an opponent; only in this way can the team maintain possession of the ball.

41. Nine-a-side (or ten-a-side) conditioned game (three-touch play) on a 60 by 40 yard playing field; the teams play their usual tactical formations. The ball must always be played on the ground. One point is awarded if a team manages to dribble the ball forward behind the end line after controlling a back pass.

42. Divide a 70 by 50 yard playing field in 2 different parts (one is 40 yards wide and the other is 30 yards wide), with one regular goal. 9 v 10 situation with different conditioned play for each side; the team positions according to it's usual tactical formation. The team in numerical inferiority gives two-touch passes and is awarded one point if it manages to dribble the ball behind the end line opposite to the goal or if it heads the ball over that line after winning possession in the offensive area. The team in

numerical superiority plays three-touch passes to approach the goal and shoot; two points are awarded if the goal is scored with the player volleying or heading the ball.

BALL POSSESSION

It is advisable to position the players according to their usual tactical formation while practicing the following exercises aimed at improving possession skills. If the coach manages to properly stimulate and motivate his players, ball possession practice should enhance:

- mutual support;
- team spirit;
- the feeling of being part of a group;
- applied technique.

Some drills can be very similar or appear as mere repetitions, but in reality they include very subtle differences which are of critical importance in the context. For instance, stimulating the players to help each other during practice to achieve the final goal allows them to indirectly encourage and motivate all members of the team. On the other hand, the exercises focused on the opposition between two specific team lines (defense v attack, midfield v defense and so forth...) considerably enhance those psychological mechanisms motivating the players to work for a common team goal.

The exercises we are going to show you in the next pages imply high-intensity work practice and can therefore replace (for those who have little time for practicing) or better complete lactic-acid power and capacity training. The coach should take this aspect into proper account, to combine these exercises with low-intensity practice which does not require further considerable tactical concentration.

Don't forget that:

a) When practicing ball possession exercises in particular, the size of the playing area should be connected to the number of players involved, their physical condition and the average technical level; the coach should therefore avoid applying our suggestions too strictly without considering his team's requirements.

b) It is important to decrease the number of passes and controls in each exercise (three-touch, two-touch play...) very gradually: only in this way can the players get accustomed to the new situation and assimilate the new experience.

c) When speaking of usual tactical disposition, we do not only refer to the arrangement of each horizontal team line (attack - midfield - defense), but we also include the vertical lines formed by the outside or central players.

d) For these exercises to be really effective, the coach should always justify the goals he wants to achieve and stimulate his players by encouraging or 'pushing' them to maintain maximum concentration as long as possible.

e) All these exercises can be particularly useful to improve the coach's personal knowledge, but should also stimulate his creativeness to create his own exercises in direct relation to his own coaching situation.

Ball possession drills

43. Eight-a-side conditioned game on a 40 yard wide playing field; place two cones on the two end lines to divide each of them in 2 equal parts. Six-a-side conditioned game (two-touch play to maintain possession of the ball) in the playing area with the outside support of 2 teammates playing in the marked zones. The outside players give one-touch passes to play the ball into the square and two-touch passes when they want to take a shot towards their teammates standing behind the opposite end line. The players operating inside the square try to win possession of the ball by intercepting the passes or the shots by their opponents standing outside the playing area (see **diagram 37**).

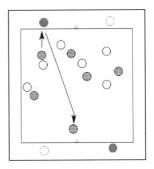

Diagram 37

44. Seven-a-side conditioned game (two-touch play) on a 70 by 40 yard playing field, divided into four rectangles by two perpendicular lines. In order to be awarded one point, the team must move in three different areas and make three consecutive passes in each one of them before moving to the next. Before attacking the opponents when moving

from one zone to another, it is necessary to wait for them to position in the same area all together. At this point, when the coach gives the starting signal, the players begin to practice ball possession.

45. Seven-a-side conditioned game (two-touch play) on a 50 yard wide square field divided into 3 parts: the central zone is 10 yards wide. Two goalkeepers are always standing in the two side areas. One point is awarded when the team makes 7 consecutive passes in their own zone. The team wins the ball in the opposing area and shoots at their own goalkeeper to start ball possession practice: the goalkeeper catches the ball (*one possible variation*: the goalkeeper must control the ball with his feet and promptly start a two-touch play action). The goalkeepers can take part in ball possession practice, but their passes are not included in the pass count (see **diagram 38**).

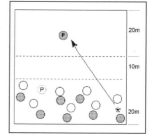

Diagram 38

46. Eight-a-side conditioned game on a 40 yard wide square field. The players are divided into 4 groups (red and green v white and blue). The red and the green players play together but with different ball possession rules (one team plays one-touch passes and the other two-touch). One point is awarded when the team makes 7 consecutive passes. Change the ball possession rules for the different colors from time to time.

47. Eight-a-side conditioned game + 2 goalkeepers on a 40 by 30 yard playing field, with another 10 yard wide area on each one of the two flanks. The goalkeepers position in the two small zones. One point is awarded if the team makes 7 consecutive passes and manages to play the ball to the goalkeeper in any position inside the zone to which he is assigned. The two goalkeepers cannot be challenged in their areas and can practice ball possession together with their respective teams (one or two-touch play). When the goalkeepers receive the ball, pass count starts from the beginning. One possible variation: two-touch ball possession before giving the pass. In this case, the goalkeepers are actively involved in the possession practice,

although they can never move outside their playing areas (see **diagram
39**).

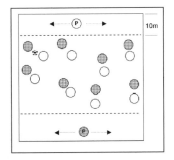

Diagram 39

48. Eight-a-side conditioned game (two-touch play) in a 50 yard
wide square area, with another 10 yard wide zone on two opposite sides of the field. For a point to be awarded, the team must
make 5 consecutive passes (the ball cannot be intercepted by
the opposition) and dribble the ball to their respective target
zones (the two 10 yard wide lanes). *Possible variations*:

- for one point to be awarded, the team can also make 5 consecutive passes and then cross the ball to the uncommitted teammate penetrating into the target area; this player cannot be
challenged in this zone and must meet the high pass by controlling the ball before it lands on the ground;
- if the player penetrating into the target area cannot meet the
pass from one of his teammates because the opponents win possession of the ball, he cannot move into the playing area until
his teammates regain possession;
- include 1 two-way player who always plays on the team in possession of the ball; in this case, one point is awarded after ten
consecutive passes.

49. Eight-a-side conditioned game (two-touch play) on a 50 by 40
yard playing field divided into three parts; one two-way player
positions in the central 10 yard wide zone. One point is awarded when the team makes 7 consecutive passes in their own possession area (one of the two 20 yard wide playing zones). When
the opponents gain possession of the ball, they pass the ball to
the two-way player, who promptly plays it back to them, so that
they can move into their possession zone (see **diagram 40**).

50. Eight-a-side conditioned game on a 60 by 50 yard playing field
divided into 3 parts: the central area is 30 yards wide. Differently
conditioned possession practice in each playing area. Three-

touch play in the central zone; one or two-touch possession in the side areas. One point is awarded after 7 consecutive passes.

51. Eight-a-side conditioned game on a 40 by 30 yard playing field divided into two equal parts; one ball with a four-a-side game in each area for ball possession. The players can move into the opposite zone provided the number of players in each zone remains unchanged (teammates switch positions). One point is awarded after 7 consecutive passes; the players can also play the ball between the two areas of the field, but in this case they must give three passes before playing the ball to their team-mates in the opposite half (see **diagram 41**).

52. Eight-a-side (or nine-a-side) conditioned game (two-touch ball possession) on a 70 by 40 yard playing field, divided into two equal parts. One point is awarded if the team manages to give 7 consecutive passes in their own possession zone. If the team wins possession of the ball in the opponents' area, they can move back to their zone by making one-touch passes.

53. Nine-a-side conditioned game on a 60 by 30 yard playing field divided into 3 equal parts. In practice: three 3 v 3 situations; two-touch ball possession or differently-conditioned play in the various sectors. The players cannot move from one zone to another; one point is awarded after 7 consecutive passes from one area to another. One point is also awarded when playing the ball through all three different zones regardless of the number of passes, provided the ball is not intercepted by the opposition (see **diagram 42**).

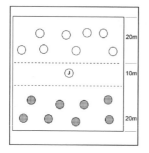

Diagram 40

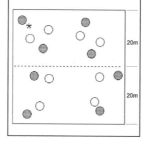

Diagram 41

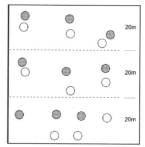

Diagram 42

Possible variations:
- the players can move outside their areas and position in another one, provided the number of players in each zone remains unchanged (change of positions between teammates);
- the players are allowed to move from one zone to another, but if the team loses possession of the ball, the players must stand where they are until the opposition gain possession. In practice, the game could develop with a 5 v 3 situation in the first zone, a 2 v 2 situation in the second, and a 2 v 4 situation in the third.

54. 12 v 6 (ball hunters) situation on a 40 yard wide square field; 3 teams of 6 players each practice ball possession. One point is awarded to the two teams when the players manage to make 10 consecutive passes, without the opposition intercepting the ball. If the 6 hunters win possession of the ball, the group whose player made the bad pass becomes 'the hunting squad' (see **diagram 43**).

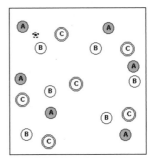

Possible variations:
- change the hunters every 2 minutes; the team who regains possession more than the others wins the game;
- differently conditioned ball possession (one-touch play for one team and two-touch for the other);
- two-touch ball possession, but the players must use both feet.

Diagram 43

TOTAL GAME

Approaching soccer in a modern way also means developing a suitable coaching method which directly results from the modern soccer philosophy. All the various components of play (dribbling, passing, heading, jumping, agility, and so forth...) cannot be split up into smaller details and coached separately. As a matter of fact, for training to be really effective, it should approach real game situations in the most accurate way possible: it should therefore include exercises (regardless of the number of players involved) where the athlete is forced to practice all the aspects (like technical skills, tactical sense, physical condition, attention, and concentration...) which allow him to successfully deal with all the problems arising from the game.

Practically, each exercise should accurately reproduce the various situations occurring during the course of a match to stimulate the athlete to use all his individual skills to solve the problems which he is faced with: this is why we speak of the 'total game'. Each exercise should enhance:

- agility skills while moving;
- the ability to anticipate the opponents' movements;
- the ability to read teammates' movements;
- the ability to anticipate the tactical development of each situation;
- ductility (that is the abilty to adapt to various tactical situations);
- the ability to be completely involved in the team group;
- the capacity to live any new experience in a conscious manner;
- the capacity to practice in relation to the final goal, that is the match;
- the ability to take the initiative;
- the ability to sublimate one's moral values and motivations;
- the physical condition.

Practice

55. 3 v 2 situation on a 40 by 30 yard playing field divided in 2 equal parts, with two regular goals and two goalkeepers; 3 attacking players try to shoot at one of the two goals in a 3 v 2 situation. The two pairs of defenders play in numerical inferiority in their respective areas and try to prevent the opponents from scoring; when they win possession of the ball or when they receive the

ball from the goalkeeper (after saving the ball or after a goal has been scored), they practice ball possession with the help of the other defending pair (4 v 3), while always remaining in their zone. The attacking players play 3-touch possession, while the defenders play two-touch (see **diagram 44**). One possible variation: 3 v 3 situation in the defensive phase, by allowing one of the defenders to move into another zone.

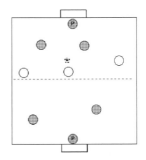

Diagram 44

56. Three attacking players and 4 defenders (2 in each area) practice on a 40 by 30 yard playing field divided into 2 equal parts; two goals defended by their respective goalkeepers. The attackers practice two-touch ball possession, beat the two defenders who are controlling the first half of the field and move into the other half and try to elude the challenge by the two other defenders to shoot at goal. Once the action is finished (goal, interception and so on...), the 3 attackers can either press the 2 defenders - who play free ball possession - to prevent them from dribbling the ball into the opposite zone, or directly withdraw in a defensive position and create a 4 v 3 situation. Two-touch play when the 4 defenders move into their offensive half (see **diagram 45**).

Diagram 45

57. Six-a-side conditioned game on a 40 yard wide playing field divided in 2 equal parts by a vertical line, with 2 goals defended by their respective goalkeepers. 3 v 3 situation in each zone; one ball. The players cannot move from one area to the other and position according to their usual tactical system (for instance: 2 defenders and 1 outside or central midfield player in each zone; or 2 midfielders and 1 forward...). The teams play two-touch ball possession and move to shoot at goal (see **diagram 46**). *Possible variations:*

• the players can move from one zone to another without upsetting the tactical balance of their teams;

- introduce 1 two-way player - who cannot strike at goal - to create a situation of numerical superiority;
- 1 or 2 players on each team are allowed to play in the two zones;
- 1 outside player on each side who plays to support his teammates, but cannot move into the playing area.

58. 7 v 6 situation on a 50 by 40 yard playing field, divided in 2 different parts: the area near the goal is 20 yards wide, while the other is 30 yards wide; one goal defended by the goalkeeper. In the 30 yard wide area: 4 v 4 situation, one team practices two-touch ball possession. When the opponents gain possession, they immediately play the ball to the two forwards moving in the other area challenged by the three defenders. The forwards maintain possession of the ball while waiting for one of their teammates to penetrate forward (in relation to the position of both the ball and the teammates) and try to shoot at goal in a 3 v 3 situation. The goalkeeper distributes the ball to one of the 3 defenders to restore the starting 3 v 2 situation. The 3 defenders play the ball to their teammates who promptly regain possession (see **diagram 47**).

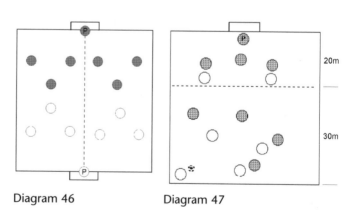

Diagram 46　　　　　Diagram 47

59. Seven-a-side conditioned game (two-touch play or differently-conditioned ball possession) on a 60 by 40 yard playing field divided in 2 equal parts, with two goals defended by their respective goalkeepers. It is important to constantly create a 5 v 5 situation in the area of the ball (2 players on each team

must constantly move into the opposite half). Once the offensive action is finished, the players can position to create different situations: 5 v 5 with high pressing (in the attacking area) to prevent any long shot or cross-field pass; 5 v 2 (or 5 v 3) because 2 or 3 players promptly retreat in the other half to perform low pressing (in the defensive zone) (see **diagram 48**).

60. Seven-a-side conditioned game in a 40 yard wide square area, with two regular goals and the relative goalkeepers. Divide the players into 6 pairs while the two remaining athletes act as two-way players. The 6 players play unconditioned ball possession (or three-touch play) while the two-way players play with two-touches. Each player can directly challenge his immediate opponent exclusively. The two-way player can support his teammates on defense by challenging any opponent; on attack, he supports his teammates but cannot strike at goal. The two two-way players can commit and challenge each other (see **diagram 49**).

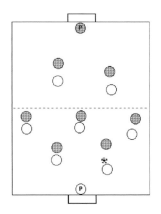

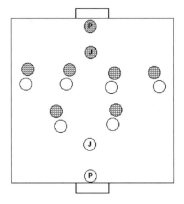

Diagram 48   Diagram 49

61. Seven-a-side conditioned game (two-touch play) on a 40 yard wide square field, with two goals and relative goalkeepers. After scoring a goal, the team cannot shoot again, but only try to win the ball and maintain possession. The situation changes when the opposition scores. The goalkeeper on the team practicing ball possession takes an active part in the offensive build up, thus creating a situation of numerical superiority. *One possible variation*: one-touch play while practicing ball possession.

62. Seven-a-side conditioned game (two-touch play) on a 40 yard wide square field, with two regular goals and relative goalkeepers. The team cannot challenge the opposition in possession, but only try to intercept the ball by attacking free spaces. The defender disturbing the opponent in possession can only act as a screen, by directing his opponent's pass. Each member of the defending team positions near his immediate opponent (1 v 1) and tries to anticipate the development of the action to be ready to intercept or anticipate the ball (mark the space and the intent to pass the ball). Challenge the attackers when they shoot at goal.

63. Seven-a-side conditioned game on a 40 by 30 yard playing field, with two regular goals defended by the relative goalkeepers. Each player on the team in possession of the ball must practice three-touch play before releasing a pass to another teammate; unconditioned play when shooting at goal. *Possible variations*:
   - the player in possession must dribble the ball and beat one opponent before passing the ball to another teammate;
   - two-touch play by controlling the ball with both the right and the left foot.

64. Seven-a-side conditioned game on a 60 by 40 yard playing field divided into 3 equal parts, with two regular goals and relative goalkeepers. In the two offensive areas the attackers practice unconditioned ball possession, while the defenders practice two-touch play. Two-touch play in the central zone. When one team reaches the offensive area, the players must all move out of the defensive zone (push up the team, distance between the different team lines). The players can move back into the defensive zone only when the opponents play the ball in that area or when one of them manages to elude the pressure in the central sector. If the team loses the ball during the offensive build up, the players standing in the central area can apply the offside tactics. Corner

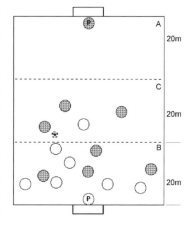

Diagram 50

kicks are taken regularly; there is no throw-in when the ball crosses theside lines, but the goalkeeper directly distributes another ball to resume the game (see **diagram 50**).

65. Seven-a-side to ten-a-side conditioned game on a regular playing field with one single goal and the relative goalkeeper. Mark out 3 horizontal lines at a distance of 30, 55 and 70 yards from the goal line respectively. The teams play according to their usual tactical dispositions. One team defends the goal, while the other defends the three lines which can be crossed only by dribbling the ball. The three lines show the three possible pressing zones (offensive, at midfield and defensive). This exercise can also include the offside tactics, if the team usually uses this tactical strategy during the match (see **diagram 51**). *One possible variation*: one of the two sides plays in numerical inferiority or with differently-conditioned ball possession.

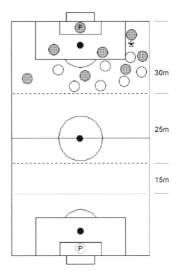

Diagram 51

66. 8 v 7 situation on a 60 by 40 yard playing field divided into 3 parts (20, 10 and 30 yards wide respectively). 5 v 5 situation in the 30 yard wide area; one team attacks to shoot at goal (two-touch play), while the other endeavors to regain possession (unconditioned play) to dribble the ball through the central zone into its offensive sector. Two attacking players and three defenders position in the offensive area (see **diagram 52**); it is possible to create a 3 v 3 situation by including the player in possession of the ball. On the other hand, the defenders can apply the offside tactics by pressing the player in possession if he is moving centrally (see **diagram 53**). It is better to avoid using the offside trap if the player in possession is penetrating on the flanks of the field.

67. Eight-a-side conditioned game on a 60 by 40 yard playing field divided into three equal parts: 2 v 2 situation in the side zones

and 4 v 4 in the central area. The players should especially concentrate on maintaining the balance of the disposition on attack; they should create 3 lines (attack - help and support - defense), by maintaining the suitable distance between the lines and position to properly occupy free spaces. It is very important to push up the team and therefore move out of the defensive zone while attacking, and retreat from the attacking area when defending. *Possible variations*:

- all the players operate in their own area and cannot move into another zone;
- it is possible to move into another area to create a situation of numerical superiority;
- it is possible to introduce one two-way player who creates a situation of numerical superiority but cannot score;
- it is possible to introduce another player operating outside the marked playing area.

68. Eight-a-side conditioned game on a 60 by 40 yard playing field divided into three parts: the two end zones are 25 yards wide and the central lane is 10 yards wide. Two 4 v 4 situations in the 25 yard areas: one team moves to shoot at goal, while the other tries to gain possession of the ball and give a long pass over the free zone to the teammates in the opposite area. In order to make the game much easier, the defending side (performing either zone or man-to-man marking) should always allow one of the opponents to move uncommitted to meet the pass by his teammates (see **diagram 54**). One possible variation: one player is allowed to enter the neutral area to create a situation of numerical superiority following the pass.

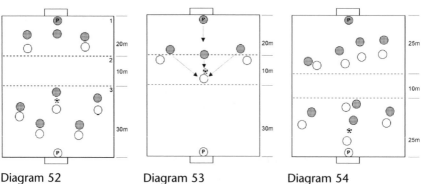

Diagram 52   Diagram 53   Diagram 54

69. Mark out a 40 by 50 yard playing field, divided into three vertical parts: two 10 yard wide side lanes and one 30 yard wide central area, with two goals defended by the relative goalkeepers. 6 v 6 situation and two-touch play in the central area; 1 v 1 and unconditioned play in the side zones (see **diagram 55**). *Possible variations:*

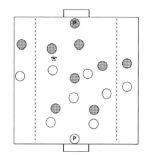

Diagram 55

- change the players operating in the side areas, while always maintaining the 1 v 1 situation (change of positions);
- the two side zones are free spaces; any player moving into one of these areas cannot be challenged by the opposition and must promptly play the ball (one-touch play) to the left by making a left-footed cross and vice versa;
- the outside players cannot disturb each other and must make either one-touch passes or two-touch crosses.

70. Nine-a-side conditioned game (two-touch play) on a 70 by 50 yard playing field divided into 3 parts (the central area is 20 yards long), with two regular goals and relative goalkeepers. The teams play their usual tactical systems. When the team wins possession of the ball in its defensive area, the players must give three consecutive passes before moving out of this zone. In this case, the opponents withdraw in the near zone without pressing. If they manage to win possession of the ball by intercepting the three consecutive passes and shoot at goal, the goal is awarded two points. *Possible variations:*

- although the players regain possession of the ball in the central zone after three consecutive passes, the opponents must withdraw in the near area without pressing;
- if the ball is kicked out of the playing area, the goalkeeper on the team responsible for the throw-in resumes the game by distributing a new ball;
- if the players intercept the ball in their defensive zone, they cannot pass the ball backward (unless the ball is passed to the goalkeeper, who is forced to promptly kick the ball back), but must give an immediate through pass;
- the players must move into another area of the field before

making the third consecutive pass.

71. 16 players position on a 50 by 40 yard playing field with two regular goals defended by the relative goalkeepers. The 16 players are divided into 4 groups wearing shirts of different colors to create an 8 v 8 situation (for instance: the red and the blue v the yellow and the green). They play the ball with the hands and always pass it to a different color; a goal is awarded only if a player heads or volleys the thrown ball. Only later can the players kick the ball (two-touch play), while always passing the ball to a different color (belonging to the same group).

72. Eight-a-side conditioned game on a 50 by 40 yard playing field divided in two equal parts. The players make 5 consecutive passes in their own defensive area before getting out of that zone and move to shoot at goal (if they win possession of the ball in the offensive area, they can directly strike at goal). When the second team gains possession (regardless of the zone), it must make 5 consecutive passes at most to strike at goal: the lower the number of passes, the higher the number of points they are awarded if they manage to score (one pass less means one point more).

73. Mark out a 60 by 40 yard playing field divided in two equal parts, with two regular goals defended by the relative goalkeepers. Three groups of 6 players each; one 6 v 6 situation in each half of the field (one team plays to strike at goal and the other to win possession of the ball). When the opponents shoot at goal (goal scored or ball behind the goal line) or after regaining possession of the ball, the defending players promptly change into attackers and try to beat both the opponents standing in their half of the field and those standing in the opposite area to take a shot at goal. In practice, six-a-side conditioned game with different roles and situations. The players who are waiting in their own half of the field position along the goal line (see **diagram 56**).

74. Eight-a-side conditioned game on a 70 by 50 yard playing field divided into three parts (the central area is 15 yards long), with two regular goals and the relative goalkeepers. 4 v 4 situation in each of the two side zones and one two-way player standing in the central area. The two-way player plays with the team in possession and can create a situation of numerical superiority in the

two offensive areas. The two-way player cannot shoot at goal but actively takes part in the offensive build up. Two-touch play, but the player controls the ball with one foot and plays it with the other. In order to move into another zone while on attack, the players must give a long pass crossing over the central area (see **diagram 57**).

75. Nine-a-side conditioned game on a 70 by 40 yard playing field divided into three parts (the central area is 30 yards wide), with two regular goals and goalkeepers. 3 v 2 situations in the defensive zones and 4 v 4 situation in the central area. While moving out of the defensive zone the three defenders (challenged by the two attackers) make three-touch passes and dribble the ball into the central area (where they play two-touch ball possession) to create a situation of numerical superiority (5 v 4). The midfield players move to favor the penetration of the three defenders. 3 v 3 situation in the offensive area, thanks to the forward penetration of one midfield player, either with or without the ball. The players should be particularly skillful at successfully penetrating forward on attack (see **diagram 58**).

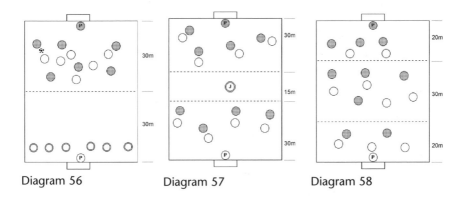

Diagram 56   Diagram 57   Diagram 58

CHAPTER SEVEN

PLANNING YOUR TRAINING SESSIONS

Training must be the result of a constant dialogue with oneself. In order for the relationship between the stimulus and adaptation to be effective, the athlete must be encouraged to endeavor to increase his efforts to adapt but, at the same time, be careful not to become over-stimulated as this would destroy his psycho-organic harmony.

Physical work (with or without the ball) is rewarded by an increase in performance, but this result requires time. In brief, an intensive period of training usually results in a fall in performance, which is defined as a period of fatigue. This, however, precedes a subsequent increase in performance which can be defined as 'super-compensation'.

Here we will briefly introduce the various qualities which must be trained in the soccer player, referring the reader to more specific texts concerning the preparation of the athlete for more useful and detailed information.

Strength: this is the quality which allows the muscle to lift or move a certain weight. It is closely linked to the muscular factor and so, through training, an increase in strength can be achieved. We can also refer to this as an increase in muscular performance. An area of the cross-zone of the muscle represents a parameter for measuring the increase in strength - an increase which can come about in two ways:

- by increasing this area
- by causing the maximum number of fibers of that muscle, even the deepest, to work.

Increase in strength can also be achieved by doing dynamic, static or plyometric exercises, with or without weights. It is always better to increase strength gradually, rather than quickly, because by doing this the results obtained last longer without creating serious problems during their development. In order to increase muscular strength, training must always be adapted to individual specialties so as not to lose sight of the other qualities which the athlete needs, such as speed, dexterity of the movement etc..

Speed: this is the ability to move as quickly as possible. Let's define three factors which determine speed:
- the ability of the muscle to contract completely in as little time as possible;
- the ability to make several movements (similar or different from each other) in a specific period of time;
- reaction time

At this point we may well ask: will a slow person always be slow? The answer to this, in part, is no. Even speed, if only to a limited extent, can be improved and increased. The increase, however, must not reach the point where the athlete's movements become unbalanced.

Sprint: this is the ability to cover a distance of several meters in as short a time as possible. This quality can be improved. However, it is important to know the cause which limits this quality in each individual in order to be able to take appropriate action. The factors which determine the ability to sprint are:
- the ability of the central nervous system to send out several impulses;
- the ability of the person to concentrate;
- the running technique and, above all, acceleration;
- muscular flexibility;
- the presence of a considerable amount of pale fibers in the muscles of the calf, thigh and gluteus;
- the power of these same groups of muscles.

Some of these qualities are influenced by training only to a very small extent and some not at all (the nervous system and the presence of fibers). Others are influenced greatly. Muscular power can be improved by specific work, flexibility by stretching exercises and other lengthening techniques and the technique of acceleration with exercises to learn how to control movement.

Quickness: Soccer, today, requires an ever increasing amount of rapid effort and movements which presume a basic speed, with or without the ball, which is becoming faster. A player is fast if he succeeds in gaining advantage from a situation in a very short period of time.

Quickness in a player is a very complex thing to train because it does not just consist of a fast reaction, a quick start or run, fast acceleration or stopping or guiding the ball quickly. Immediate perception of a situation (tactical perception) and immediate exploitation of chances which occur, in fact, are all equally important parts of a player's quickness qualities.

All quickness exercises should be carried out when the athlete is at peak physical freshness.

Resistance: this is the quality which allows a player to prolong physical effort over a period of time. We must point out the difference between: **specific resistance**, i.e. the ability to bear an amount of muscular work approaching peak power for as long as possible (for a period of time which will, in any case, be limited); and **general endurance** which is the ability to prolong average to heavy muscular work for a long time (N.B. not all tests agree on this terminology to define the different types of resistance).

Increase in these qualities is closely linked with improvement in the functions connected with the production of energy, the transport and utilization of oxygen in the blood, disposal of the substances of fatigue and the efficiency of the respiratory system.

In order to increase endurance, a joint type of training must be followed which bears in mind that aerobic work is more economical and profitable than anaerobic.

To increase specific resistance, the various systems (cardio-respiratory and muscular) must be subjected to more intensive work (with respect to what has been carried out up till now) over a short period of time, but repeated and separated by longer pauses of recovery (due to the amount of oxygen which is used).

Coordination; this is the ability to adapt the strength, duration and amplitude of muscular contraction in order to carry out joint athletic movements.

It is also important for the central nervous system to be able to eliminate all movements which are superfluous, restraining and which cause friction on the muscles which do not participate directly in the movement. The apparatus which is responsible for the co-ordination of movement is, in fact, exclusively nervous, involving the cerebral cortex, the connections of the central and peripheral neurons at the level of the spine, peripheral nervous receivers, the sight apparatus and the labyrinth.

Training improves coordination because it improves co-relations between the various parts of the nervous system and, through improved functional synergy, it has a positive influence on gestular harmony, freeing it from associated movements and creating the habit of exact patterns of movement.

Obtaining good coordination of movement cannot help but take into consideration the ability to learn the various sequences of the movement itself, at least during the initial phases of training. These capacities depend on limits set individually by the highest structures of the central nervous system.

Current research and know-how teaches us that between six and twelve is the age (this may vary due to climate and social environment) when the factors responsible for human coordination (the basis of any future motor performance) can best be developed. During this period, however, there are fluctuations in the response of these factors to training stress.

A psycho-motor curriculum which, during this period, has not given sufficient stimulus to some of the fundamental factors, which are at the root of these motor functions, will have repercussions on future motor performance. The greater the level of performance requested, the more this lack will be obvious. The technical-tactical aspect, especially in soccer, is the one which will feel the effect of any such gaps the most.

We refer you to the specialist book *The Complete Handbook of Conditioning for Soccer* by Raymond Verheijen (heartily recommended) for more detailed information about these topics.

GUIDE TO LENGTHENING (STRETCHING)

Muscular lengthening is one aspect of the training process which should not be neglected and can be achieved easily through methodical stretching exercises.

The main purpose of lengthening is to relax the muscles

involved, making them flexible. Benefit from this is felt both by the joint surfaces and by the musculature connected to them, causing them to relax, and developing their flexibility.

Lengthening should be an important part of the daily life of an athlete because in sporting activities a sufficient level of muscular flexibility and joint mobility is necessary for many reasons. The most important are:

- to reduce muscular tension and to foster the sensation of relaxation in the whole body;
- to achieve greater amplitude of movement due to increased joint mobility because of less resistance from antagonist muscles (which are the ones which must be lengthened to increase movement);
- to achieve greater fluidity when making a joint movement because there is no hindrance due to resistance from antagonist muscle groups.
- by improving flexibility and increasing predisposition for movement, muscular injuries can be prevented;
- a flexible muscle is faster (improving kicking power).

Stretching also helps improve recovery; after running, by supplying oxygen to the muscular fibers, it will restore them and decrease rigidity.

There are, however, certain rules which must be followed when doing lengthening exercises. The first rule consists in starting the exercises after a period of general activity which must increase as the athlete gets older. The second is that these exercises must be carried out slowly and gradually.

It is a good idea to bear in mind that it should take five seconds to go from the start to finish position and vice versa. The position of maximum stretch will be reached through gradual, constant and systematic exercises during which the athlete will be asked to pay attention to the muscles which are being stretched.

HOW TO ORGANIZE A TRAINING PROGRAM

The macro-structure of a training program, after careful analysis and assessment of the work carried out during the previous season, can be divided into different periods:

1. **transitional**
2. **preparation**, divided into three stages:

- general
- fundamental
- special
3. **pre-competitive**
4. **competitive**, which also can be divided into:
   - the first competitive period;
   - special or revision period;
   - the second competitive period;
   - a special or revision period;
   - the third competitive period.

These periods vary depending on the level at which the teams play, the duration of the season, any tournaments and the climatic conditions in which training takes place. These also influence how the special and revision periods are handled.

TRANSITIONAL PERIOD

This is the period between the end of the league and the beginning of the pre-season period. It must not be a period of total inactivity. Rather, it is a good idea to re-commence physical activity after a period of recovery (which must not exceed half the period of the player's holidays). With regard to this we present some programs which allow the athlete to arrive at the start of the pre-season in acceptable psycho-physical condition. Great care must be taken in interpreting the instructions given for this period because the work requires the maximum participation of the athlete as he is responsible for training himself during this period more than at any other time.

Summer preparation (one week - program to be carried out before the pre-season): during this week four sessions will take place, if possible in a relaxing environment (the beach, woods, hills...), and the aims of this program are to gradually get used to working again and to everything involved in training (protracted effort, copious perspiring, painful muscles and joints, the wish to stop working, rebuilding motivation...). When values of cardiac frequency are quoted at 140-150 beats a minute you have reached maximum frequency. You are, in fact, advised not to take into account the "standard beat", because you would risk making errors in evaluating the work being done.

The sessions take place for two-day periods with a day of recovery between. In the graph below the height of the rectangles represents the amount of work which should be done.

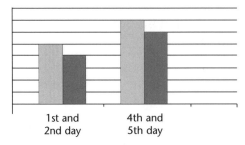

1st and
2nd day

4th and
5th day

First session:
- 30 minutes of running with at least 15 minutes of continuous running;
- 10 minutes of stretching;
- 8 lengthening jumps along 80 to 100 meters at 80% of maximum speed (depending on the distance to be run) with a recovery period of 90 seconds, between one set and the next.
- 5 minutes of exercises for the abdominal and dorsal muscles + relaxation of the spine.

Second session:
- 45 minutes of running of which at least 25 are continuous, with pulse rate at about 140-150 beats a minute (while running introduce some turning, changes of direction, and feints in order to imitate as closely as possible the movements made during an actual game);
- 10 minutes of stretching, 10 lengthening jumps along 80 to 100 meters at 80% of maximum speed, with a recovery period of 90 seconds between sets;
- 5 minutes of stretching and relaxation exercises for the spine.

A day of rest must be introduced before the third session.
Third session:
- 45 minutes of running of which at least 30 are continuous, with pulse at about 140-150 beats a minute;
- 10 minutes of stretching;
- 10 minutes of fartlek which consists of running at the same pace as the previous run introducing some zones of lengthening

jumps along 150 - 200 meters so as to bring pulse up to about 150-160 beats a minute, then returning to the normal running pace until the pulse returns to 130 beats a minute;
- 10 minutes of stretching;
- 10 lengthening jumps along 80-100 meters at 80% of maximum speed, with a slightly shorter recovery period than before (1 minute 15 seconds);
- 5 minutes of exercises for the abdominal and dorsal muscles + relaxation of the spine.

Fourth session:
- 35 minutes of uninterrupted running with pulse at about 140-150 beats a minute;
- 10 minutes of stretching;
- 10 minutes of fartlek as on the day before;
- 5 minutes of stretching and relaxation of the spine.

Summer preparation (two weeks):
This program is structured over three weekly sessions to be organized on alternate days during two consecutive weeks.

First week

First session:
- 10 minutes of stretching
- 10 minutes of mobilization of the spine;
- 5 x 10 abdominals, with 30 seconds recovery between series, plus 2 x 10 dorsals, with 30 seconds recovery between series;
- 5 minutes of joint mobility exercises for the most important regions of the body;
- 5 minutes of stretching and preparation for work (because strength work will be carried out, the musculature must be prepared through small jumps, running jumps, rolling jumps...);
- 3 x 5 squat jumps with recovery of 2 minutes between series;
- 3 minutes of stretching;
- 3 x 50 meters in lengthening jumps, at a speed of 60% of maximum speed, with 60 seconds recovery;
- 5 minutes of relaxation of the spine;

- 3 x 5 counter movement jumps, with recovery of 2 minutes between series;
- 3 minutes of stretching; 3 x 50 meters in lengthening jumps, at 60% of maximum speed, with 60 seconds recovery;
- 5 minutes of relaxation of spine;
- 15 minutes of running with variations in rhythm;
- 5 minutes of stretching.

Second session:
- 10 minutes of stretching;
- 10 minutes of mobilization of the spine;
- 6 x 10 abdominals, with 30 seconds recovery between series;
- 3 x 10 dorsals, with 30 seconds recovery between series;
- 10 minutes of general warm-ups and preparation for work;
- 5 x 100 meters, at 70% of maximum speed, varying the frequency of the pace during the run and with a 90 seconds recovery;
- 3 minutes of stretching; 5 x 150 meters, at 70% of maximum speed, continually varying the running direction, with a 120 seconds recovery;
- 5 minutes of stretching;
- 15 minutes of running, varying the rhythms.

Third session:
- 10 minutes of stretching;
- 10 minutes of mobilization of the spine;
- 7 x 10 abdominals with 30 seconds recovery;
- 10 minutes of joint mobility exercises for the most important regions of the body and preparation for work;
- 4 x 5 squat jumps, with 2 minutes recovery between series;
- 3 minutes of stretching;
- 4 x 50 meters in lengthening jumps at 60% of maximum speed, with 60 seconds recovery;
- 3 minutes of stretching;
- 4 x 5 counter jump movements;
- 3 minutes of stretching;
- 4 x 50 meters in lengthening jumps at 60% of maximum speed, with a 60 seconds recovery;
- 5 minutes relaxation of the spine;

- 20 minutes continuous running, changing the rhythm at will;
- 5 minutes of stretching.

Second week

During the second week the work-load increases, as long as the work done during the first week has progressed well. The program proposed below should be expanded with warm-up exercises and mobilization exercises for the spine respecting the methods, times and recovery periods given previously for each exercise.

First session:
- 8 x 10 abdominals;
- 4 x 10 dorsals; 5 x 5 squat jumps:
- 4 x 50 meters at 70% of maximum speed;
- 5 x 5 counter-movement jumps;
- 25 minutes of running with variation in rhythm (if possible on an undulating track).

Second session:
- 8 x 10 abdominals
- 4 x 10 dorsals;
- 8 x 100 meters at 70% of maximum speed;
- 6 x 150 meters at 70% of maximum speed, varying the running direction frequently;
- 25 minutes of running, varying the rhythm.

Third session:
- 8 x 10 abdominals;
- 5 x 5 squat jumps; 5 x 50 meters with long jumps;
- 5 x 5 counter-movement jumps;
- 30 minutes of running with variation in rhythm (if possible on an undulating track).

Summer preparation (three weeks): this program is structured over three weekly sessions to be organized on alternate days. The work load is characterized by an increase in the intensity of the first two weeks and by a decrease in the final one.

First week

First session:
- 10 minutes of stretching;
- 10 minutes of mobilization of the spine;
- 5 x 10 abdominals and 2 x 10 dorsals, with 40 seconds recovery between series;
- 10 minutes of general warm-ups (invent runs and exercises);
- 5 minutes of stretching;
- 4 x 60 meters of long, alternate jumps (right-left-right trying to make as few jumps as possible), with 90 seconds recovery;
- 3 minutes of stretching; 4 x 60 meters of very fast jumps (resting the foot on the ground for a very short time), with 2 minutes recovery;
- 5 minutes relaxation of the spine;
- 8 x 8 seconds running at 80% of maximum speed (at this time of preparation), varying the direction constantly, with 1 minute recovery in between the sprints;
- 5 minutes of stretching and muscular relaxation.

Second session:
- 10 minutes of stretching;
- 10 minutes of mobilization of the spine;
- 5 x 10 abdominals and 3 x 10 dorsals, with 40 seconds recovery between series;
- 10 minutes general warm-up;
- 5 x 100-meter lengthening-jumps, varying the frequency of the pace, with complete recovery;
- 6 x 25 seconds at 60% of maximum speed, constantly varying the running direction, with 2 minutes of recovery between sprints;
- 5 minutes of stretching and muscular relaxation.

Third session:
- 10 minutes of stretching
- 10 minutes of mobilization of the spine;
- 4 x 10 abdominals, with 40 seconds recovery;
- 10 minutes of general warm-up exercises;
- 3 x long jumps from a standing position landing on one foot

followed by lengthening-jumps for 10 meters + 1 minute of stretching;
- 3 x alternate triple jumps + 1 minute of stretching;
- 3 x consecutive triple jumps + 1 minute of stretching;
- 3 x alternate quintuple jumps;
- 5 minutes of relaxation of spine;
- 20 minutes of continuous running with changes of rhythm;
- 5 minutes of stretching and muscular relaxation.

Second week

During this week the amount of work increases, continuing the same kind of exercises during the training sessions. The following changes will be made.

First session:
- 5 x 60 meters of long jumps;
- 5 x 60 meters of fast jumps;
- 10 x 8 seconds, varying running direction, bringing the speed up to 85% of maximum, with 1 minute recovery.

Second session:
- 8 x 25 seconds, varying the running direction, bringing the speed up to 65% of maximum, with 2 minutes recovery.

Third session:
- 4 x long jumps from standing start;
- 4 x alternate triple jumps;
- 4 x alternate quintuple jumps;
- 25 minutes of running with changes of rhythm.

Third week

During the third week the work load will be the same in the first week. The same exercises, therefore, must be repeated.

PREPARATION PERIOD

The pre-season, within the sphere of soccer activities, is very important because it influences the whole season. This phase is dedicated to a basic preparation developing simultaneously physical and technical-tactical and character preparation. It is during this period that the team is formed as a group under all aspects. The parallel development of these factors is helped by the fact that the coaches are in constant contact with the players and are able to organize training days with several sessions. It should be borne in mind that during the first weeks the volume of work is greater than the intensity, gradually changing so that the work intensity is greater than the volume towards the end of the preparation period. During the season, on the other hand, volume and intensity should become balanced.

The length of the preparation period varies according to the schedule, the availability of the players and the category to which they belong. The coach, when planning the period, must bear in mind the locality and the ground where the physical exercises will be carried out. He also has to give the players a description of the various cycles into which the pre-season activity is sub-divided, the objectives to be gradually pursued, and the means and methods for achieving them. By so doing, he will develop in the player a greater awareness and therefore a better sense of responsibility. This way of proceeding is important because the emotional influence on the performance capacity become more and more crucial. So, pointing out to the players the aims, objectives and the work expectations and demanding from them the will to achieve high levels of performance will strengthen even more the sense of responsibility and their aspirations.

General stage
This is divided into two working cycles, the **introductory** cycle and the fixation cycle.

The introductory cycle, to be carried out in the best possible climatic and logistic conditions which the team can offer, is aimed at achieving high work loads and greater physical and organic efficiency. The work to be carried out in this period is that of building the musculature in general (aimed at activating the various muscular regions, but with a greater attention paid to those used during the performance) and building the organs with an increase in aerobic capacity but without neglecting the lactic acid capacity. Specific and capillary work must also be carried out on joint mobility, muscular flexibility, relaxation of the spine and on the tarsus tibia articulation. The ball will also be introduced with technical exercises (both conceptual and applied), games, and global and technical-tactical exercises.

The part concerning psychological preparation is dedicated to helping the various components of the group to get to know each other and developing a relationship with the press and fans to whom a correct level of attention must be paid.

The fixation cycle. The aim of this cycle is to build up the organs and will concentrate on a further increase in the aerobic capacity and above all the aerobic power, with interval work. Muscular exercises therefore will be increased in general, using the same means as in the previous cycle. Work with the ball will be aimed at applied techniques, through various technical and tactical games, a series of short sided games on large and small pitches, tactical work and in the introduction of one or two not very demanding games. One part of the work will then be dedicated to acrobatic exercises and to training paths aimed at increasing coordination and reaction speed.

The part concerning psychological preparation is dedicated to overcoming the difficulties associated with a large work load and in further developing inter-personal relationships with teammates, the coaches, the coach, and other team officials.

Fundamental stage

This stage differs from the previous one as its contents are aimed at solving tasks of lactic capacity through interval work, fast specific strength (active flexible reflex strength), work to maintain lactic acid acid power and general musculature. Still, it is necessary to continue with all the other exercises already started. Specific agility exercises will then be increased, with or without the ball, in order to acquire movement habits typical to soccer players.

Work with the ball will include:
- technical (systematic, intensive and extremely demanding) exercises;
- a complex technical-tactical preparation;
- combinations;
- standard situations;
- game concepts;
- short sided games on small pitches;
- short pressure games;
- possession of the ball;

- matches (increasing the level of the teams being played against).

With regard to psychological preparation, attention must be given to:
- the relationship between teammates;
- reciprocal knowledge;
- the group spirit;
- the spirit of sacrifice;
- reciprocal help and respect;
- dedication to the development of the group, on and off the pitch;
- adapting to competition;
- adapting to the opponent;
- behavior on the pitch;
- the ways of carrying out the tasks given by the coach, during a match.

Special stage
In this stage the contents are absolutely specific and the intensity will be gradually increased, as the volume of the work load decreases. The methods used, in addition to those dedicated to specific speed strength exercises (active flexible reflex strength) are impulse exercises, sprints over short distances, exercises for increasing agility, and stops and starts. Then simple, structure speed (dry), start speed, sprint speed, speed connected to dexterity with or without the ball, and speed of thought must be developed. Lactic capacity (short term, but of the maximum intensity possible so as not to be alactic) and all the other components dealt with in the previous stages must be gone over again.

The technical contents will become totally specific: combinations, patterns of play with several players, team patterns, re-start plays, games, short pressure games, play concepts, zone work, and speed of thought by means of games and exercises. The intensity of the commitment will then be increased gradually and this will be consolidated by playing friendly matches or tournaments with teams of equal levels.

With regard to psychological preparation, all the work is targeted at strengthening the qualities developed in the previous period.

Incentives must then be introduced depending on when the league begins.

Everyone has his own kind of preparation

We are now going to propose two preparation models dedicated to those who can work on undulating ground and to those who do not have this possibility. Do not forget also to carry out a battery of tests, both on the pitch and in the training or weight room in order to have a complete picture of the condition of the team and of the individual players. In this way it is possible to make up a targeted and rational program of pre-season preparation.

The following proposal, obviously, is only a useful idea which **each coach must personalize** (the times taken, for example, must be established on the basis of the condition of the athletes and the ground on which they run) on the basis of his knowledge of the team, his convictions, the equipment available and of the place where preparation takes place.

The work loads suggested below refer to the preparation of a team of top conditioned players and must therefore be adapted to your own athletes.

First day

Morning:
- 10 minutes of stretching;
- 15 minutes of joint mobility exercises for the most important regions of the body (free exercises and games);
- development circuit composed of 12 stations (calculating the availability of 24 players working in pairs alternately - when one works for 20 seconds, the other rests for 20 seconds) to be carried out twice with a maximum pause of 3 minutes between the two series carrying out active recovery with stretching (these work loads are suggested for a top conditioned soccer player weighing 75 kilograms):

first station - bend the legs (with the legs slightly apart) until a 90° angle is formed at the knee (put a wedge under the heels and wear a belt to protect the spine) with a 25 kilo weight on the shoulders;

second station - lying on the back bend the top part of the body and the lower limbs simultaneously;

third station - starting from a supine position stretched out on a bench (forming an angle of 90° between the top part of the body and the thighs) and the feet crossed and raised, extend and close the arms rhythmically using a 25 kilogram weight (bench);

fourth station - starting from a prone position (stretched backwards) resting on the palms of the hands bring the legs together and then jump up high (with a weight jacket weighing 4 kilos);

fifth station - starting from the prone position with the arms stretched out at the front, stretch the top part of the body upwards and then return to the floor (this exercise should be carried out carefully as it can damage the spine);

sixth station - starting lying on your back with the legs forming a triangle with the floor and the feet, and using a 3 kilo medicine ball, held in the hands half-stretched out in front, bend the upper part of the body forward (up and down) and twist to the right and left;

seventh station - start off in a standing position on a 5 centimeter-high plank with the heels hanging over, and with a 10 kilo weight or jacket, raise yourself onto the tips of the toes rhythmically;

eighth station - starting from a sitting position (or erect with the lower limbs slightly bent), with the arms stretched out along the sides and with two 6 kilo weights in the hands (the palms of the hands are pointing backwards), bend the forearms (bring the weight level with the chest) and at the same time rotate inwards (the palms arrive at the chest);

ninth station - starting from the prone position with the arms (stretched out) forming a 90° angle with the sides and lifting the top part of the body, pass a medicine ball, (3-kilo ball), from one hand to another (passing it along the floor) twisting the torso (this exercise too can damage the spine);

tenth station - starting from an erect position with a weight (jacket) of 4 kilograms, skip on the spot;

eleventh station - starting off laying on your back, with the legs forming a triangle with the ground and the feet, do some abdominals keeping a 3-kilo medicine ball behind the nape of the neck (the arms are bent and in line with the shoulders);

twelfth station - starting from the prone position with the palms of the hands resting on the ground (at the side of the shoulders) spring up and clap the hands before returning to the ground.
- 5 minutes of relaxation for the spine;
- 10 minutes of warm-ups for aerobic exercises (slight stretches, changes of direction...);
- 2 x 1 kilometers on a slightly undulated circuit, with a maximum pause of 3 minutes between series;
- 4 kilometers on a very undulated circuit;
- 5 minutes of stretching;
- 10 minutes of quickness and reactivity exercises with small obstacles and speeds;
- 5 minutes stretching and relaxation of the spine;

Afternoon:
- 10 minutes of stretching
- in a 20 x 20 meters square arrange two teams with one ball for each player (filling the spaces, guiding the ball to the right, to the left, inwards, outwards, passing the ball between players of the same team, passing the ball between players of different teams, passing the ball high after a first touch, passing the ball after a stop);
- in a 40 x 40 meter square, with two teams with one ball each (give the ball to a teammate in various ways - pass the ball to teammate - pass the ball to teammate, triangle with him and pass - triangle with teammate who approaches and passes);
- in a 40 x 40 meter square, 2 teams with only one ball (pass the ball to a different player than before - head the ball and pass to a different player);
- in a 40 x 40 meter square, one ball for each player (guide the ball, and on a signal from the coach, come out of the square quickly - pass the ball and, on the signal, guide the ball quickly - head the ball and, on the signal, quick guide - dribble with exchanges and, on the signal, stop and move out quickly);
- in a 65 x 40 meter rectangle, 2 teams each with a ball (possession of the ball with 2 touch-play - possession of the ball using only the left or right foot - possession of the ball with 2 touch-

play alternating the feet);
- in a 65 x 40 meter rectangle, 2 teams and 4 posts placed at 10 meters from the goal line, turned towards the outer game space (game with 2 touch-play alternating the feet);
- 5 minutes of stretching and relaxation of the spine.

Second day

Morning:
- 10 minutes of stretching;
- 15 minutes of joint mobility exercises for the most important regions of the body (free exercises and games);
- development circuit to be carried out twice (first series 20 seconds of work and 20 seconds of recovery - second series 30 seconds of work and 30 seconds of recovery) with a maximum pause of 3 minutes between the two series carrying out active recovery with stretching;
- 10 minutes of quickness, agility and reactivity exercises with and without equipment;
- 10 minutes of warm-up for aerobic work;
- 4 kilometers on a very undulated circuit, with 7 minutes of maximum pause with relaxation exercises;
- 2 kilometers on a very undulated circuit, with 4 minutes of maximum pause;
- 1 kilometer on a slightly undulated circuit;
- 10 minutes of quickness and reactivity exercises with equipment and changes in pace;
- 5 minutes of stretching and relaxation of the spine.

Afternoon:
- 10 minutes of stretching;

Technical-tactical work
- in a 30 meter square in which flags have been placed, with a ball at the start (guiding the ball and slalom), one ball per two players (guiding, slalom and passing - dribbling, stop, slalom and passing - dribbling, trapping with the chest and head, slalom and passing);
- in a 30 meter square, practicing psycho-kinetic technique in pairs;

- in several 10 meter squares play 4 v 2 to get possession of the ball;

Team and zone tactics:

- in a 40 x 50 pitch, divided into 2 parts by the center-field line, divide the team according to the tactical formation and move according to commands (forwards, backwards), in reference to 3 balls put on the goal line (in the game space), maintaining distances between zones; in the same pitch the team moves around taking the 4 players behind the goal line as reference points (2 at the side and 2 in the center) who kick the ball back and forth to each other. The team will move backwards and forwards, staying compact, and to the side, forming diagonals;
- still on the same pitch, using the same 4 players and the same movements, the previous exercise is repeated, but the players can kick the ball inside the block. At this point the whole team will attack the ball zone and will then kick the ball back to the 4 external players, shortening the pitch by moving forward towards them;
- the same exercise is repeated, lining up the other 2 reference points on the half-way line of the defense, when the 4 kick towards the reference points the whole team attacks them;

Technical-tactical work:

- in a 40 x 60 meter pitch, 2 teams play with 1 ball with their hands and win a point when they pass the goal line with 1 header;
- on the same pitch the players play with their feet and 3 touch-play and win a point when they take the ball past the goal line (the ball must stay close to the ground);
- on the same pitch the players play with their hands, but the passes must be bounce passes (the ball can be taken only after it has bounced on the ground) and a point is won when the goal line has been passed with a header;
- on the same pitch the players play with 3 touch-play, with the ball still close to the ground and win one point when they kick the ball over the goal line after a last pass made backwards;
- 6 flags are positioned on the same pitch along the goal line and the players play with 2 touch-play;
- 5 minutes of stretching.

Third day

Morning:
- 10 minutes stretching;
- 10 minutes of preparation for work doing psycho-kinetic exercises with the ball;
- 4 x 1 kilometers on a slightly undulated circuit, with 3 minutes recovery between series;
- 10 minutes of stretching and abdominal, dorsal and upper limb exercises;
- 4 x 1 kilometers on a slightly undulated circuit, with 2 minutes 30 seconds recovery between series;
- 10 minutes of quickness, agility and reactivity exercises (with or without equipment);
- 5 minutes of stretching and relaxation of the spine.

Afternoon:
- 10 minutes of stretching;
- in a 30 meter square 4 teams move (each with one ball) filling up the spaces. They must do the following exercises: pass the ball to the teammate who is moving quickly - pass in a triangle to the player to make a last pass to a third teammate - give the ball to a teammate and follow the ball - give the ball to a teammate and go to the other side;
- in the same square 2 teams are formed composed of players wearing 2 different colored shirts and they repeat the same exercises as in the previous exercise;

Physical work:
- 5 x 5 minutes of zigzag climbing with 1 minute of recovery between series and 3 minutes of recovery at the end (stretching);
- 4 x 7 seconds of zigzag climbing with 90 seconds of recovery between the series and 3 minutes of recovery at the end;
- 3 x 10 minutes of zigzag climbing with 90 seconds of recovery between series;

Technical-tactical work:
- in two 30-meter squares the players play, with 2 touch-play, 4 v 4 plus 1 utility player and the goal must be scored first in 3 small goals (made with flags and 6 meters wide) set up in the

center of the field and defended by 1 goalkeeper;
- on the same pitches 5 v 4 is played with 1 large goal (defended by a goalkeeper) and 3 small goals on the opposite side (the 4 players play 4 touch-play and defend the large goal, while the 5 players play 3 touch-play and defend the small goals);
- 5 minutes of stretching.

Fourth day

Morning:
- 10 minutes of stretching;
- 10 minutes of joint mobility exercises for the most important regions of the body;
- development circuit (30 minutes of work per station and 30 seconds of recovery), 2 series with a 3 minute pause in-between;
- 10 minutes of agility, quickness and reactivity exercises;
- 10 minutes of warm-ups for aerobic work;
- 3 kilometers on a very undulated circuit + 5 minute pause with stretching;
- 2 kilometers on a very undulated circuit + 3 minute pause with stretching;
- 2 kilometers on a very undulated circuit + 5 minutes of agility and quickness exercises;
- 5 minutes of stretching and relaxation of the spine.

Afternoon:
- 10 minutes of stretching;

Technical-tactical work:
- on a 60 x 40 meter pitch, 2 teams with 1 ball per pair (guide and, when signaled, pass to teammate - dribble and, when signaled, stop and pass to teammate - head pass and, at a signal, pass to teammate);

Team and zone tactics:
- on a 40 x 50 meter pitch, a team, laid out according to its tactical formation, kicks the ball around (keeping to their positions and distances) and when the coach calls, 1 player (who becomes the reference point) moves to re-create the defense block;
- the previous exercise is repeated, but on the signal from the

coach, the player in possession of the ball becomes the opponent and the whole team moves in order to defend;
- the previous exercise is repeated, but this time the reference point is the player to whom the coach passes a new ball;
- the exercise is repeated again but, on the signal the team moves out of the play area and concludes the game, first freely and then guided;

Technical-tactical work:
- on a 60 x 40 meter pitch, with 2 small goals set up at the side of both main goals (defended by the goalkeepers), 2 teams play and the goal is valid in all the goals but with different scores according to the way the goal is scored (with the head, the foot, with 1 touch-play...);
- on the same pitch, divided into 2 zones and without goals, 2 teams play with 2 touch-play to possess the ball in their own defensive zone;
- in the same field, with 2 normal goals (defended by goalkeepers) and 4 small goals on the side lines (2 per side), 2 teams play. They can play 1 touch-play at the large goal and 2 touch-play at the small ones;
- on the same pitch, but with four 6-meter wide goal (formed by flags) set up in the center and defended by 2 goalkeepers, 2 teams play with 2 touch-play per goal which is valid in all the goals;
- 5 minutes of stretching.

Fifth day

Morning:
- 10 minutes of stretching and 10 minutes of joint mobility exercises for the most important regions of the body;
- development circuit (first series 30 seconds of work per station and 30 seconds of recovery, 5 minutes of stretching and relaxation of the spine - second series 30 seconds of work per station and 30 seconds of recovery, speeding up all movements);
- 5 minutes of relaxation of the spine;
- 10 minutes of warm-ups for aerobic work;
- 5 x 1 kilometers on a slightly undulated circuit, with 2 minutes 30 seconds of recovery between series + 8 minutes of

rest with stretching;
- 5 x 1 kilometers on a slightly undulated circuit, with 2 minutes 30 seconds of recovery between series;
- 10 minutes of agility, quickness and reactivity exercises (with or without equipment);
- 5 minutes of stretching and relaxation of the spine.

Afternoon: friendly game (the players are used according to their athletic condition).

Sixth day

Rest
We have proposed a complete work plan for the first week (to which appropriate changes can be made). For the next pre-season days we are going to illustrate morning preparation work, while, with regard to technical-tactical sessions during the afternoon, we refer you to the exercise routines proposed in the previous chapters, according to the tactical formation of your team and the specific requirements which you will become aware of. With reference to continuing team and zone tactical training, we will also indicate the days on which this should be introduced, pointing out that teaching progress must follow a logical plan depending on the learning level of the team.

Seventh day

Morning:
- 10 minutes of stretching + 10 minutes of joint mobility exercises for the most important regions of the body and preparation for strength work;

Cometti method (circuit with 11 stations to be repeated 4 times - if the press or calf machine is not available):

first station - 8 squats (with a wedge under the feet and a belt to protect the spine) with a 45 kilogram weight (go down into half squat position slowly and come up at an even speed);

second station - go into a half-squat position and maintain it for 8 seconds;

third station - 6 counter-movement jumps (fast bends downwards followed by jumping up);

fourth station - jump 5 obstacles (90 centimeters high) with the feet together;

fifth station - jump 6 obstacles quickly one after the other, alternating the take-off foot + 5 meters of sprint;

sixth station - 2 minutes of circuit including development exercises for the abdominals and lower limbs combined with stretching;

seventh station - go up onto the tips of the toes 8 times with a 35 kilogram weight (there will be a 5 centimeter plank under the front part of the foot and when descending the ground must never be touched by the heels);

eighth station - go up onto the tip of the toes and maintain the position for 8 seconds (with a 5 centimeter plank under the front of the foot);

ninth station - jump 6 obstacles, with the feet together, without bending the knees;

tenth station - rapid series of alternate jumps (to the right and to the left - at maximum speed) over six circles laid out on the ground (to the right and left of an imaginary 8-meter long line) + 5 meters of sprint;

eleventh station - 2 minutes of development exercises for the dorsals and abdominals combined with stretching.
- 10 minutes of agility, quickness and reactivity exercises (with or without equipment);
- 12 minutes of fartlek with 1 ball between two players working over the whole pitch (10 seconds of rapid passes on the spot + 50 seconds of slow running with passes + 20 seconds of 1 v 1 guide and follow + 40 seconds of slow running with passes + 3 minutes of rapid passes on the spot + 30 seconds of slow running with passes + 40 seconds of 1 v 1 to take possession of the ball +20 seconds of slow running with passes) x 3 series; 3 minutes of rest;
- 10 minutes of fartlek;
- 1 minute of running at 80% maximum speed + 1 minute of slow running x 5 times + 3 minutes of rest;

- 12 minutes of fartlek with 1 ball between two players working over the whole pitch: 15 seconds of rapid passes on the spot + 45 seconds of slow running with passes + 30 seconds of 1 v 1 guide and follow + 30 seconds of slow running with passes + 30 seconds of rapid passes on the spot + 30 seconds of slow running with passes + (15 seconds of 1 v 1 to gain possession of the ball; 15 seconds of slow running with passes x 2) x 3 series;
- 5 minutes of stretching and relaxation of the spine.

Afternoon: technical-tactical work and introduction of the team or department tactic.

Eighth day

Morning:
- 10 minutes of stretching
- 10 minutes of general warm-ups with the ball;
- 4 x 5 obstacle jumps with counter-movement jumps; changing direction with reactivity exercises;
- 4 x 5 obstacle jumps with feet level + changing direction with pace and quick sprints of 5-10 meters;
- lay out 10 circles along an imaginary line, alternating to the right and left, and carry out 4 repetitions of jumps (alternate - only to right - only to the left - with the feet together) + changing direction with skip;
- 4 x 5 obstacles to be jumped with the feet together (legs stretched out) + changing direction with skip and quick sprints of 5-10 meters;
- 8 minutes of stretching and relaxation of the spine;
- 10 minutes of preparation for next work (stretches - running with turns...);
- 2 x 700 meters + 2 x 600 + 2 x 500 + 2 x 250 (with recovery times between the sprints equal to the time of the path-work 1:1);
- 8 minutes of stretching and relaxation of the spine;
- 2 x 250 + 2 x 500 + 2 x 600 + 2 x 700 (work 1:1);
- 5 minutes of stretching and relaxation.

Afternoon: technical-tactical work

Ninth day

Morning:
- 10 minutes of stretching;
- 10 minutes of warm-ups with the ball;
- exercises for the abdominals, dorsals and upper limbs;
- training for zone tactics (respecting the teaching progress);
- 10 minutes of agility, quickness and reactivity circuit exercises with small equipment;
- 2 x 6 x 10 meters of guiding the ball at speed with 5 minutes of recovery between series;
- 5 minutes of stretching and relaxation of the spine.

Afternoon: friendly match.

A sequence to be followed:
Team and zone tactics training must be followed, on the next day, by exercises to improve technical-tactical play. Two days later this work is checked during a match in which an attempt is made to apply the techniques learned during the previous training period both by the team itself and the individual zones. This work philosophy is adopted during the whole preparation.)

Afternoon: friendly match.

Tenth day

Morning:
- 10 minutes of stretching + 10 minutes of joint mobility exercises for the main regions of the body and preparation for strength work;

Cometti method (10 station circuit to be repeated 5 times - when the press and calf machine is not available):

first station - assume the half squat position and maintain it for 8 seconds with a 45 kilo weight on the shoulders (with a wedge under the feet and a belt to protect the spine);

second station - 8 squats (with a wedge under the feet and a belt to protect the spine) with a 45 kilo weight go down into the half squat position slowly and jump evenly;

third station - plyometric work (starting in the half squat position , on a 40 centimeter high bench, jump down softly and slowly, without forming an angle less than 90° between the thigh and calf, then jump up again stretching out the legs x 6 times);

fourth station - jump 5 obstacles (90 centimeters high) with the feet together + skip and 10 meter sprint;

fifth station - 2 minutes of circuit including development exercises for the abdominals and lower limbs combined with stretching:

sixth station - go up onto the tips of the toes and maintain the position for 8 seconds (with a 5 centimeter plank under the front part of the foot);

seventh station - go up onto the tips of the toes 8 times with a 25 kilogram weight (a five centimeter plank under the front of the foot, without touching the ground with the heels when coming down);

eighth station - jump 6 obstacles, feet together without bending the knees;

ninth station - rapid series of alternate jumps (to the right - to the left - at maximum speed) on six circles laid out on the ground (to the right and left of an imaginary 8-meter long line) + 5 meters of sprint;

tenth station - 2 minutes of development exercises for the dorsals and abdominals combined with stretching.
- 10 minutes of agility, quickness and reactivity exercises (with or without equipment);
- 5 minutes of preparation for next work (light stretches, running with turns, running with changes in speed...);
- 700 + 600 + 250 + 250 + 500 + 600 + 700 over slightly undulated track (work 1:1);
- 5 minutes of stretching and relaxation of the spine.

Afternoon: technical-tactical work and team and zone tactics (respecting the teaching program)

Eleventh day

Morning:
- 10 minutes of stretching + 10 minutes of general warm-ups;
- plyometric work (4 x 5 jumps from a 40-centimeter high bench + jumping 1 90 centimeter obstacle + 3 meters of skip - after the last obstacle sprint of 10 meters at maximum speed);
- 4 x rapid series of alternate jumps (to the right - to the left - right/right + left/left - at maximum speed) over eight circles laid out on the ground (for a length of 10 meters to the right and to the left of an imaginary line) + changing direction with changes in pace (with and without equipment);
- 4 x jumping 6 obstacles (90 centimeters height) with the feet together + changing direction with skip + interrupted skip + sprint of 5 meters at maximum speed;
- 4 x jumping 6 small obstacles with the feet together without bending the knees + changing direction with quickness with obstacles, changes in pace + sprint of 10 meters at maximum speed;
- 5 minutes of stretching and relaxation of the spine;
- 5 minutes of preparation for work (lengthening-jumps, running with turns...);
- 2 x 200 + 300 + 400 + 300 + 200 + (work 1:5, or a recovery time equal to 5 times work time);
- 5 minutes of stretching and relaxation of the spine.

Afternoon: technical-tactical work.

Twelfth day

Morning:
- 5 minutes of stretching
- 10 minutes of exercises with the ball; abdominal, dorsal and upper limb exercises (increasing the load with respect to the previous days);

Training for team and zone tactics;
- 2 x 6 exercises of agility, quickness and speed with ball over 5 and 10 meters, with complete recovery.

Afternoon: friendly match.

Thirteenth day

Rest

Fourteenth day

Morning:
- 10 minutes of stretching + 10 minutes of joint mobility exercises for the most important parts of the body and preparation for strength work;

Cometti method (11 station circuit to be repeated 5 times - if press and calf machine is not available);

first station - 8 squats (with a wedge under the feet and a belt to protect the spine) with 55 kilogram weight (go down into half squat position slowly and come up gradually);

second station - go into half squat position and maintain it for 8 seconds with a 55 kilogram weight on the shoulders;

third station - 6 counter movement jumps (small bends downwards followed by a jump upwards);

fourth station - jump 6 obstacles (90 centimeters high) with the feet together (at equal obstacles go into a squat);

fifth station - jump 6 small obstacles quickly alternating the take-off foot + 10 meters of sprint;

sixth station - 2 minutes of circuit including development exercises for the abdominals and lower limbs combined with stretching;

seventh station - go up onto the tips of the toes 8 times with a 35 kilos weight (with a 5 centimeter plank under the front part of the foot, without touching the ground with the heels when coming down);

eighth station - go up onto the tips of the toes and maintain the position for 8 minutes with a 30 kilo weight on the shoulders (with a 5 centimeter plank under the front part of the feet);

ninth station - jump 6 small obstacles (some cones are placed between the second and the fifth obstacle and these must also be jumped over), with the feet together and without bending the knees;

tenth station - rapid succession of alternate jumps (to the right - to the left - at maximum sped) over 6 circles laid out on the ground (to the right and left of an imaginary 8 meter long line) + 5 meters of sprint;

eleventh station - 2 minutes of development exercises for dorsals and abdominals combined with stretching.
- 10 minutes of agility, quickness and reactivity;
- 8 minutes of fartlek with the team divided into 3 groups running slowly around the perimeter of half the pitch (at a signal one of the three groups reverses running direction and goes towards the following group - at 80% of maximum speed, calculated on the group average - once they catch the other group they also change direction and run after the third group, and so on);
- 3 minutes of stretching;
- 12 minutes of fartlek with the ball;
- 3 minutes of stretching;
- 6 minutes of fartlek at a slow run both along the long and short side of the pitch and quickness work with and without the ball (for 6 seconds) each time the corner flag is reached, or where the 4 work stations are positioned;
- 5 minutes of stretching and relaxation of the spine:

Afternoon: technical-tactical team and zone work (following the teaching program once the players have shown that they have understood the type of work proposed).

Fifteenth day

Morning:
- 10 minutes of stretching;
- 10 minutes of general warm-up and preparation for strength work;
- climbs: 5 x 20 meters at maximum speed (in equal climbs replace running with jumping)
- 3 minutes of stretching;

- 5 x 30 meters at maximum speed (in equal climbs replace running with jumping);
- 5 minutes of stretching and relaxation of the spine;
- 5 minutes of preparation for work (stretching, changes of direction...);
- 350 + 300 + 350 + 200 + 150 meters (work 1:5);
- 7 minutes of stretching
- 100 + 150 + 200 + 300 meters (work 1:5);
- 5 minutes of stretching and relaxation of the spine:

Afternoon: technical-tactical work

Sixteenth day

Morning:
- 10 minutes of stretching;
- 10 minutes of ball exercises; abdominal, dorsal and upper limbs work;
- training for team and zones tactics;
- 5 minutes of preparation for work;
- 6 x 50 meters at maximum speed, with 1 minute 30 recovery between sprints;
- 5 minutes of stretching;
- 6 x 30 meters at maximum speed, with 1 minute recovery between sprints;
- 5 minutes of stretching and relaxation of the spine.

Afternoon: friendly match.

Seventeenth day

Morning:
- 10 minutes of stretching + 10 minutes of joint mobility exercises for the most important regions of the body and preparation for work;

Cometti method (11 station circuit to be repeated 5 times - if the press and calf machine is not available);

first station - 8 squats (with a wedge under the feet and a belt to protect the spine) with a 55 kilo weight (go down in half squat slow-ly and come up gradually);

second station - 6 x counter-movement jumps (slow bends down-wards, followed by a jump up with the feet together and the legs stretched);

third station - 6 counter movement jumps (go down on one leg, soften and then jump up, alternate the leg on which you go down);

forth station - jump 6 obstacles (90 centimeters high) with the feet together;

fifth station - jump over 6 obstacles in rapid succession alternating the take-off foot + 10 meters of sprint;

sixth station - 2 minutes of circuit including development exercises for the abdominals and lower limbs combined with stretching;

seventh station - go up onto the tips of the toes 8 times with a 35 kilo weight (a 5 centimeter plank under the front part of the foot, without touching the ground with the heels when coming down);

eighth station - jump 6 small obstacles (cones are introduced between the obstacles and these must also be jumped over), with the feet together, and without bending the knees;

ninth station - hopping over 5 balls placed in a line with 3 meters between each one (2 hops on the same foot between one ball and the other - right right + left left + right right...);

tenth station - rapid succession of alternate hops (right-left at max-imum speed) over 6 circles laid out on the ground (to the right and left of an imaginary line 8 meters long) + 10 meters of sprint;

eleventh station - 2 minutes of development exercises for abdom-inals and dorsals combined with stretching.
- 5 minutes of stretching and relaxation of the spine;
- 10 minutes of agility, quickness and reactivity exercises (with small equipment);
- 5 minutes of preparation for work;
- 6 x 100 meters (at 85% of maximum speed), with 65 seconds recovery between sprints;
- 6 minutes of stretching;
- 6 x 100 meters (at 85% of maximum speed), with 70 seconds

of recovery between sprints:
- 6 minutes of stretching;
- 6 x 100 meters (at 90% of maximum speed), with 65 seconds recovery between sprints;
- 5 minutes of stretching and relaxation.

Afternoon: technical-tactical work and team and zone work.

Eighteenth day

Morning:
- 10 minutes of stretching;
- 10 minutes of general warm-ups with the ball and preparation for work;
- 5 x jumping 6 small obstacles with the feet together without bending the knees + changing direction with quickness and agility (with equipment);
- 6 x counter-movement jumps, going down onto one leg + changing direction with skip + 5 meter sprint at maximum speed;
- 5 x jumping 6 obstacles with the feet together + changing direction with changes in pace + 3 meter sprint at maximum speed;
- 5 x hops over 5 meters + 5 meter sprint at maximum speed (in this exercise the recovery time must be complete) + changing direction with quickness and agility work in circles;
- 5 minutes of relaxation of the spine;
- 5 minutes of preparation for work;
- 6 x 50 meters at maximum speed, with 90 seconds of recovery between sprints;
- 6 minutes of stretching;
- 6 x 30 meters at maximum speed, with 1 minute of recovery between sprints;
- 6 minutes of stretching;
- 6 x 10 meters at maximum speed, with 1 minute of recovery between sprints;
- 5 minutes of stretching and relaxation.

Afternoon: technical-tactical work.

Nineteenth day

Morning:
- 10 minutes of stretching;
- 10 minutes of exercises with the ball;

Training for team or zone tactics;
- 6 x 5 meters at maximum speed with the ball, with complete recovery;
- 6 x 10 meters at maximum seed with the ball, with complete recovery;
- 5 minutes of stretching and relaxation.

Afternoon: friendly match.

Twentieth day

Rest

Twenty-first day

Rest

From this moment on, physical work should be carried out in the afternoon and technical-tactical work in the morning, because the latter now requires a clear head as it takes on more importance. Physical work should now be aimed at achieving greater quality and intensity rather than quantity.

Twenty-second day

Morning: technical-tactical training.

Afternoon:
- 10 minutes of stretching + 10 joint mobility exercises for the most important regions of the body with the ball and preparation for work;

Cometti method - (10 station circuit to be repeated 4 times - if the press and calf machine are not available);

first station - 3 squats (with a wedge under the feet and a belt to protect the spine) with a 65 kilo weight on the shoulders (go down into half squat slowly and come up quickly);

second station - plyometric work (starting in a half-squat position on a 40-centimeter high bench, jumping downwards, softening and slowing the bend, forming an angle of 130° between the thigh and the calf, then springing up to jump a 90 centimeter obstacle x 4 times, after jumping the obstacle, skip);

third station - 3 squats (with a wedge under the feet and a belt to protect the spine) with a 65 kilo weight on the shoulders (go down into a half-squat slowly and come up quickly);

fourth station - jump 6 obstacles (90 centimeters high) with the feet together + skip and 5 meter sprint;

fifth station - 2 minutes of circuit including development exercises for the abdominals and lower limbs combined with stretching;

sixth station - go up onto the tips of the toes 3 times with a 40 kilo weight on the shoulders (with a 5 centimeter plank under the front part of the feet and without touching the ground with the heels when going down);

seventh station - jumping 4 small obstacles with the feet together, without bending the knees + changes in pace;

eighth station - going up onto the tips of the toes 3 times with a 40 kilo weight on the shoulders (a 5-centimeter plank under the front part of the feet and without touching the ground with the heels when going down);

ninth station - skipping over 6 small obstacles + sprint of 10 meters;

tenth station - 2 minutes of development exercises for dorsals and abdominals combined with stretching;
- 5 minutes of relaxation of the spine;
- 10 minutes of agility, quickness and reactivity exercises (with equipment) and preparation for work;
- 2 x 100 meters at maximum speed, with 70 seconds pause;
- 2 x 150 meters with 2 minutes pause;
- 2 x 200 meters with 3 minutes pause;
- 6 minutes pause with stretching;

- 6 x 50 meters at maximum speed with 50 seconds pause between series;
- 5 minutes of agility, quickness and reactivity exercises;
- 5 minutes of stretching and relaxation.

Twenty-third day

Morning: technical-tactical and team and zone tactics work.

Afternoon:
- 10 minutes of stretching + 10 minutes of general warm-up exercises with the ball and preparation for work;
- 6 x long jumps, starting with the feet together and landing on one foot without stopping the action (continue walking and go to the end of the line to wait for next turn);
- 4 x 20 meters at maximum speed, with complete recovery;
- 6 x alternate triple jumps with feet together at the start, landing on one foot without stopping the action;
- 4 x skips + 10 meters of sprint at maximum speed, with complete recovery;
- 6 x consecutive triple jumps (3 times only on the right foot and, the next time, 3 times only on the left;
- 4 x changes in pace + 20 meters of sprint at maximum speed, with total recovery;
- 6 x alternate quintuple jumps;
- 4 x small obstacles for quickness;
- 3 x 4 jumps (between 8 cones) + 10 meters of sprint at maximum speed;
- 8 minutes of play with the ball;
- 3 minutes of stretching;
- 2 x 6 minutes of fartlek + 3 minutes of pause;
- 2 x 8 minutes of fartlek with the ball;
- 5 minutes of stretching and relaxation.

Twenty-fourth day

Morning: technical-tactical work.

Afternoon:
- 10 minutes of stretching + 10 minutes of warm-ups with games;
- abdominals, dorsals and upper limbs, in pairs with medicine ball;
- 10 minutes of exercises with the ball;
- 10 minutes of agility, quickness and reactivity exercises with the ball;
- 9 x 100 meters with 60 seconds pauses between series;
- 7 minutes of stretching and relaxation;
- 9 x 100 meters with pauses of 60 seconds between series;
- 5 minutes of stretching and relaxation.

Twenty-fifth day

Morning:
- 10 minutes of stretching + 10 minutes of general warm-ups with games with the ball;

Training for inactive balls and for team and zone tactics;
- 10 minutes of agility, quickness and reactivity exercises with equipment;
- 6 x 10 meters of sprint at maximum speed with different start positions (feet skipping, turned...), with complete recovery;
- 6 x 5 meters of sprint at maximum speed, with various starting positions on the ground (sitting, supine, prone...) with complete recovery;
- short scrimmage.

Afternoon: friendly match.

Twenty-sixth day

Morning:
- 10 minutes of stretching + relaxation work for those who played the whole match:
- 3 x 4 minutes of continuous running with the pulse around 150 beats a minute (we remind you that this value is just an indication and refers to 60-70% of the value of the cardiac frequency of the individual athlete), with a pause of 3 minutes (stretching) between each series;

- 10 minutes of stretching and relaxation of the spine;
- differential work for the others.

Afternoon: technical-tactical work.

Twenty-seventh day

Morning:
- 10 minutes of stretching;
- 10 minutes of start-up with the ball with games;
- training for inactive balls;
- 10 minutes of stretching and relaxation.

Afternoon: friendly game.

Twenty-eighth day

Rest

Twenty-ninth day

Morning: technical-tactical work and team and zone tactics.

Afternoon:
- 10 minutes of stretching;
- 10 minutes of joint mobility exercises for the most important regions of the body and preparation for work with the ball;
- abdominals, dorsal and upper limbs;
- 10 minutes of agility, quickness, reactivity and impulse exercises;
- 3 x 10 meters hopping + 10 meters of fast hops;
- 3 x various skips;
- 3 x jumps with feet together over 6 obstacles;
- 4 x changes in pace;
- 3 x jumps with feet together over 6 small obstacles + 6 low cones;
- 4 x reactivity exercises;
- 3 x free squat jump;
- 10 minutes of games with the ball;
- 3 x 10 meters at maximum speed, with complete recovery;
- 3 minutes of stretching;

- 3 x 20 meters at maximum speed with complete recovery;
- 5 minutes of stretching and relaxation of the spine;
- 5 x 20 + 20 meters of run and come back with the ball, with 20 seconds of recovery between the series;
- 4 minutes of stretching;
- 3 x 3 x 5 + 5 + 10 + 10 meters of run and come back with the ball (work 1:4);
- 5 minutes of stretching;
- 3 x 30 seconds of creative running (in half-field, the players run zones at maximum speed changing direction, stopping and starting again...);
- 5 minutes of stretching and relaxation.

ALTERNATIVE WORK

We propose an alternative program which, in practice, on certain days changes the dry running work. This model is indicated for those who do not have undulating ground available and whose needs can be met by changing work rhythms frequently.

This program has been inspired by some interesting articles published by **Giorgio Rondelli** in the magazine **Correre**, and the ideas have been adapted to suit the requirement of preparing a soccer team.

In the model which follows, therefore, only running work is indicated (involving the days when this is changed), while all the other exercises are the same as those described in the previous program.

During the first week, by slow work, we mean a run of aerobic capacity at 60% maximum speed, while by fast work we mean an effort at 70-80% of maximum speed (of the distance to be covered).

First day
3 x 2000 meters divided as follows: 400 slow + 400 fast + 400 slow + 400 fast + 400 slow, with 6 minutes of recovery between series.

Second day
5000 meters divided as follows: 2000 slow + 1000 fast + 1000 slow + 1000 fast + recovery of 10 minutes + 3000 meters divided as follows: 500 slow + 500 fast + 500 slow + 500 fast + 500 slow + 500 fast.

Third day
5 x 1 kilometer (work 1:1/2 - recovery for half the time it took to cover the distance) + 8 minutes recovery + 5 x 1 kilometer (work 1:1/2).

Fourth day
4 x 2000 (in the first and third series alternate 1000 slow meters and 1000 fast meters; in the second and fourth, 500 slow meters and 500 fast meters), with a recovery of 6 minutes between the series.

Seventh day
(From this day on the fast zones should be run at 80-90% of maximum speed over the distance to be covered and the medium slow zones at 70%).

2000 meters divided as follows: 1200 slow + 800 fast + 8 minutes recovery + 1500 meters divided as follows: 1000 slow and 500 fast + 8 minutes of recovery + 800 meters divided as follows: 500 slow + 300 fast.

Eighth day
1000 meters divided as follows: 300 fast + 400 medium slow + 300 fast + 8 minutes recovery + 600 meters divided as follows: 200 fast + 200 medium slow + 200 fast + 6 minutes recovery + 5 x 400 meters divided as follows: 100 slow + 100 fast + 100 slow + 100 fast, with 3 minutes recovery between the series.

Tenth day
2 x 800 divided as follows: 400 slow + 400 fast, with 8 minutes recovery between the series + 8 minutes recovery + 2 x 400 divided as follows: 200 slow + 200 fast, with 6 minutes recovery between the series + 6 minutes recovery + 2 x 200 divided as follows: 100 slow + 100 fast, with 4 minutes recovery between series.

Eleventh day
3 x 600 divided as follows: 50 meters in jogging + 150 sprinting + 50 in jogging + 150 sprinting + 50 in jogging + 150 sprinting, with 6 minutes recovery between series.

Fifteenth day

2 x 3 x 500 meters fast, with recovery carrying out 300 meters of slow running between the sprints and 6 minutes of recovery between the series + 100 slow + 300 fast.

PRE-MATCH PERIOD

This period includes work which is organized according to the days available between one match and the next. Technical-tactical, finishing-off training must allow the athlete to express increasingly improved performances, thanks to growing dynamism, and therefore must include and emphasize all those exercises developed during the previous period (combinations, patterns, inactive balls, zone work, short pressure matches, speed of thought and action...).

As for psychological preparation, all the work is aimed at increasing motivation in view of the League standings.

Contents will become global, although specific work which will be necessary will not be overlooked. In addition to further improving the qualities trained during the previous period (strength, active speed, flexibility, reflexes, impulse exercises, completion of speed, agility and quickness of thought and action, dexterity...), the methods must also include going over all the other qualities developed during the various preparation periods, bearing in mind the work load involved in the matches to be played.

IN-SEASON PERIOD

The work during the season is divided into monthly-cycles and micro-cycles. By micro-cycles we mean planning weekly work. This programming can include one or two peaks (which correspond to the days in which the athletes' minutes work load is at the highest).The single-peak micro-cycle usually plans the most demanding session for Wednesday when matches are played on Saturday.

The double-peak micro-cycle, only for professionals, includes two double sessions on Wednesday and Thursday.

An interesting idea could be that of planning one micro-cycle with just one peak and two double sessions, on Tuesday and Thursday, reserving the second just for technical-tactical work.

By monthly cycles we obviously mean planning the monthly work.

Limited training time

Rationalizing training means managing the time available as well as possible, according to one's requirements. Some coaches at the youth or club level only have a maximum of 6 hours training a week which they must exploit in order to improve the players both individually and collectively, on a technical, tactical, athletic and character level.

In this context it is absolutely vital to organize and structure one's work, because, as coach, in addition to the chronic problems caused by lack of time, you will also have to face the many other problems typical of the sector in which you work:

- training which takes place in the evening (artificial light, intensive cold...);
- the area where you work (not always suited to requirements, small, uneven surface...);
- available materials (few and not always corresponding to requirements);
- irregular attendance and lateness;
- physical, and above all, psychological tiredness of the players after a day's work or study.

The coach will have to adapt himself to these and many other difficulties, trying obviously to get around them with work which, without changing the objectives and without improvising, will make it possible to optimize the organization of each individual session.

The coach must, above all else, prevent loss of motivation in the players (a very important factor in obtaining their regular attendance) through the stimulus given by well-organized work and without pointless pauses; this may be tiring but, at the same time, it is enjoyable. The coach must never lose sight of the human relationship with the individual and with the group, or respect and consideration for the players.

Training, however, must not be organized into tight compartments (operate on different aspects at different times) because the match is the expression of many different factors. Consequently, if work is to be productive, the exercises must reflect these aspects as globally as possible.

The presence within an exercise of several characteristic elements of the game will make it possible to increase the performance of the individual and the group rationally and in a balanced manner.

Working with the ball, without neglecting dry work which in some cases is indispensable, also because it is almost impossible to carry out these exercises with the ball **(we refer you to specific texts with regard to this part of the session)** - in addition to making exercises more enjoyable and in keeping with the type of activity (the ball is the main object) will also improve technical qualities and will not lower the level of the players' ability.

The Monday Session
If your first weekly training session falls on a Monday, physiology tells us that 36-48 hours are usually enough for an athlete to recover the energy expended during a match (on condition that he has rested enough and has followed a correct diet). We propose therefore a kind of work whose requirements are very similar to those of a real game.

Start-up: after warming-up (for a long or short period depending on the season: summer - winter) through stretching, with or without the ball, and small, general warm-up movement, start-up will be carried out through movements with the ball involving technical movements to be carried out, either individually or in pairs, on small pitches and with the introduction of simple tactical notions (filling spaces...). It is important to introduce changes of rhythm in these exercises.
1. all the players move about in a square (25 x 25 meters) guiding the ball in various patterns (suggested by the coach):
   * exchanging the ball when they pass each other;
   * stopping one in front of the other and exchanging the two balls;
   * exchanging balls when they pass each other, making guided stops (for example, lifting up the ball and making various stops);
   * defending the ball in situations of 1 against everyone and 1 v 1 (trying to steal the ball from each other - to hit the opponent's ball - to hit the opponents with the ball in various, pre-established parts of the body...).
2. as an alternative to the previous point: 2 teams play with their hands (head goal) in a pitch with or without goals (line defense). A bounce on the ground or head goal could also be requested,

alternating a hand pass with a head pass or a hand pass with a foot pass... .

3. another alternative could be: play using the hands (header into the goal or passing a line) and when the other team wins the ball, the players play with their feet. They must, however, free themselves from cover in the spaces in order to be able to receive the passes without the ball touching their opponents (the goalkeeper must save). This is a method to train peripheral vision and movement without the ball.

Physical conditioning: if included in the program, we now go on to aerobic and capacity work with or without the ball (or other qualities could be trained). The length of the exercises varies according to the program and is divided into 4 - 6 - 8 - 12 minute periods repeated a number of times so as to reach an overall time of 16 - 36 minutes of work.

4. fartlek for 8 minutes with one ball for each player composed of: 10 seconds of fast ball guiding + 50 seconds of slow running (with or without the ball) + 30 seconds of fast ball guiding + 30 seconds of slow running (with or without the ball) + 15 seconds of fast ball guiding + 15 seconds of slow running with the ball x 4 times). All of this is repeated twice (reaching the total 8 minutes).

5. fartlek for 8 minutes with the ball in pairs composed of: 5 seconds of play 1 v 1 + 55 seconds of slow running exchanging the ball + 10 seconds of play 1 v 1 + 50 seconds of slow running exchanging the ball + 20 seconds of play 1 v 1 + 40 seconds of slow running exchanging the ball + 30 seconds of slow running exchanging the ball. 2 series are carried out.

6. fartlek playing short games; on a 40 x 40 meter pitch, with goals and goalkeepers, with 2 teams playing. The first part of the exercise (4 minutes) - is a normal game where everybody must be moving (no player must stop, because anyone 'caught' will have to run round the field decreasing the number of players in the team) then - for the recovery of the exercise (4 minutes) - every player who passes the ball must change his rhythm (with the ball) for 5-10 meters.

7. on a 40 x 40 pitch (with only one goal defended by one goalkeeper) one team attacks and the other defends. The attacking

team, which loses the ball or kicks the ball into the net (whether they score or not) must run quickly (change of rhythm) and touch the goal line where the goals are and then prepare to defend. The team which wins the ball leaves it and runs quickly (change of rhythm) to pick up a new ball on the goal line without goals, and then starts an attacking phase.

This procedure does not only train the teams to defend and attack but it is also a physiological exercise.

Situational exercises: after this work the coach goes on with proposing situational exercises (lasting 20-30 minutes) the aim of which is to solve playing problems (with the help of the coach). Groups of 2, 3, or 4 players (of an equal, lower or higher number) play against each other. In this context, too, according to the frequency at which they play, the coach must chose exercises which are suitable for achieving the desired physical objectives.

8. an example of alactic power and capacity training:"duels' are carried out with final conclusions. On a 30 x 30 meter pitch with goals and goalkeepers, players play 2 v 2 or 2 v 2 + utility player (who plays with the team in possession of the ball but cannot score any goals) or 3 v 3 or 3 v 3 + utility player... The game evolves (each time a goal is scored the players leave the pitch and line up behind the goal line on the opposite side to where they started, in the meantime other players enter and have further duels).

Theme games: we now go on to theme games in which the coach asks the player to try to win by respecting certain rules. The teams line up according to their tactical formation and objectives (aimed at improving their own formation and their opponents who they will confront in the match).

9. on a pitch divided into three zones, with goals and goalkeepers, the players play 9 v 9 (3 v 3 in each zone). This balance must be kept at all times (players never changing zone but interchanging with each other). The touches vary according to the zones (for example: two touch-play in the defensive phase - 3 in center-field - free when attacking).

10. on a 50 x 40 pitch, divided vertically into three parts (with the outer parts the shortest 10 meters), the players play 2 v 2 on

the external bands (free touches) and 4 v 4 in the central band (2 touch-play). 2 goals and 2 goalkeepers, or 2 goals with goalkeepers and 4 small goals on the outer bands.

11. on a pitch with goals and goalkeepers 2 teams play against each other. They start playing with 3 touch-play, but the team which scores a goal decreases by one touch. Playing with less than the expected touches, the goal is worth double points.

12. on a pitch with one goal and goalkeeper, two teams play against each other (one team with less players). The team with the most players defends the line and plays with 3 touch-play (and can defend the goal only with the head), the other team defends the goal (where it can score freely) and plays with 2 touch-play.

N.B. to finish off the session (if possible) it is useful to do some abdominal, dorsal and upper limb work through individual or pair exercise. At the end, stretching exercises and relaxation of the spine should always be done.

The Tuesday (and/or Thursday) Session

The second weekly session needs a longer recovery time and therefore attention must be paid to not hold it too near the time of the match. In this training session various characteristic aspects of the game which influence each other, helping increase performance, must be proposed simultaneously. Because, at an amateur level it is necessary to:

- train the physical part (the players must keep up certain rhythms for the whole 90 minutes of the game);
- to overcome those deficiencies which have become evident during various matches;
- to give a tactical aspect to the team;
- to constantly exercise technical movements;
- to take into consideration the character aspect of each individual player and of the problems of the group.

Training must tend to perfect or to maintain all these aspects simultaneously. If you have the possibility of holding three weekly training sessions, the second should follow your program. We propose three alternative sessions in which the following main aspects are trained:

- general or specific development;
- lactacid capacity or power;

- alactic capacity or power;

Obviously during each session a mixture of work will be carried out, but this will have one main characteristic. The coach will therefore be able to use, as an approximate plan, the three alternative sessions which we propose, inserting them into his own monthly program and adapting them to the situation in which he operates.

With a predominance of general or specific development
After the usual start to proceedings, we propose a warm-up with the ball.
Start-up
13. in a 30 x 30 meters square, the players, divided into pairs (one ball per pair) move around freely to fill up the spaces.
They do the following exercises:
- guiding the ball and on a signal passing it to the teammate;
- dribbling and on a signal stopping and passing the ball to the teammate;
- head passing and on a signal stopping and passing to a teammate, freeing themselves from marking outside the square.
14. as an alternative to the previous exercise routine: in a 30 x 30 meter square 4 teams play (different colors), each with its own ball, and follow the following exercise routine:
- they fill up the spaces passing the ball from one teammate to another;
- they fill up the spaces passing the ball from one teammate to another. The player who receives the ball lifts it up and stops;
- the ball is passed between teammates, but if it is passed to a player with a different color the latter has to return it;
- a triangle is formed with a player with a different color and then the ball is passed to a teammate (same color);
- at a signal, the teams must quickly form groups in the four corners and continue dribbling and passing;
- at a signal in each corner the players form groups of 4 players of different colors and they continue playing with the ball.
15. as an alternative to the previous exercise routines: in a 30 x 30 meter square one team does technical exercises with

their opponents standing still (at regular intervals they exchange tasks).

16. as an alternative to the previous exercise routines: in two 10 x 10 meter squares the players play 4 v 2 with various kind of touch-play. Or they play 3 v 1 only with the head.

Physical conditioning: dry, general or specific development work is carried out (see specialized texts) according to the established program.

Situational exercises: which provide for possession of the ball (objective of periodization: lactacid capacity and power).

17. in a 40 x 40 meter square 2 teams play with 2 goalkeepers. They take possession of the ball and when they reach a seventh consecutive pass they win a point if the ball is passed to their own goalkeeper (who must play it with his feet). The goalkeepers move freely inside the square and can obstruct each other (stopping the pass) and participate in possession (playing with the feet).

18. as an alternative to the previous exercise routine: on a 70 x 50 meter pitch, divided into four parts, the players play 8 v 8 with 2 touch-play getting one possession of the ball. They play in one zone and only after 3 consecutive passes are they allowed to move into another (they must all move to that zone to start a new possession of the ball). The changes of zone are counted and the team which has the most wins.

Theme games

19. an 11 v 11 match is played with several rules: when the players are in their own half of the pitch they play with two touch-play; in the other with as many touches as they like; they try to score by crossing; the pitch is divided into three parts in which the center-field must be passed over. Other variations are introduced according the specific requirements of each formation.

20. an alternative to the previous exercise routine: on a 70 x 40 pitch divided into three zones, with 2 goals defended by goalkeepers, the players play 8 v 8 with 2 touch-play. In the 2 defensive zones, before coming out, the players must make 3 touch-plays. The attackers must press, but at the third touch of the

opposing team they must immediately return to the central zone (losing a zone). The team which wins the ball in the defense zone must make 3 touch-plays before being able to get out of it.

With a predominance of lactacid capacity or power.

After the usual period of activity and start-up, if the session is to have a predominance of lactacid capacity or power, a short match of 10 minutes is played in preparation for work.

Physical conditioning: dry work or work with the ball, following these exercise routines:

21. playing on half of the pitch (1 ball for each player) and, at the coach's signal, each player, for a pre-established time, carries out all the movements of a match at almost maximum speed (creative running: guide, stop, change of direction...). Recovery is carried out guiding the ball at a slow run 5 x 7-10-12 seconds with a micro-pause of 40 seconds between the zones of the run and 2 minutes recovery between the series (1 minute of stretching and 1 minute of slow running).

22. an alternative to the previous exercise routine: 10 x 7 seconds with 1 minute recovery between the series.

23. an alternative to the previous exercise routines: 8 x 10-20-30 meters over a previously prepared track carried out at maximum speed, with recovery of 10 seconds after each distance and 90 seconds between series.

24. an alternative to the previous exercise routines: run and come back with the ball 2 x 5 x 20 + 20 meters with a 40 seconds pause (after each repetition of 20 + 20 meters) and 2 minutes recovery between series.

25. an alternative to the previous exercise routines: in a triangle of 50 x 25 meters 8 players do 2 relay races, guiding the ball (at maximum speed) and passing it over to their teammate every 25 meters.

26. an alternative to the previous exercise routines: 7 v 7 match with 2 goals defended by the respective goalkeepers, 3 pairs of players (fixed) form, who play against each other and 1 two-way player for each side who can intervene, in help, both during the offensive and defensive phases, but who cannot score (the two-

way player is changed every 2-3 minutes).

N.B.: one or more exercises may be repeated. These repetitions must be broken up by active recovery periods (short games without rules or technical exercises) which replace the situational exercise routines.

Theme games

27. an 11 v 11 match is played with several rules: the players must score within 7 passes; they must always pass forward, otherwise the ball passes to the opponents; each time a player passes backwards, a deep throw will be given. Other variations can be introduced according to the specific requirements of the formation.

28. as an alternative to the previous exercise routine: in a rectangle measuring 60 x 50 meters players play 8 v 8 with 2 goals defended by goalkeepers and two small goals (3 meters wide) set up on the middle line of the play rectangle. The teams must defend first the small goals and then the main goals.

Finish the session with the usual stretching work, relaxation of the spine and relaxation exercises.

With predominance of alactic capacity and power

A period of action and start-up is carried out.

Physical conditioning: dry work or ball work is carried out. In this case pattern training is carried out, with scoring, without opposition (the players are asked to carry out the exercise routine at maximum speed).

29. 3 players work at a time + the goalkeeper. A, B and C start 20 meters from the penalty area. Guiding the ball, B places himself on the side line and receives the ball, then he crosses to the center allowing C to enter at the first pole and A at the second. This exercise routine not only involves technical work (heading, throwing, crossing, shooting...), but it also involves physical and tactical work and is repeated 6 times with crossing from the right and 6 with crossing from the left (the players must change starting positions each time). Recovery is the same as the time waited before re-starting. Before the next exercise, 3 minutes of stretching and technical exercises.

30. A, B and C position themselves at 30 meters from the penalty

area. B passes to A who chips to C on the side line. C crosses to allow A to move to the first pole and B to the second. The exercise is repeated 6 times with a cross from the right and 6 times with a cross from the left and the players must change starting positions each time. Recovery time is the same as the waiting time before re-starting.

Before the next exercise, do 3 minutes of stretching and technical exercises.

31. Working with 4 players, D and C position themselves at about 40 meters from the penalty area. D passes to C, who, in turn, passes to B, positioned several meters further back: B chips to A (who is in the start position and at the same level as B) on the side line and crosses to allow D to enter on the first pole, C on the second, and B in the center. The 3 players form an offensive triangle. The exercise is repeated 4 times with crosses from the right and crosses from the left and the players must change starting position each time. Recovery time is the same as the waiting time before re-starting.

Situational exercises

32. in a 30 x 50 meter rectangle, divided into 2 parts vertically, the players play 4 v 4 with small goals (6 feet wide) and one ball in each zone of the pitch. They play with 2 touch-play and score 1 point each time they pass the ball through a goal (from either side) as long as the ball comes straight from a teammate. The following variations may be made to this exercise:
   - the players play with just one ball and in fact an 8 v 8 situation takes place (4 v 4 in each zone of the pitch) in which the players must stay on their respective sides of the pitch;
   - playing still with one ball 8 v 8, but the players can exchange between each other as long as the number of players on each side of the pitch does not change (4 v 4).

33. as an alternative to the previous exercise: in a 60 x 40 meter rectangle, divided into 3 parts with the central zone 10 meters wide, the players play 9 v 9 with 2 goals defended by the goalkeepers and 4 small goals (6 feet wide) placed on the 2 lines between the center-field zone. Two 4 v 4 situations of 2 touch-play in the widest zones take place, while in the central zone a 1 v 1 free game is played (the players playing 1 v 1 change every

90 seconds). The players can score in any of the 4 small goals or in the 2 main goals.

Theme games

34. in a 60 x 50 meter rectangle, divided into 2 parts, the players play 9 v 8 with a goal defended by a goalkeeper and 6 small goals (4 on the goal line and 2 on the center line). The 8 players defend the goal and can score in the small goals. The 9 defend the small goals and can score normally in the large goals.
35. an alternative to the previous exercise routine: in an 80 x 50 meter rectangle, divided into 3 parts with a wider central part (40 meters), the players play 8 v 8 with 2 regular goals defended by the goalkeepers. All the players place themselves in the central zone and an 8 v 8 game starts with 2 touch-play. When one team succeeds in taking the ball over the line of the offensive zone, where they cannot be opposed, they must score in 3 passes playing with 1 touch-play (to score, in the offensive zone they can use only 3 players).

The Friday session

If a third session is held the day before the match, the coach must take a sensible attitude towards it. The reason for this is that the body needs this period to recover its reserves of energy.

After a period of activity and start-up (by playing games which do not rely on the physical condition, but with the ball), the session is dedicated to reactivity and to sprints with complete recovery times. This further possibility can be exploited to try out re-start play situations, zone play or movements and to psychologically prepare the players for the match.

36. divide the players into pairs (with one ball), and with the cones placed at a distance of 10 meters from each other, the following exercises are carried out:
   • one player gives the ball to his opponent (with whom he forms a pair) and before the latter can make two touches on the spot, after receiving the ball, he must sprint over to him and reach him. If he succeeds he scores 1 point (the two players constantly exchange roles);
   • one player gives the ball to his opponent and before the latter can lift up the ball and head it 2 times, he must reach

him. If he succeeds he scores 1 point (the two players constantly exchange roles).

37. an alternative to the previous exercise: in a 10 x 10 meter square the players position themselves at the sides. On a signal, they must quickly run to 4 balls situated at the center and then guide them quickly to the corners (the players divided into groups of 4 alternate and before doing the exercise again recovery must be complete).

At this point the coach will assess which other exercises to introduce, if any, before the match.

ADVICE TO THE READER

A. the size of the areas proposed in the various exercise routines can be changed to suit the number of players available as can the training space available.

B. the number of touches suggested in the various exercise routines is considered to be optimal. Each coach may change this at the beginning to suit the level of his own players.

C. During the exercise routines, when possible, the players should always be positioned according to the tactical formation adopted by their own team and according to the characteristics of the opponents formation which they are to meet (assuming they know it).

D. the duration of the various exercise routines must be adapted to the time available for training and to the fitness of the players.

E. the coaches must give their own interpretation to the exercise routines because it is not possible to make suggestions which suit every situation.

CONCLUSION

All the different sports disciplines, and soccer in particular, are aimed at stimulating the growth of the athlete both at a physical level and from the psychological and social points of view. In this context, and in relation to the main goals he wants to achieve, the coach should:

- develop his theoretical, technical and practical knowledge concerning all the different themes he constantly deals with while coaching soccer (always keeping himself up to date);
- remember that each player has his unique character and personality (unique nature) and to approach each athlete accordingly;
- overcome the conflict between teacher and student and discover that teaching - in this case, coaching soccer - means providing the athlete with useful suggestions, reference points, special criteria, information and knowledge;
- realize that he is working in a team context;
- use a suitable mental approach in which what you tell your players prevails over economic and ideological interests.

In this particular context, the coach should specifically concentrate and work to:

- improve the technical and tactical skills of each player;
- justify everything he is coaching and communicating to his players;
- suggest suitable solutions helping the athlete to trust and become completely aware of himself, his talent, his desires and roles within the group; these aspects are key in the development of constructive interpersonal relationships, both within and outside the team group;
- successfully control interpersonal relations and the active involvement in the team experiences as well as assume one's own responsibilities.

In practice, the coach is the man who is responsible for leading the team or individuals towards specific goals. People and goals are therefore the two key factors on which a coach must successfully carry out his coaching role.

Team rules

The team is a complex group, the coach cannot neglect all the mechanisms and rules regulating team life as well as all the elements necessary to manage the group as a whole. Each team has its own structure, special goals and relationships to other groups (society, mass-media, supporters and so forth...). Moreover, the team is a dynamic system whose peculiar organization develops through a series of behaviors, interpersonal relationships and constant changes.

All the situations occurring within a team should be investigated carefully; not only as a consequence of each subject's personal actions, but especially in direct connection with the general relationship system inside the team: players' condition, goals, general atmosphere, rules and moral values regulating the team.

Each team meets for a specific purpose and consequently develops their own structure and teaching method including different control systems to achieve the final common goal and stimulate team cooperation.

Team cohesion can be enhanced by every factor exalting team values over personal needs: this means that it is fundamental to help the athlete to understand that personal benefits directly result from successful team performance. Each single member enhances his personal cohesion when the whole group:
- successfully pursue their goals;
- are threatened from outside;
- are in direct competition with other groups;
- operate with a system of special rewards (either material or not) based on cooperation rather than competition.

Inner cohesion and cooperation can be threatened by such elements as differences of power inside the group or the creation of smaller sub-groups. When one of the sub-groups plays a key role inside the team, the situation can become very risky and considerably influence the behavior of the other members.

Likes and dislikes between single players or between the leaders of the various sub-groups can also hinder and threaten team cohesion. When the group is organized in this way - hierarchical levels and various sub-groups - the lack of dialogue and mutual communication obviously prevents any form of cooperation.

Therefore, it is evident that cohesion is the key element of the whole group, since it helps each individual to enhance his self-esteem, self-confidence and moral approach, since all the members can mutually support each other.

The coach can work to maintain this favorable situation by using suitable reliable communication tools and never forget that his players' receptive ability specifically depends on the cohesion of the team as a whole (the ability and willingness to listen to information coming from outside) and the context in which the message is conveyed.

This is the reason why the coach should be responsible for stimulating mutual dialogue and team cohesion inside the group, by approaching the players both at their level (observing the reality with their eyes and taking an active part in their group) and with a neutral disposition by acting as a fair judge in some cases.

The modern coach

He should always set two main goals:

* coach his players to react to all the different situations occurring during the course of a match by themselves (thanks to the technical and tactical solutions experienced while practicing);
* coach his athletes to play without being constantly controlled and stimulated from outside.

For the coach to successfully achieve these goals, he should especially work on personal needs and values like independence, evaluation, self-esteem, personal fulfillment, success and so forth. Only by stimulating these important needs can he achieve his goals. The coach must perfectly know his players in order to coach them in the best way possible and should never forget that the players directly influence the final success or failure of the team by means of their individual behavior. Unfortunately, many coaches have based their soccer knowledge on personal attitudes and experiences without developing a truly effective coaching method, allowing them to properly approach their players and assistants and convey the necessary skills in the best way possible.

The coach does not need to be a magician, but should:

motivate - by means of his enthusiasm and personality (by keeping his players' efforts into proper account and working with them to achieve the final success); motivated players are increasingly stimulated to face new situations and constantly pursue the final goal, since motivation is directly connected to personal need;

communicate - his ideas and the desire to struggle for the final goal. The performance is considerably influenced by the players' personal feelings and disposition and by their team sense. The coach - the appointed leader - is an effective member of the group and his personal technical, tactical and psychological attributes become key elements if he manages to convey them to the team to develop mutual contact and an effective coach-athlete communication. In this way, each player can enhance his own personality in a much wider team context;

teach - which means above all correcting the players and correcting himself, since human adaptability is not a mere conviction, but a real challenge and responsibility;

work - very hard and improve himself to improve the others, by experiencing his job in strict connection to his personal development and to the growth of his athletes.

The coach should not follow special trends, but only stimulate his creativeness to develop personal solutions which can be tested and improved through constant experience.

Moreover, he needs to approach time properly and never forget that the team is an entity projected into the future, beyond his personal experience. The real professional coach constantly works for the development of the club; this approach is not always immediately profitable for the coach himself, but his professional skills inevitably emerge as time goes by.

The professional development of the coach can only be achieved in the long term by trusting one's own 'adaptability' and constantly keeping up to date. The coach should regularly investigate new coaching methods but also improve his psychological approach to the reality (to constantly refine his ability to manage every single player and the group as a whole). As a matter of fact, it is fundamental to approach everybody in the same way, since each member of the team could be useful in achieving the common final goal.

In the end, the coach should carefully improve his relationship with himself, since self-esteem plays a key role in the figure of the leader (his self-esteem often stimulates the respect from and towards other people). The coach who does not hold himself in high esteem obviously conveys his weaknesses and anxieties to his players and this is absolutely harmful for the group.

Coaching Books from REEDSWAIN

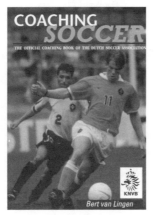

#785:
Complete Books of
Soccer Restart Plays
by Mario Bonfanti and
Angelo Pereni
$14.95

#154:
Coaching Soccer
by Bert van Lingen
$14.95

#177:
PRINCIPLES OF
Brazilian Soccer
by José Thadeu
Goncalves
in cooperation with Prof. Julio Mazzei
$16.95

#185:
Conditioning
for Soccer
Dr. Raymond Verheijen
$19.95

#244:
Coaching the 4-4-2
by Maziali and Mora
$14.95

#787:
Attacking Schemes
and Training
Exercises
by Eugenio Fascetti and
Romedio Scaia
$14.95

Call REEDSWAIN 1-800-331-5191

Coaching Books from REEDSWAIN

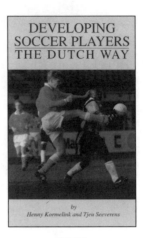
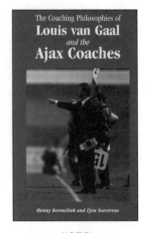

Notes

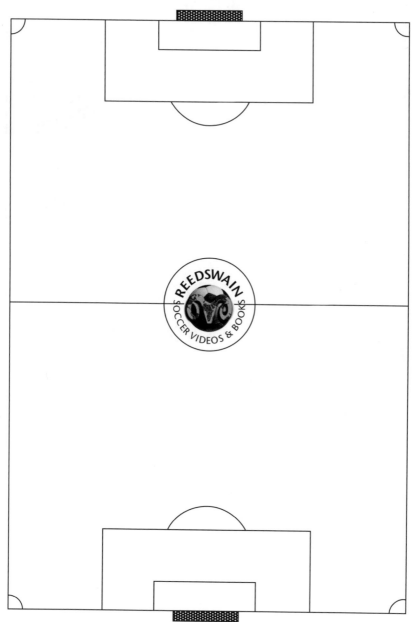

REEDSWAIN BOOKS and VIDEOS
1-800-331-5191 • www.reedswain.com

Notes

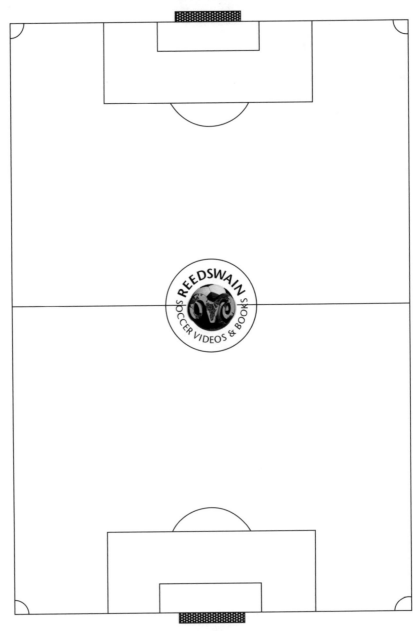

REEDSWAIN BOOKS and VIDEOS
1-800-331-5191 • www.reedswain.com

Notes

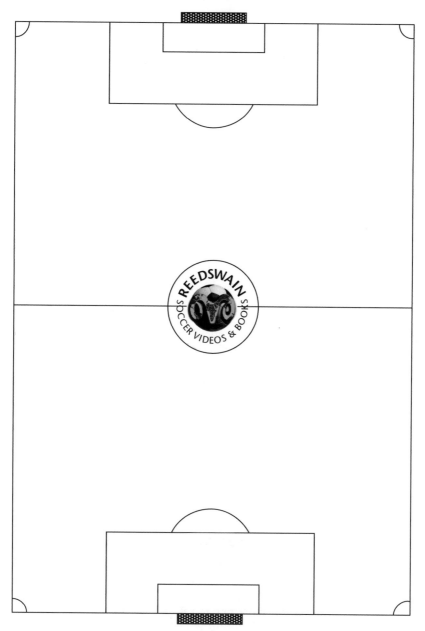

REEDSWAIN BOOKS and VIDEOS
1-800-331-5191 • www.reedswain.com

REEDSWAIN BOOKS and VIDEOS
612 Pughtown Road
Spring City, Pennsylvania 19475 USA
1-800-331-5191 • www.reedswain.com